Information and Decision
in Behavioral Economics

Schriftenreihe Arbeit und Bildung des Heinrich-Vetter-Forschungsinstituts e.V.

Hrsg.: Franz Egle und Carl-Heinrich Esser

Band 5

PETER LANG
Frankfurt am Main · Berlin · Bern · Bruxelles · New York · Oxford · Wien

Information and Decision in Behavioral Economics

Adam Biela

PETER LANG
Internationaler Verlag der Wissenschaften

Bibliographic Information published by the Deutsche Nationalbibliothek
The Deutsche Nationalbibliothek lists this publication in the Deutsche Nationalbibliografie; detailed bibliographic data is available in the internet at http://dnb.d-nb.de.

The publication of this work was supported
by a grant from the Alexander von Humboldt-Foundation.

ISSN 1869-182X
ISBN 978-3-631-63380-9

www.peterlang.de

TABLE OF CONTENTS

FOREWORD

This monograph was completed during the stay of Professor Adam Biela from the John Paul II Catholic University of Lublin in Poland, at the Hochschule der Bundesagentur für Arbeit in Mannheim and the University of Mannheim in the summer of 2011. His research visit had been funded by the Humboldt Foundation.

The volume is an interdisciplinary attempt to analyze decision making in dynamic decision situations. It represents the result of many years of scientific activities and is firmly set in the decision-making research tradition of Mannheim which is characterized by a strong association of economics, social psychology and vocational counselling. Although the title might suggest concentrating on the narrow problem of information seeking and decision making, the monograph begins with a reflection on the philosophy of science and development of science. Biela uses a metaphor that nowadays it is necessary for science to breathe its both "lungs" simultaneously: the narrow-specialist approach that extends the research horizon of the particular disciplines and helps to develop knowledge and enable the progress of civilization, and the integrative approach that vertically supports the internal communication of the accumulated knowledge and enables a reflection on science or its branches as a system. The coexistence of the two trends of development in science, i.e., the narrow horizontal one and the integrative vertical one, may be observed in four areas of the methodology of science: 1) in the conception of science itself, 2) in the systematization of science, 3) in the concept of a scientific paradigm, and 4) in the development of scientific concepts (Biela 1991).

Although the narrow-specialist trend is necessary for the development of civilization and science, it also brings risks seen in the ever more difficult communication among professionals not only of different disciplines, but even of the different research approaches within the same one. A counterbalance to this difficulty in communication is the integrative trend in science. The main idea of the latter trend is that a specific aspect, object or scheme of research becomes common for representatives of various disciplines. In his monograph, Biela shows that the contemporary social sciences and economic science may be seen as a case of the latter trend. In his behavioral approach to information seeking in decision making, he represents the integrative trend in economic and social sciences. Information and decision belong to the key concepts that enable to understand situations where people play various roles, of a social, professional, political, economic, spiritual or existential character. Biela illustrates the theoretical reflections, normative models and descriptive regularities with examples from his behavioral experiments or from the macroeconomic-level observations from his parliamentary work.

The monograph is organized into five chapters. First, the methodological basis for a behavioral interpretation of decision-making is presented. That is why at the beginning Biela presents the development of the concept of a decision situation, from an ordered triple, through an ordered quadruple, to an ordered 5-tuple. This development in the study of decision making and information seeking in decision situations is described as a result of cooperation of formal logicians, mathematicians, economists and psychologists. The author suggests a behavioral approach as a methodological tool that integrates and develops decision sciences and information sciences. Therefore, decisions, treated as human behavior, are analyzed in light of the axioms of game theory formulated by J. von Neumann and O. Morgenstern.

After discussing the decision making situation as human economic behavior, i.e. explaining the behavioral economics approach in decision making, Biela analyses the issue of information seeking in a dynamic decision situation where one may identify the problem of a decision whether to invest in obtaining new information in order to reduce the risk of the final decision. Here, the question of optimality of this decision is articulated. The situation of seeking new information is presented as a communication system, and the related economic problem of the decision whether to invest is also discussed. The presented models of the optimal decision concerning the investment in obtaining new information base on the criteria of the theory of optimal decision.

The Author's interest in decisions concerning an investment in obtaining new information, refers to the question whether in terms of the economy it is legitimate to invest in searching for new information in a given economic decision situation, and if so, how much to invest. To present this issue in a wider context, Biela proposes the behavioral and cognitive interpretation of the pragmatic methodology of accounting developed originally by Ronek (1995) as an appropriate one to analyze the costs and benefits related to searching for and obtaining new information in a given decision situation. Biela points to the particular value of this methodology for analyzing the relationship between the incurred primary costs and the useful goods which are an effect of activatingg the primary input (through the process of manufacturing or rendering services), at the macro- and microeconomic level. Considering the reasons why it is difficult to determine how adequate or comparable the costs and their effects are, the proposed methodology questions the procedures used for determining adequacy and comparability and suggests that the difficulty is caused by incorrect assumptions of the accounting methodology (arguing that neither the costs incurred nor those of manufacturing proceed according to the accepted accounting periods). The author also points out that the pragmatic methodology suggests that production costs should also reflect other costs derived from the primary input – and not include only the consumption or use of the initial resources in the total input calculation, without considering other factors, such as the cost of the decision maker's risk or the cost of obtaining information. Biela underlines that from a behavioral perspective, there appear abandonment costs or lost benefits of the option not chosen, which is a new behavioral cost category within the primary input, but not qualifying as consumption. His behavioral interpretation of accounting places investment in searching for new information within this category. Such interpretation of behavioral accounting leads the Author to a conclusion that the primary input (an accumulation of economic potentiality at the macro and micro level) should be updated by including the above activity. He also observes that the pragmatic-behavioral approach in accounting brings economics closer to the interdisciplinary field of decision theory.

Biela discusses the concept of an economic decision situation and the problem of optimality of the decision to invest in searching for new information in a dynamic decision situation, which he follows by a review of behavioral studies on human behavior in dynamic decision situations where there is a possibility to search for new information. He notes that these studies belong to the mainstream of behavioral economics and concern the decision situation understood as a dynamic stimulus situation that affects the decision maker, and that these studies base on the descriptive and normative models of searching for new information in the decision process (these models are broadly used in research on information seeking in behavioral economics). The monograph presents the Author's own systematization of studies on economic behavior within the stream of research on informational processes in a dynamic decision situation, alongside with the basic research outcomes. He refers to *information seeking* and *information purchasing, gathering, reaching* and *obtaining,* to define the informational function, as well as *revision of opinion,* where each of the terms focuses on a different aspect of finding information, and he points out that *informational activity* and *information processing* seem the most adequate and complementary to expressing the totality of information processes in a dynamic decision situation.

The monograph accepts the viewpoint of behavioral economics as a theoretical approach to analyze the behavior of decision makers in economic situations that are of interest to the various fields within economics and management studies. The author stresses that in decision situations on specific issues of investment, finances, management strategy, marketing or consumer-issues people rarely apply normative models known in economics, but rather use their own cognitive schemas, originating in intuitive cognition and everyday language. Based on his own research, Biela provides examples of such cognitive regularities, called fallacies (or cognitive biases), including those connected with conjunction and disjunction, and indicates the need to consider them in the analyses of economic phenomena.

The focus on the search for probabilistic information in the paper is based on the assumption that the rationality of decisions depends on the information resources available to the decision maker. Thus, the Author analyzes various descriptive and normative models and experimental results, also observing how decision-makers behave when seeking information in decision situations, and points to two of such models that describe a sequential search for probabilistic information. The first model described here, an intuitively simple one to use, created by A. Biela, enables to sequentially analyze the optimality of each new investment to buy new probabilistic information in a dynamic decision situation, while the other model, cheaper to use (by E. Micał and A. Biela), is a combinatorial version of the first one and allows to evaluate the utility of a given informational cycle without having to perform a calculation after each step of the investment cycle.

A distinct element in Biela's methodological analysis is a reflection on the significance of experimental methods in economic sciences, illustrated with examples of experiments on decision making in various areas of economic life, where he notes that introducing experiments into economics makes it a more empirical and methodologically strict science. His interest focuses on experiments on seeking information in a dynamic decision situation where the decision maker is able to undertake investment activities that involve purchasing new information to reduce the uncertainty of the decision situation. A clear added value of such approach is that adopting a more integrated perspective of behavioral economics, economic sciences come closer to the reality of economic life of actual people, who perceive the reality around them in their own cognitive categories.

The behavioral approach also allowed the Author to integrate certain theoretical concepts used in different scientific disciplines, such as the concepts of *information* and *decision* in the first part and the concepts of *information* and *energy* in the final part. Such integration enabled him to create the original conception of *energy-decision-information,* for which the formulated equation shows that information is a function of energy as an actualization of mass-energy in an act of decision making by the operator, i.e. the decision maker operating with energy.

Finally, another value of the monograph is that from the reviewed literature one may learn not only about the contribution of American authors, but also of ones from Europe (such as Polish and German authors) into decision making and information seeking in behavioral economics.

In conclusion, the analyzed monograph offers a general view on the cognitive and applied potential of the behavioral approach in economic and social sciences. This potential lies mainly in the theoretical and methodological possibilities of the behavioral concepts, research methods, and particularly experimental studies. The author suggests to continue the explorations on information seeking in specific areas of decision making, for example on choosing one's profession or employment after graduation, perceived as an economic decision of long-term socioeconomic consequences not only for the individual, but also for his or her family, local community, employer, region, state and macrostructures such as the European Union. For example, although in Poland the budget expenditures on higher education are successively increasing, however, in order to assess the efficiency of this investment in human capital in a more comprehensive way, one should rather ask if and where the graduates get employed and actualize the accumulated resources they have gathered, how efficient their transition from school to the labor market is, and what their income to the state budget is. From this perspective, state expenditures on higher education in Poland fail to result in unemployment, and graduates, often specialists whose education was very costly, are not prevented from emigrating abroad for work; hence, considering the economic criteria, the present policy causes that human capital is not actualized efficiently by the country, as the high investment from the state budget does not bring back income, which is irrational from the macroeconomic perspective. Obviously, the described phenomenon also concerns other countries, especially Spain, Portugal, Greece, but dissatisfaction of graduates with the employment possibilities is also expressed in France and other western countries. Thus, certain states raise questions on the rationality of their integration with the European Union if their investment in human capital through education is not efficient in the sense that their graduates seek employment abroad, yet still do not find the satisfactory conditions to fully actualize their professional potential there, as it is not fully suitable for the foreign market, and would be far more efficient if it could be actualized in their home land. Biela's behavioral-economic model for information seeking and decision making, may be used for dealing with the above issues, using a pilot study for graduates (Post-Graduation-Work-Learning), a macroeconomic stimulation of the costs and benefits of such project, and a quasi-natural experiment on post-graduation work learning in a given region. His conclusion, grounded in the cognitive and behavioral economics approach to information seeking and decision making concerning graduates is rather optimistic, as – he argues – it is possible to avoid wasting public funds that had been invested into education if the graduates are employed within a relatively short time after graduation. The above issue was discussed more comprehensively by Biela at his Colloquium on "Post-graduation work learning: a quasi-natural experiment" at the Hochschule der Bundesagentur für Arbeit in Mannheim which took place on June 22, 2011.

We are convinced that this monograph provides important incentives for further research as well as for the training and qualification of career guidance counsellors. We especially welcome the international character of the work and particularly its contribution to the dialogue of the German-Polish scientific community.

Bernd-Joachim Ertelt and Eduard Gaugler

Mannheim, May 2012

Introduction

In the development of science over the centuries two trends may be observed. The first one is the trend of narrow specializations, manifested in the emergence of newer and newer theoretical approaches to the same object of research, as well as in the emergence of ever new academic disciplines to study completely new objects of research. Reasoning by analogy, and following the idea of division of labor by Durkheim (1964), the narrow-specialist current in the development of science may be called a scientific division of labor into ever new areas and fields for a more adequate understanding of the truth about the reality in which the human being is interested. The narrow-specialist path of development has resulted not only in a richer understanding of the reality, but also in enormous practical achievements in the developed areas of basic research and application. This is visible in the development of technology and civilization in various fields of social and economic life (including health and social care, transport and communication, agriculture and nutrition, biotechnology, trade, finance, various areas of management, education, defense, sports and recreation).

Apart from the undoubted civilization benefits of the narrow-specialist development for the progress of science, one may, however, also observe risks resulting from the given science developing only in a selected direction. One of such signals of danger is the growing difficulty in communication among professionals representing various schools and academic approaches, even within a single scientific discipline, not to mention those of differing disciplines. This is evident at scientific conferences, where narrow-thematic symposia of representatives of one discipline are run parallel. As a response to this difficulty in the world of science, in addition to the mainstream narrow-specialist growth, it is also developing within a different second trend, which may be called *integrative path of science development* (Biela 1991).

What is the key idea of the integrative trend in the development of science? The essence of this trend may be considered a specific aspect or scheme of research which is common not only for representatives of one scientific discipline, but may also be object of analysis for representatives of various scientific disciplines.

In the development of science one may thus metaphorically speak of the "two lungs", which scholars should breathe simultaneously: the narrow-specialist one, which extends the horizon of research and involves the development of knowledge and the progress of civilization, and the integrating one, which vertically and internally deepens the communication with the accumulated knowledge and reflects on its system. The coexistence of these two trends of development, i.e. the narrow-specialist one horizontally and the integrative one vertically, may be observed e.g. in four areas of methodology: 1) in the concepts of science itself, 2) in the systematization of science, 3) in the concept of the scientific paradigm, and 4) in the development of scientific concepts (Biela 1991).

The methodology of science and the philosophy of science distinguishes three main conceptions of science: 1) the classical conception, formulated by Aristotle based on the science-founding question: *why?,* 2) E. Kant's conception, which poses the question: *what are the a priori forms of understanding the human mind?,* and 3) the positivist one, formulated by Comte, which asks: *how does a given phenomenon take place?* (Kaminski 1998). The first conception has set both maximalist and integrative goals for science: to determine the *raison d'etre,* the rationale of a fact/phenomenon observed, independently from the different aspects of analyzing this fact. The integrating factor within this conception is the *raison d'etre* of the particular scientific fact. In turn, the conception of Kant, which is the foundation of modern cognitive sciences, states that the object of science are actually *a priori* forms of cognition in the human mind, which – although may differ individually between people – in their essence are common to all (Biela 2007). It is the *a priori* forms of the human mind that are the base for the integration of science.

The positivist conception enables the development of still new research approaches and the emergence of new disciplines. The scholar has the full freedom to penetrate new research areas, and need not necessarily worry about the communication between them. The relationship between the conception of science and the economic thought was developed more broadly by A. Biela, by discussing the relationship of human capital and intellectual capital with the economic and moral good (Biela 2007).

The second area where the narrow-specialization and the integration trends clash or harmonize in scientific development is the emergence of new disciplines and the attempt to systematize them. The emergence of new disciplines is the most common manifestation of the narrow-specialization development tendency. However, also new disciplines emerge, which are a sign of the integrative trend. An example of such integrative disciplines are disciplines developed in the 40's and 50's, such as information theory (Shannon and Weaver 1949), cybernetics (Wiener 1965, 1971), game theory, which began in the 40's and developed later, (Neumann, Morgenstern, 1944), or the theory of data, developed in the 60's, (Coombs, 1964). These disciplines have proposed new approaches to the objects of scientific analysis: the theory of information – the flow of signals in the communication model, cybernetics –control in the systems moving in the environment, the theory of data – processing the primary measurements into relational structures, and game theory – the behavior of the players in the situation called game.

Another example of the integrative trend are the types of science based on an integrative approach to research (e.g. social sciences, behavioral sciences) or an integrative object of study (e.g. life sciences, brain sciences, information sciences). In the first case, the integrative dimension is the methodological scheme of the relation which is the object of analysis. For the social sciences, which include e.g. sociology, economics, pedagogy, psychology, management science – the integrative center are the interpersonal relationships, recognized by each of these disciplines in a specific aspect. For the behavioral sciences the axis of their integration is the pattern of relationships of *S-O-R,* where: *S* - *stimulus,* O - mediating variable, *R* - reaction, interpreted as a given behavior. Behavioral sciences include e.g. psychology, sociology, economics, behavioral medicine, behavioral biology, behavioral physics, computer science, etc. In the latter examples of sciences, the center of integration is the object of analysis itself, i.e. life – for the life sciences, the brain – for the brain sciences, information – for information sciences.

The third manifestation of the integrative or narrow-specialization trend is a/the different scope of the concept of *paradigm,* whose meaning was defined in the methodology of science by T. Kuhn (1962). According to him, a paradigm – understood as a vision with a mental breakthrough – has so far been elaborated only by the natural sciences, where the most obvious example is the heliocentric paradigm of Copernicus. The humanities, to Kuhn, have not yet elaborated their paradigm. A potential paradigm – understood as above – in the social sciences is indicated by A. Biela, who considers the inspiration of the so-called new economics, proposed by Ch. Lubich. This proposal, called by Biela *the paradigm of unity* has been indicated in more detail for economics and psychology (Biela, 2006). Such approach may be described as integration within the natural sciences or the social sciences around the paradigm.

Another example of the integrative approach in the search for a new paradigm for the economic sciences is a proposal to understand the object of economic analysis as a decision-making process and as making a series of decisions by the subjects/entities of social and economic life. This proposal was presented for the first time by K. Kłosiński in his work concerning the reflection on the rationality of human decisions (Kłosinski 1995). T. Żylicz, who defines economics as *the study of human choices,* sees the methodological status of economics as a science in a similar way (Żylicz, 2009, s.132). Such proposed approach to the object of economics as a science, which may be described as one of decision-making, economic analysis should be understood as an economic version of decision analysis.

Moreover, both presented proposals of the new integrative paradigm in economic science may be considered jointly, because decisions, as an object of economic analyses, may be made with a view to maximize the usefulness or value of an action, with regard not only to the welfare of an individual, but also in the context of the whole social environment and natural heritage, by the principles set out in the paradigm of unity, which is essentially expressed in maximizing the common good (Biela, 2006). Meanwhile, there are also opposite tendencies to define the term *paradigm* in a narrow sense, e.g. in education, economics and psychology, this term is used to determine how to conduct research based on a specified schema. The latter approach represents the narrow-specialist trend of development within these disciplines.

The fourth of these manifestations of the integration trend in science is the development of scientific concepts and their conceptual integration. The basis of this integration is to analyze the relational nature of concepts, which results in the construction of new concepts in one discipline by analogy from another discipline. The base of this inference is the correspondence of relationships which are the essence of the concept in one discipline to the relationships in another discipline. An example here may be economic concepts derived from the theory of marginal utility[1].These concepts have been transferred into economics through reasoning by analogy from the concepts introduced by psychologists involved in psychophysical laboratory research where participants differentiated the intensity of sensory perception[2].

Another manifestation of the integrative trend is to combine concepts that emerged and developed independently, even within the separate disciplines, through discovering of a deeper relationships between them. An example of such manifestation of the integration is the present monograph. Remaining in the integrative stream of development in behavioral sciences, the monograph formulates its research problem in the following question: what is the relationship between the concepts of *information* and *decision* in terms of behavioral economics? Practically, it is meant to indicate: 1) what is the optimal model of investing in finding new information by a decision-maker in a dynamic decision situation?, and 2) how

---

[1] The concept of marginal utility was developed by C. Menger and W.S. Jevons, and then extended by V. Pareto, according to whom utility is the degree of achievement of the business.

[2] It is a study initiated by Weber and Fechner at the Laboratory of Psychology in Leipzig in 1970s and 1980s, followed later by all the psychological laboratories in the world that elaborated a strict methodology for measuring the difference in sensory threshold, low threshold sensory and the upper limit of sensory.

does the decision-maker actually behave in such decision-making situation, i.e. how realistically is he or she able to bear the cost of searching for new information?

Having answered the above questions, the monograph will also seek to obtain information on two issues: firstly, whether the terms: *information* and *energy,* taken from different disciplines, may be integrated conceptually, and secondly, how far would the behavioral approach be useful in integrating these concepts.

Altogether, the aim of the monograph is to analyze the relationship between such basic concepts as *information, decision, mass* and *energy* on the basis of the approach proposed by behavioral economics. The integration of concepts belonging to different disciplines is of course not a goal in itself, but aims to create a basis for non-eclectic links between these disciplines, and thus a more effective cooperation between them in solving many important problems of both theoretical and practical matter. To achieve this, the structure of the book is planned as follows.

Chapter 1 presents the decision-making situation in terms of behavioral economics. First is presented the evolution of the concept of *decision situation* as ordered triples, fours and fives orderly structured. Then the decision situation will be discussed in terms of game theory and behavioral economics, after the presentation of the behavioral economics as a theoretical approach in economics.

Chapter 2 will discuss the problem of optimality of the decision to invest in finding new information in a dynamic decision situation. After the initial outlining key elements of the structure of the processes of searching for information will be presented the same problem of investment decision seeking new economic information. This problem will be elaborated for a specific payoff matrix from the viewpoint of the ten following decision *criteria: maxmin, maximax,* the criterion of Laplace, Hurwicz criterion, the criterion *β,* the criterion Savege'a (also known as *minimax*), *SEU, SEV, EU, EV.*

The next Chapter 3 will be structured on the basis of the literature related with behavioral studies on the search for new information in a dynamic decision situation. This review will cover the most commonly used normative and descriptive models in researches, systematization of the research situations, the research techniques and results obtained. In a special manner will be dealt with experimental research on the typical economic decisions, with particular emphasis on experiments by V. Smith, and on the behavioral regularities called as cognitive fallacies (*cognitive biases*), on which the study conducted, among others D. Kahneman.

Chapter 4 presents the author's own game experimental trial as an empirical model of the situation looking for a new probabilistic information in a dynamic decision situation. For this situation have been developed two versions of the optimal search for information: a sequential model and a combinatorial model. Although these models are mathematically equivalent, but are not identical behaviorally for decision-makers. They indicate when it is optimal in the sense of the criterion the EV, to complete the process of finding a new probabilistic information in the analyzed decision situation.

The last chapter proposes the conceptual integration of the four concepts: *information, decision, mass,* and *energy* - based on behavioral approach. On the basis of the analysis will be provided the energetic-decisional equation of information as a behavioral approach towards the integration of the above concepts.

Chapter 1

The decision situation in an economic approach

Decision theory is an example of an interdisciplinary integration around the topic of decision. The field was created thanks to the achievements of authors representing philosophy, logic, economics, psychology, sociology and mathematics. The group of decision theory founders, including logicians and mathematicians, initiated the theory and the axioms of economic behavior, and it for use in economics. Firstly, one should mention J. von Neumann and O. Morgenstern (1944), who developed the game theory and the – already classic in the literature – utility theory, formulated in an axiomatic way, typical for deductive systems in logic and mathematics.

The list of authors who have contributed to the development of decision theory is long. Let us mention only some of the significant academic centers in this field. One of the most significant research centers for the development of decision theory was the University of Michigan in Ann Arbor. The pillar of this center was C.H. Coombs (1964) – the creator of the theory of data and the base of research on behavioral decisions. This center may be called the American school of the interdisciplinary theory of decision. To the authors whose thoughts had roots in an interdisciplinary reflection and research on behavioral decisions belong: W. Edwards, who after leaving Ann Arbor developed a decision research center at the University of California, H. Raiffa, who created a research center on decisions at the Harvard University Business School in Boston, A. Tversky, D. Kahneman and P . Slovic – who organized the center of Decision Research in Eugene, Oregon, J. Lingoes, Roskam and L. E. Guttman – who developed the methodology for testing decision-making with multidimensional scaling at Ann Arbor, cooperating with J.B. Kruskal of Bell Laboratories at Murray Hill, New Jersey and R.N. Shepard (1962, 1972) from Stanford University (Biela 1995).

Other American authors who have contributed to the development of decision theory, outside the Michigan center, are, among others: K.J. Arrow – the Nobel Prize winner in economics in 1972 (risk analysis), H.A. Simon – the Nobel Prize winner in economics in 1978 (the relation between decision and thinking), G.S. Becker – the Nobel Prize winner in economics in 1992 (economic theory of decision as human behavior), R.D. Luce and H. Raiffa (1964: preferences, utility, subjective probability), L.J. Savage (statistical decision theory), F. Mosteller and P. Nooge (experimental measurement of the utility of money).

Outside the USA, to the development of decision theory also contributed authors from European countries and Japan. Some of them are also mentioned in the present chapter.

First, one should examine the evolution of the concept of *decision situation* itself, from the so-called ordered triple to an ordered 5-tuple, where to a well-structured set – containing alternative activities, hypothetical states of the world and the function of utility – is added a probability distribution on a set of hypothetical states of affairs and a set of new information possible to be gained. Next, the issue of decision is presented in economic terms, and against this background we will discuss decision in terms of game theory and behavioral economics.

1.1. The evolution of the concept of a decision situation

One of the fundamental concepts of the decision theory – the *decision situation* – like the theory of decision as such, arose as a result of a cooperation between three disciplines: economics, psychology and mathematical logic (and more precisely, the set theory). The latter term has been the source of *a well-ordered set,* i.e. one where the order of the elements in the set is determined by definition and cannot be changed. This means that the fixed sequence of elements of a well-structured set is a feature belonging to its nature, i.e. to the essence of the set in question.

G.S. Becker (1990) and other economists contributed an economic approach to human behavior to the concept of a *decision situation*. Psychologists, in turn, extended the concept of a *decision-making situation,* giving it a relational character, as an interaction between the subject, called the *decision maker,* the environment where the subject is currently located or may hypothetically be standing.

To the development of decision theory contributed mostly economists cooperating with psychologists, both in solving theoretical-conceptual problems, as well as in applied research. A classic example would be a professor of psychology at MIT, Cambridge, H.A. Simon, who specialized in the psychology of thinking, including his *General Problem Solver* (*GPS* – see his publications with Newell (1962), and Newell and Show (1963)), artificial intelligence (Simon 1969) and decision-making problems in economics and behavioral sciences (Simon, 1959)[3]. Simon's contribution to experimental economics and the application

[3] The phenomenon of conservatism in such cases are treated by F. Bujak (1972). Evaluation of simple events are, according to the author, more conservative than in the case of complex events. The literature (Kietliński, 1972; Strojna, 1974) also emphasizes that the result of assessing the likelihood of events (and hence the degree of conservatism) in static decision-making situations, depends on whether the decision maker has an impact on the outcome of an event or not. If the decision

of his research results in behavioral finance in economics is treated more extensively by authors representing the mainstream of behavioral economics (Caginalp et al 2004).

Among the authors who contributed to the development of decision theory, three were Nobel Prize winners in economics, awarded since 1969; however, the list of the winners in economics who contributed to economic theory through the development of certain aspects of decision theory and applying then into economic analysis, is much longer. James M. Buchanan (1986, USA) was awarded for his contributions to new methods in the analysis of economic decisions. Harry M. Markowitz, William F. Sharpe and Merton H. Miller (1990, all from USA) – received a joint Nobel Prize for developing tools to determine the weighting of the risks and benefits associated with decisions related to investing. In 1994, John Nash, John C. Harsanyi (USA) and Reinhard Selten (Germany) – were awarded for developing the theory of games. Then, in 1995, Robert E. Lucas, Jr. – received the Nobel Prize for the application of decision theory and decision analysis in macroeconomic research, while in 1996 two authors were awarded parallel, James A. Mirrles (UK) and William Vickrey (USA) for the development of the theory of economic incentives by introducing the elements of decision theory into this field.

It is significant in the development of behavioral economics that, in the first decade of the twenty-first four Nobel Prizes in economics were awarded for introducing creative elements of decision theory into economics. Thus, already in 2001, three American authors, George A. Akerlof, A. Michael Spence and Joseph E. Stiglitz – jointly received the prize for enriching the market analysis with the elements of decision making and information processing, and particularly with a behavioral analysis of market decision-making in the conditions of asymmetry of information available to market participants. A year later, in 2002, two American authors were awarded parallel: Daniel Kahneman – for integrating the results of psychological research on the so-called cognitive abnormalities (cognitive biases) with economic analysis, and Vernon Smith, for introducing behavioral experiments on a larger scale as a tool for empirical analysis in economics. The next two Nobel prizes in economics were: in 2005 – to Robert Auman and Thomas Schillong, for their contributions to game theory, and in 2007 for Leonid Hurwicz, Eric S. Maskin and Roger B. Myerson – for their contributions into theories of economic planning through tools derived from decision theory. These facts clearly indicate that the theory of decision, decision analysis and

---

maker's action has any effect on the same event, then he or she is willing in some cases overestimate the probability of events in relation to the likelihood of an objective, while others do not underestimate this probability.

behavioral economics are the leading trends in the development of modern economic theories, methods of economic analysis and empirical research in the economic sciences.

Extremely significant for the development of interdisciplinary cooperation, especially between psychologists and economists in research on decisions, are the international conferences *Subjective Probability, Utility and Decision Making* (*SPUDM*), held every four years. These conferences have resulted not only in the development of decision theory, but also in concrete solutions for applying the decision theory concepts to economic problems, environmental protection, new technology, organization and management (see, among others: Sjöberg, Tyszka, Wise (eds.) 1983, Vlek, Cvetkovich 1989). Two of these conferences were held in Warsaw (in 1977, organized by J. Kozielecki – the promoter of decision theory in Poland, a student of H.A. Simon and W. Edwards, and in 2008, organized by T. Tyszka), which indicates a meaningful contribution of the Polish authors into the development of research on decisions[4].

A characteristic feature of the Polish contribution to the development of research on decisions is its interdisciplinarity. Already since the 1960s and 1970s decision analysis has been an object of interest for logicians and mathematicians (Szaniawski 1974, Greniewski 1969, Greń 1972; Kaźmierczak 1973; Kofler 1968; Lerner 1971) economists (Lange 1971; Kłosiński 1983, 1995, 2007, Sadowski 1963, Szeloch 1991, 1996, Adamus 2008, 2009, 2010) psychologists (Kozielecki 1981; Tyszka 1968, 1970, Tyszka and Grzelak 1974; Chlewiński 1975, 1979, Biela 1976; Bujak 1971, 1974, Walesa 1972, 1975, 1988). The result of this interdisciplinary collaboration was a number of new concepts, research trends and applications. One example may be working on optimizing decisions (Lange 1971), the theory of a decision-making situation (Kłosiński 1983), the pragmatic concept of information (Szaniawski, 1974), the development of decision making (Walesa 1972, 1975), the concept of momentous decisions in life (Walesa 2005, 2011), the concept of a group decision (Chlewiński 1975).

One may now talk about a broad "entry" of the decision-making trend in European research within the following areas: decision-making in managers (Gaugler 1962, 1993; Kirsch 1988; Mączyński 1996), multidimensional decision-making strategies and multi-criteria decision support (Łukasik-Goszczyńska 1974, Skulimowski 2009, Adamus and Gręda 2005), multidimensional data analysis (Adamus and Rzońca 2008), decision making and

---

[4] During the conference SPUDM in 1977, the author of this book was invited to deliver a *major paper* on the theoretical and experimental achievements in the field of decision theory at the Catholic University of Lublin. Speech presented by A. Biela, Z. Chlewinski and Cz.Walesa (1983), was entitled *Developmental Aspects of Decision Making,*

implications for careeer guidance (Ertelt and Ruppert 2011), analysis of costs, risks and opportunities associated with the Polish accession to the euro area (Adamus 2008), creativity of managers (Szopiński 2004), goal-oriented behavior (Zaleski 1987, 1991), the functioning of the labor market (Rożnowski 2009), border lines of risk taking (Makarowski 2008), international economic relations (Kłosiński 2006) and financial decisions (Jajuga 2004). With such broad interdisciplinary collaboration, the boundaries between the particular disciplines not only did not disappear, but the methodological awareness deepened the need for further cooperation in the broad area of research on human decisions in situations of work, in social systems, economics and political activity. This awareness is most accurately expressed in the title of a synthetic monograph by T. Tyszka (2010): *Decisions. The psychological and economic perspective,* in that it is the human being who makes decisions in various situations throughout his or her life, which is unique and unrepeatable, but above all, it is only one.

An example of interdisciplinary collaboration between persons involved in researching these issues within the broader theory of decision is a biannual *Decyzje,* edited by T. Tyszka in Poland and devoted to the problems of decision making, especially on economic and social issues, including information about the Nobel Prize winners in economics and their contributions to decision-making and decision theory[5]. An event stimulating the development of decision theory and its applications in Central Europe is an interdisciplinary international conference *Human being and decisions,* first held at the Catholic University of Lublin 17-19 November 2009. This conference is an aftermath of the initiative of K. A. Kłosiński and A. Biela – former members of the Decision Making Seminar, led in 1925-1990 by Klemens Szaniawski (a logician, a world expert on decision-making) at the Polish Academy of Sciences, Department of Praxeology. Other participants of this seminar (T. Tyszka, G. Lissowski, Z. Chlewiński and Cz. Walesa) were members of the scientific committee at the Lublin conference. A two-volume collection of contributions, edited by K. A. Kłosiński and A. Biela (2009), includes sections on decision theory, rational decision, philosophical and theological aspects of freedom and determinants of decision-making processes.

How should the decision-making situation be understood, in the context of cooperation with psychologists and economists with logicians? The decision situation is a mental state of the decision maker in his or her the particular motivational conditions. He or she often experiences behavioral difficulties on a macroeconomic scale (e.g. a policymaker may consider how to determine the structure of the state budget, how to shape the tax system

---

[5] See e.g. *Decision,No* 2 and 11 The latter number includes the development of M. Malawski (2009) on the contribution of R. Auman in the theory of games.

in the coming year, what relations to enter with the neighboring countries, or whether it is profitable to bind with only one supplier of natural gas or rather to diversify the sources) or on a microeconomic scale (e.g. how restructure the company in the current market situation, for which consumer or target group market to aim in the company's production profile, what kind of investment to make to improve the company image), as well as on the level of an individual household (e.g. how to meet the housing needs of one's family, how to deal with commuting of the working family members, where to spend the family holidays, etc.).

The deductive theory of decision-making situations by K. A. Kłosiński

An advanced outline of the theory of a decision situation in terms of the logical-formal apparatus of was presented in Polish literature by K.A. Kłosiński (1983). The starting point for his theoretical ideas were both inspirations from operational research, as well as from the H. Greniewski, E. Kofler, and N. N. Worobiew (1969) definition of a *decision situation,* which integrates the concepts: *a game of chance, strategic game,* and *deterministic model.* To define the concept of a *decision situation,* Kłosiński uses a contextual definition (through axioms), which is a system of postulates, theorems and lemmas, formulated in a formal-deductive way. This system presents a classification of decision situations, whose common features are the following: 1) in these situations, there are at least two decision makers who are in the relationship of compliance or antagonism regarding the outcome of the decision, 2) each decision maker has exactly two alternatives of (yes or no), 3) the set of results of each decision maker consists of two elements (success or failure). In his analyses, he distinguishes the following decision situations: 1) $\hat{C}$ -type situations, where the number of decision makers is arbitrary, but not less than 2, and each decision maker selects the alternative action only once, 2) C-type decision situations, where there are only two decision makers, 3) C*- type decision situation, where in addition to the two decision-makers, there is also known a so-called map, which is a complex function of the successes and failures of both players. For these three types of decision situations, Kłosiśński developed a deductive system of statements forming the first part of his theory.

The other part of the Kłosiński's theory concerns only decision situations of type C (for two decision makers), assuming that the decision may be taken a multiple number of times. This part he calls the *algebra of complex decision-making situations.* It uses elements of the algebra of sets, propositional calculus and a typological theory of electrical networks and has the form of an axiomatic system. The last part of this theory is an application of the deductive system into decision-making situations, where the other partner for the decision maker is called “the nature”. Kłosiński’s theory in a very precise way articulates certain concepts of decision analysis, such as *rozmaitość decyzyjna* [variety of decision-making], consistence, antagonism, map and atlas of successes and failures, decision situations with a need to establish the decision-making power or the possibility of exerting pressure. The author also points to the usefulness of its formal analysis tools to interpret the various situations of economic, social and political conditions. These interpretations may also find an application to analyze current situations of economic decisions.

Situations of momentous life decisions

The object of decision analysis may also be issues not directly related to economics. Decisions may also apply to health problems, environmental conditions, social welfare, cultural and national heritage. These and other related issues are also of interest to economists. An example here might be analyses within the *real life economy* (see e.g. Ekins and Max-Neef 1992) and the research within the so-called new economy stream (e.g. Ekins (ed) 1990). Authors who develop a broader conception of economics based on axiology and the concept of *sustainable development* include J. Davies et al (2008), T. Żylicz (2009) and F. Piontek (2001, 2007).

Decision analysis may also include one’s most significant decisions in life, such as the choice of a spouse, reproductive decisions, the choice of one’s profession, the choice of priesthood or a convent life. Not every existential decision situation may be a subject of economic analyses, because the factors taken into account by the decision maker are difficult to operationalize in economic values. However, there are economists, like G.S. Becker (1990), who dare to – successfully – perform an analysis of optimization processes considering certain decision-making situations of a momentous character in life, such as the choice of one’s partner to marry, the decisions on the number of offspring, or altruistic actions. In this context, the state of the decision maker’s interaction with the environment constitutes a definite type of decision-making situation on a microeconomic, macroeconomic or individual household scale. The decision situation may concern activities, operations, tasks, problems of a daily and commonplace type (e.g. consumer decisions in a shop) or existential choices which have lifelong consequences for the decision maker or other people.

In Polish literature, momentous decisions in life are the object of interest for Cz. Walesa (1988, 2005, 2011). In a synthesis of the characteristics of a momentous life decision he states that it: 1) consists in selecting by the decision maker, from the set of possible actions, the one that is of particular importance his or her life and brings significant meaning for its further course, 2) appears in the decision maker's consciousness as a moment which is highlighted and critical in the course of his or her life, affects its restructuring, and gives it sense, 3) is an event of momentous consequences, thanks to which the decision maker's further life may have a specific course, designated by this decision; 4) gives effects which then yield a series of further decisions, 5) is generally a meta-decision of a relatively great regulatory power – and becomes a conscious direction to achieve an important long-term aim, 6) is constantly maintained and confirmed, and transferring a future aim into the continuous "now", 7) is a consequence of one's life experiences to date, and simultaneously it is a factor influencing further experiences, 8) is a mechanism which regulates the course of human life, and includes the sense of life, beliefs, worldview, and the leading ideas in life, 9) concerns not only the decision maker, but also other people (including a transcendental reality), 10) points to new paths of development for the decision maker, as it extends beyond what he/she has and who he/she is currently, 11) essentially is of a final, transgressive character, and sometimes applies to an irrevocable and final choices.

1.1.1. The decision situation as an ordered triple

In order to continue our discussion about decision situations, I propose to adopt an approach of the logical theory of sets, which has the advantage that, apart from the actual content of decision, it enables to make generalizations in a way which is convenient for our purpose. In Polish literature on decision theory, a decision-making situation (*DS*) was originally defined as an ordered triple (Szaniawski 1971; Kozielecki 1981): $DS \stackrel{df}{=} \langle D, H, u \rangle$, whose elements are: $D = \{d_1, \ldots, d_i, \ldots, d_n\}$ – a finite set of possible actions; $H = \{h_1, \ldots, h_j, \ldots, h_m\}$ – a finite set of possible things that determine the outcome of the action; u – the real-valued function, called utility, determined with a Cartesian product defined on $D \times H$ (the *u* symbol should not be confused with the *U,* which often designates decision problem itself – which implies that *U* may be used interchangeably with the *DS,* since *DS*=*U*).

Hence, the decision problem *DS*=*U,* usually presented with a corresponding payoff matrix of $n \times m$ fields, where the rows are the options, strategies, or alternative actions (1...*n*), and its columns are hypothetical states of the world envisaged by the decision maker (1...*m*). On the intersections of the rows and columns are the corresponding values of the utility function u_{ij}, defined with the Cartesian product of *DxH,* as shown in Table 1.1.

Table 1.1. Payoff matrix *U* of a decision situation *DS*, determining the usefulness of the various alternatives of the decision maker's actions (d_i) in a case when a certain state of affairs occurs (h_j.).

H / D	h_1	h_2	...	h_j	...	h_m
d_1	u_{11}	u_{12}	...	u_{1j}	...	u_{1m}
d_2	u_{21}	u_{22}	...	u_{2j}	...	u_{2m}
...	...	...	...	...	...	...
d_i	u_{i1}	u_{i2}	...	u_{ij}	...	u_{im}
...	...	...	...	...	...	...
d_n	u_{n1}	u_{n2}	...	u_{nj}	...	u_{nm}

This definition recognizes only formal elements of the decision situation. However, we may ask a question: How does the constitution of the semantic content of the decision situation as an ordered triple take place $\langle D, H, u_{ij}\rangle$? To answer this question, we should indicate which variables constitute the elements of this ordered triple.

In the literature, *decision situation* is even identified with the external determinants of the decision, or with environmental stimuli. Thus, in a macroeconomic environment these are global stimuli (e.g. the collapse of certain markets, an international banking crisis, etc.). This understanding of the *decision situation* is not the most accurate, as it ignores the role of the subjective (internal, not objective) determinants of the decision.

Considering the decision situation, we always have in mind a person who co-creates this situation. In the case of economic decisions it is important to define who is the actual decision maker in a certain situation, macro- or microeconomic. Although not in every context the decision maker is indicated clearly enough, it is almost always possible to determine who is the subject (decision maker) of a certain situation. If the decision maker actually exists, then, the decision situation whose subject he or she is, is a real situation (the reality may be understood objectively or subjectively). The decision-maker may exist just as an ideal or hypothetical being, also in terms of fulfilling the conditions of certain postulates of an economic policy or economic theory. Examples here may be: the ideal decision-maker in the classical school of A. Smith's political economy, where the public is treated as a collection of loosely related individuals and the state's role is quite limited, while the role of the free market is dominant, or in terms of the J.M. Keynes school, which assumes that the main cause of low production and unemployment is inadequate investment, driven mainly by the state as the regulator of the labor market and the momentum of the economy, or the ideal decision-maker who fulfills the rationality axioms of the classical utility theory formulated by von Neumann and Morgenstern. In the case of such ideal or hypothetical decision-makers as above, the situation will then be referred to as an ideal or hypothetical decision situation. These situations may be the content of games simulating the behavior of the decision makers who aim to reach the economic goals assumed by the given economic theory.

What is, then, meant by the phrase "to be in a situation of decision-making A subject (decision maker) is said to be in a certain decision situation only when he or she "creates" the situation in the given circumstances. Thus, analyses show that the determinants of a decision situation should also be sought in the subject him/herself, i.e. in the decision-maker. This seems intuitively reasonable, as different people may perceive the same conditions as different decision-making situations. However, on the other hand, the determinants of a decision situation must also be sought in the set of variables which are the given conditions, i.e. external stimuli (global economic conditions, legal provisions, the economic environment).

In the light of the findings adopted, the decision-making situation should therefore be understood as a function of two variables: 1) a set of the subject's determinants, which are the competencies and other dispositions of the decision maker, and 2) a set of external determinants of the economic situation. What are, then, these sets of determinants? The elements of the sets of subjective determinants may be interpreted as disposition systems available to the macro- or microeconomic decision-maker (talents, abilities or personality traits). They are structures that may be recognized by factor analysis or other statistical methods (e.g. Guilford 1961 and Cattell 1957). The examples of such systems of available dispositions may be: the ability to reason convergently and divergently (on behavioral, numerical or semantic material), emotional and motivational dispositions, personality traits, etc.

This understanding of the determinants of subjective factors (i.e. the decision maker's disposition systems), may be interpreted in the sense of S. Leśniewski's (1930) system of logic as elements of a mereological set. Indicating the mereological nature of the set of the decision maker's dispositions (established in the system of mereology by Leśniewski), seems to be closer to the economic theory and practice than the distribution understanding of this set (i.e. stated according to the classical set theory). The mereological understanding namely permits to interpret the set of the decision maker's available dispositions as a system with a structure which on one hand acts as an integrated whole, and on the other hand, each element of this structure has a relative functional autonomy[6]. The integrating function in this system seems to be played by certain groups of abilities, e.g. the so-called factor of general intelligence (Raven, 1995), the factor of social or emotional intelligence.

According to the above definition of a decision situation as an ordered triple, ($DS^{df}=\langle D, H, u_{ij}\rangle$) we may distinguish the following groups in the overall set of the decision maker's available dispositions:

1) the decision maker's ability to determine the set of possible actions *D;*

2) the decision maker's ability to determine a set of possible states of affairs *H;*

3) the decision maker's ability to assess the usefulness of the given action considering the possible states of affairs – $u\ (d_i,\ h_j)$.

In the Bayesian decision-making situations (Jeffrey, 1965), we should also distinguish the ability to determine of the probability distribution on set *H.*

How to understand the above types of abilities that create the subject's indicators of the decision-making situation? First of all, we should note that the elements of the distinguished groups of psychological dispositions are not only cognitive abilities, but also social skills and emotional-motivational dispositions based on human needs that are mentioned in economic theories. Without the latter dispositions it would be impossible for the decision makers to determine their semantic content of the ordered triple $\langle D, H, u_{ij}\rangle$. They would be helpless in determining the usefulness of actions considering the possible states of affairs or hypothetical states of the world.

The above dispositions of the decision maker must be understood as systems with a hierarchical structure, where each ability (e.g. perceptual ability, analytical thinking, etc.) is independent from the other ones, but it is also subject to the integration function within the whole system. This function lies in the fact that the given entities of abilities, without losing their functions to manage specific systems, are also subordinate to the higher groups of dispositions. For example, the abilities of perception, analytical thinking, etc., without losing their specificity, are also subject to the superior group of abilities, responsible for establishing the set of possible actions or states of affairs, or for assessing the usefulness of action considering the possible states of affairs. Through the integrating activity of the brain, the superior groups of abilities are in turn subordinate to the central system of dispositions which is responsible for the decision maker's functioning (Biela 1976, p. 23).

---

[6] Mereological interpretations of a set available to the decision maker sufficiently explains the holistic nature of the behavior of the decision maker in a situation of economic decisions, opposing to the atomistic treatment of its structure.

The concept of competence by J. Raven (1985) is also valuable theoretically and useful in application in research on economic decision making. This author draws attention to the need to integrate the decision maker's abilities and behavioral economic analysis, as his understanding of the competencies integrates the intelligence and the related cognitive processes with the emotional-motivational attitude and the values accepted by the decision maker.

In light of this interpretation of the subjective (decision maker's) determinants, the external determinants of the decision situation in question should be understood according to $DS^{df} = \langle D, H, u_{ij} \rangle$ as a set of stimuli of the given decision situation that allows the decision maker to: 1) determine the set D of possible actions – such as what economic policies to accept, 2) establish the set H of possible states of affairs that determine the results of actions – e.g. what may be predicted that would happen on the global, national, regional or local market, 3) evaluate the usefulness of action due to states of affairs - $u\ (d_i, h_j)$ - for example what may be gained, and what to lose business to take certain actions when certain events occur.

The set of stimuli of the given decision situation, which constitutes the field of economic activities, may generally be interpreted as a mereological one (i.e. such, where each part of a given element is also an element of the set), as each part of a stimulus possible to be distinguished, available to perception, e.g. visual, is also an element of the given set of stimuli, as it is available to perception also at the level of the whole set. An example here may be natural resources (natural gas, coal, marble, gold, sand, drinking water), where each part of the set of the given resource is also an element of this set. However, the already processed natural resources, through investment and work, generally become designates of names of manufactured goods, no longer belonging to the mereological sets, but rather to collective ones (e.g. chair, car, hair dryer), because no part of such goods is by itself an element of the set of the given type of goods (e.g. car wheels are not yet obviously a car).

The above analyses show that the elements of the ordered triple $\langle D, H, u_{ij} \rangle$ are a function of a specific set of abilities of the decision maker, and a strictly defined set of external stimuli elements which are in a specific interaction with the decision maker as the subject of the decision situation. Hence, the formation of the decision situation should be understood as the formation of elements of this triple in the decision maker's mind, which is present there as a cognitive representation of this situation. Adapting the J. Deway's (1997, first ed. 1910) classic conception of problem-solving phases to decision analysis, the primary phase, which initiates the decision situation, would be here the state defined by him as the "sensation of difficulty".

The primary phase, initializing the decision-making situation, is seeing the problem of decision. According to J.P. Guilford (1961), the course of the phase of noticing the problem depends on the specific group of abilities, called "sensitivity to problems". From the perspective of the external determinants of the decision situation, a condition for the primary phase to take place is a set of stimulus elements whose perception: 1) justifies stating the decision problem, and 2) enables noticing this problem. The result of the primary phase, which initializes the decision situation, is indicating and justifying the very possibility stating the decision problem. A more precise formulation of the decision problem takes place only later, in the following phases of formulating the decision situation in the decision maker's mind. A more detailed description of these subsequent stages of constituting the decision situation are found in Biela (2001).

1.1.2. The decision situation as an ordered quadruple

Various types of decision situations are distinguished in the literature, regarding the characteristics of the given sets *D* and *H*. When the sets are complete, i.e. they cover all elements which are possible to determine, the decision situation is referred to as "closed" (see: Kozielecki 1969). If a given set *D* or *H* is incomplete – the decision situation is defined as "open" (in the sets of *D* and *H*). The criterion to effectively determine whether an item is outside the set or not may be of an objective character – if it bases on reasoning of a logical, pragmatic, praxeological or economic type, etc. – or subjective, if it is used by an actual decision maker. Therefore, situations which are objectively open or closed remain as such subjectively only when the objective criterion is simultaneously a subjective criterion[7]. The decision maker in a decision-making situation, defining the sets *D* and *H*, predicts the consequences of actions considering the possible states of affairs. To Jeffrey (1965), if the conditions of the decision situation permit the decision maker to determine the probability distribution on the set of *H* and the utility function *u* defined on the Cartesian product of *D x H,* then the situation may be called a Bayesian, and the decision problem formulated in this situation is also called Bayesian. The decision situation in these conditions may be described as an ordered quadruple $<D, H, \{p(h_j)\}, u_{ij}>$, where *D, H* and u_{ij} denote the same as in the

[7] There may also be open to situations subjectively, or objectively, closed, or vice versa.

case of an ordered triple, and *{p(h_j)}* is the probability distribution determined by the decision maker on the set of hypothetical states of the world h_j, belonging to set *H* (where *j* ranges from 1 to *m* from the set *H*). The balance of gains and losses predicted by the decision maker concerning the choice of a given alternative action depends on the defined probability distribution.

In a Bayesian decision situation the decision maker may determine an objective probability distribution on the set *H* in the case when there are objective statistics or there exist logical or content-related reasons which undoubtedly enable to determine such distribution. In the case of macroeconomic decisions they may be, for example, data generally available from a statistical yearbook. For an insurance company deciding on the price of the premiums for vehicle owners, statistical data is collected by institutions involved in road accidents, taking into account the drivers' age, marital status, etc. This data helps to differentiate the premiums according to the risk categories of the insurance holders.

In the case when it is impossible for the decision maker to determine an objective probability distribution on the set of hypothetical states of the world in an economic decision situation, there is the possibility of determining this distribution by an expert or experts familiar with the analyzed decision-making situation from their professional or personal experience. These experts may be people who have participated in or observed decision situations which were analogical to the current one. In a special case, the decision maker him/herself may decide and be regarded as an expert, qualified to assess the probability of hypothetical events as a consequence of the decision, if he or she has already made similar decisions before, participated in their making, or was their observer. In the situation of assessing the probability of events by an expert or experts, the probability distribution on the set *H* determined in this way will be referred to as *subjective probability.* To distinguish the objective probability from the subjective probability, the latter one is called φ (*psi*) in contrast to *p*.

If in the decision-making situations an expert team is available to estimate the probability each of them independently, a methodological question arises: how to integrate the individual expert estimations? In such case, one should determine the weighted sum by weighing the probability of each individual assessment of an expert examiner by the level of competence attributed to the expert – which may be represented as: $\varphi h_j = \sum_{e=1}^{l} p\left(h_j\right)_e \ w_e$ where *e* is any individual expert (and takes numerical values from 1 to *l*), while w_e is the weight of the given expert's competence in assessing the probability distribution of hypothetical states of the world belonging to the set H in the decision situation *DS*. The weight of an expert's competence may be determined by evaluating his or her competence on an interval rating scale or by the method of multidimensional scaling (Biela 2001).

If the decision maker defines the utility payoff matrix U, it gives him or her the basis to formulate the criterion for decision-making (i.e. the procedure or principle of making the decision). According to Szaniawski (1971), when the decision problem is formulated, the decision-making criterion enables to distinguish the subset D of optimal actions, i.e. the best actions in terms of this criterion. This subset may have one or more elements. Chapter 2 will deal with this issue in more detail.

1.1.3. The decision situation as an ordered 5-tuple

In situations of a Bayesian type where the utility function has been established and the probability distribution on the set of hypothetical states of affairs $\{p(h)\}$ is known, a decision maker is able to subsequently take additional steps to modify the original distribution, called *a priori distribution.* In these situations, the modified distributions of probability, thanks to the new gained information are called *a posteriori distributions.*

The situations where the decision maker is able to modify the probability distribution on the set of states of affairs are called *dynamic situations* (Edwards 1971, Kozielecki 1981). In these situations it is possible to search for new information to reduce the uncertainty of the decision (Edwards and Slovic 1965).

A *dynamic decision situation* (*DDS*) is usually understood as an ordered quadruple (Edwards 1962). Using formal language, the situation (*DDS*) may be defined as $DDS \overset{df}{=} \langle D, H, \{p(h_j)\}, u_{ij}, I\rangle$. According to this definition, from the formal perspective, a condition necessary to constitute a dynamic decision situation, to the ordered quadruple we must add the finite set $I = \{i_1, ..., i_r\}$, whose elements are activities which enable obtaining new information in the utility of the activities or about the of the states of the world. The decision maker may therefore base on this information to modify the set of alternative actions, the set of hypothetical states of affairs, the probability distribution of the states of affairs, or to modify the utility matrix of the possible actions or modify. The primary utility function and the probability distribution $\{p(h_j)\}$ is defined as *a priori,* and after a modification, influenced by new information – as *a posteriori.*

A further examination of the content of a dynamic decision situation proposed in the literature, however, leads to a conclusion that, from the formal side, it is not quite correctly called an ordered quadruple, as actually we are dealing here with five elements of a set which is well-ordered in the following way: $DS = \langle D, H, \{p(h_j\}, u_{ij}, I \rangle$, where $D, H, \{p(h_j)\}$, and u_{ij} take the same denotations as in the previous equations which define the decision situation, and I is a set of new information available to the decision maker in this situation which enables to transform this distribution from *a priori* to *a posteriori.*

Every activity of the decision maker who seeks information that would allow him or her to modify each of the elements of the definitional set in a dynamic decision situation, as an ordered 5-tuple – hence, as the original set A – of the possible options for decision-making, the original set H – the hypothetical states of the world, the initial probability distribution of the hypothetical states of affairs $\{p(h_j)\}$ or the usefulness of the original payoff matrix u_{ij},, we define as *informational activity.*

What are the subjective (related to the subject) and objective (related to the object) indicators of this activity in dynamic decision-making situations? Any acquisition of information takes place in a particular communication model. Hence, the answer to the question about the subjective and objective indicators of activity requires an analysis of the communication model: the signal source – decision-maker. In such context then, the informational activity should be considered as a function of elements of this model. This model determinates the basic course of the informational activity, that is, or what subsequent decisions, in which order, will the decision-maker take in order to obtain new information in the given decision situation.

In some decision situations, a necessary initial stage is that the decision maker makes cognitive efforts to "discover" elements of a communication model existing in reality. This "discovery" means identifying a specific system of code, i.e. the relationship between the signals and the corresponding states of affairs (states of the source)[8]. Not in all situations the communication model: the source-signal – decision-maker does not exist actually (i.e. not only potentially) in all situations. In certain situations, in the preparation phase, the decision maker aims to "construct" the communication model that would allow him or her to obtain information[9]. In certain situations, the problem of "constructing" the communication model with an information source that would allow the decision maker to continually update

[8] 'Discover' the code is, among others. explore the regularities of macroeconomics and microeconomics reality. For example, a market analyst "discovers" code learning relationship between the size of the advertising costs for the product and the effects of the sad le of this product on the market.

[9] For example, a market analyst who uses the test apparatus in the form of empirical tools (questionnaires, surveys) and tools of statistical inference, "constructs" the communication system with the tested reality (Biela, 1973b).

information about the situation of decision-making, is more complex than the decision problem itself.

An outline of the conception of integrating competences and talents of the decision maker which are required for the effectiveness of his or her functioning in a dynamic decision situation, understood as an ordered 5-tuple, was outlined by Biela (1986), in the context of a discussion that took place in the journal *Behavioral and Brain Sciences,* as a part of the discussion of the concept of triarchic intelligence, whose author is R. Sternberg. This discussion included a proposal of the components of intelligence based on the definition of *DS* as ordered 5-tuple.

1.2. The decision in the approach of game theory and behavioral economics

Having discussed what a decision situation is, we will now take a look at decision itself as an act of choice, which takes place in the particular decision situation. It might seem surprising, but the very nature of the decision is still relatively little known. We only know that it is a moment of a "cut" of thoughts through a set of possible actions in a decision situation, and fulfilling one of them in the form of behavior known as a choice (*choice behavior*). This is accompanied by experiencing risk associated with the possibility of success or failure, as in the case of each game, where the winning or losing is to some extent random.

However, since the dawn of time people have always tried to get used to the risk of their decisions. One of the forms of coping with this risk was to raise their competences concerning decision-making situations. Another well-known form of coping is the deification of risk and randomness. The ancient Romans worshipped the goddess Fortuna. Near Rome, a huge temple was built to her honor, whose ruins may still be seen today. An example of a more contemporary deification of risk and randomness is the growing popularity of games of chance. This popularity reached its peak in August 2009 in Italy, where a randomly chosen lucky winner was to receive the cumulated amount of tens of millions of euros. Not only the Italians were then "infected" with the faith in their own winning of the lottery, but the lottery shops near the borders were also visited by "pilgrimage" of lottery tourists from abroad, which was also an example of a new *collective behavior* related to the expectation of winning the lottery.

This section will look at how to approach decision, as a choice, from the perspective of an economic approach called behavioral economics. In this context, we will then try to read the insights associated with the axioms of game theory, also known as the classical theory of utility. These insights will allow us to recognize more profoundly, what decision is, as a rational human behavior.

1.2.1. Behavioral economics as a theoretical approach and its methodological proposal for the economic sciences

Behavioral Economics is one of the theoretical approaches in modern economics, which grew up on the basis of American pragmatic philosophy developed by W. James, J. Dewey and Ch. S. Peirce, and the behavioral sciences, whose precursor was J.B. Watson, and whose methodological clarification was made by B.F. Skinner and E. Tolman.

What was the behavioral revolution in science about? The attractiveness of the proposal of the behaviorists was to offer a simple scheme of research which is easy to apply and enables effective interdisciplinary integration of research results. This scheme was first proposed by the founder of behaviorism, Watson himself (1930), as $S \rightarrow R$, where S represents a stimulus affecting an organism, while R is a reaction to this stimulus. An example here may be a stimulus of advertising affecting a human being, and a reaction R of this human being when he or she purchases the advertised product. Thus, the consumer's decision involving the selection of a particular product in a shop, would be a result of a direct impact of the advertising stimulus.

The scheme $S \rightarrow R$, proposed by Watson, was a direct criticism of the contemporary psychology in his time, as an empirical science based on the introspective or retrospective method. In its original form, as formulated by Watson, however, this criticism did not outlive its creator, and found no followers in the USA or abroad, to the extent that Watson did not have his direct followers. It seemed too simplistic, mechanistic, deterministic, reductionist and hence too extreme to enable a continuation. It was called extreme behaviorism and was left without direct continuation.

Nevertheless, American philosophy, pragmatic-based, would not let pass unnoticed the idea of the new regimen of practicing not only psychology, but also other disciplines and scientific fields. This scheme established itself in American science in the form of the so-called moderate behaviorism schema $S \rightarrow O \rightarrow R$, where S and R are understood as in the scheme proposed by Watson, and O is an intermediate variable between the independent variable (interpreted as the stimulus) and the dependent variable, i.e. the human response to that stimulus, i.e, his or her behavior in certain situations (e.g. a decision situation.)

In American behaviorism appeared numerous theories interpreting what the mediating variable *O* is. First, organismic interpretations dominated, i.e. a biological-physiological explanation of the relationship between *S* and *R* through learned habits, controlled by the human body. Then, a teleological interpretation followed (*purposive behaviorism*), formulated by E.C. Tolman (1995), who states that the system of goals existing in the mind is the intermediate variable, which in a complex manner converts the neural impulses from the perceived stimulus (*S*) into human behavior (*R*) that would allow to achieve the desired purpose. In case of the decision situation, we would say that it is about achieving the goal of a maximized utility function: $u_{ij}=u(d_i,h_j)$.

Currently, American behaviorism has already moved towards neobehaviorism, and is dominated by interpretations of the intermediate variable *O* as cognitive schemes, which e.g. may have the form of a system of concepts about the reality (such as the concept of the labor market, the capital market, the market of goods and services), cognitive scripts (e.g. the script of behaviors of an effective manager in a difficult situation for the company), prototypes (e.g., a prototype of a mission of a company which was successful on the market). Moreover, the cognitive trend has dominated the interpretation of the variable *O* to the extent that at present the behaviorist approach in the USA is called as a behavioral-cognitive approach.

The methodological novelty in behaviorism proposed by B.F. Skinner was the the concept of a *black box.* This concept is a conscious declaration of an epistemological agnosticism in behaviorism. Its author, having participated in discussions between proponents of different interpretations of the intermediate variable *O,* came to the conclusion that science will never unequivocally indicate the mechanism of the mediation between the stimulus and the response to this stimulus. In this situation, he drew the conclusion that the most fair and scientific approach is to declare that the reality of the variable *O is* a "black box", and impossible to be learned about by science, and suggested to call it this way.[10]

A common feature of all behavioral theories, called theories of learning, is that they explain the relationship between the stimulus and the reaction through the mechanism or process of learning. The optimism of learning theories lies in the fact that they indicate that the behaviors which are expected and desired, in school, social, and economic situations, may be learned by the developed methods and techniques of optimal learning.

Another characteristic feature of behavioral theories is their interdisciplinary "expansion". They have proposed a new methodology for various scientific disciplines as

[10] The theoretical concept of *black box* found practical application in the construction of a plane serving *the black box* analysis of the circumstances that contributed to the accident airplane.

behavioral sciences using the simple scheme *S-O-R*. Each of the disciplines for which the behaviorist schema is attractive seeks to clarify, simplify, and make its research more application-oriented, also enabling a more effective interdisciplinary communication of research results. Hence, each of these disciplines – preserving its specificity – defines its object of research, its purpose and methods, i.e. constitutes its methodological status based on the behavioral pattern. This established the pattern of behavioral sciences, including disciplines such as behavioral psychology, behavioral sociology, behavioral pedagogy/education, behavioral economics, behavioral management science, behavioral political science, behavioral medicine, behavioral archeology, etc.

Having reviewed the genesis of the behavioral approach in science, we will now focus on the theoretical proposal of behavioral economics. The object of interest of behavioral economics is the economic behavior of the participants of economic life, i.e. of individuals and legal persons. These are behaviors in various economic situations: macroeconomic, microeconomic, local, regional, global, concerning private households, the labor market, the stock market, the market of goods and services. For each of these situations, behavioral economics determines: the structure of the stimuli which trigger certain behaviors, typologies of responses of the subjects who react to the stimuli, the optimal or desired behaviors of the subjects in terms of specific goals and individual or social criteria.

An example here may be a behavioral economic analysis of consumer behaviors from the perspective of benefits from the purchase of goods for an individual consumer or his/her family (in the case of family purchases). The system of stimuli (*S*) affecting the consumer is the reality of the market situation, including: the existing network of shops available to the consumer, the system of advertising goods that are the subject of purchase (especially, attractively advertised price reductions on these goods), the brands and trademarks of products in stores, the packaging of the products, the current sales or special incentives to buy the product in the given store. A consumer behavior is e.g. to bypass certain whole segments, shelves or goods, due to the exposed stimuli in the form of the packaging, advertising or sales of the products, while stopping at other segments, shelves or goods. The final effect of the decision making process of the consumer in a supermarket is a shopping cart loaded with more or less necessary goods and making a payment at the cash register.

In a macroeconomic context, a typical stimulus (*S*) for businesses, i.e. producers or service providers, is the tax system (its nature, a linear or threshold structure, its clarity and social logic, its acceptability). A typical economic behavior (*R*) is then the type of the taxpayers' response to the stimulus in the form of a regular payment of taxes, tax evasion, irregular paying taxes, a bankruptcy of a business because of an excessive tax burden, etc. In the situation of the labor market the system of the stimuli (*S*) is the infrastructure of the state assistance for job-seekers, especially labor offices. An alternative stimulus for unemployed persons is, however, also the black market, also called the "grey zone". An unemployed person mostly analyzes offers from both the formal labor market, as well as the black market, to make a choice based on both.

In the three above economic situations it is relatively easy to indicate stimuli-situations that affect humans as consumers, taxpayers, and unemployed people. It is also possible to see the types of human reactions to certain stimuli. To determine both the structure of the stimuli as well as the response to them, is for behavioral economics a relatively more simple task than to indicate which alternative actions are beneficial, and even more so, which ones are optimal, and for whom. One must bear in mind that the optimal choices of consumers not necessarily mean behaviors which are beneficial for producers or traders. Optimal behavior of taxpayers, in turn, may be not the most beneficial for the state budget. If an unemployed person chooses to receive unemployment benefits, and still finds "black" employment, then such state is evidently not beneficial for the public finances. A problem to be solved is therefore to find such balance in the market systems, so that the balance of the gains and losses of the economic partners is acceptable for them in long run. This perspective in behavioral-economic analyses is in my opinion, at least to a certain limited extent, proposed by behavioral economics.

The current interest in the approach suggested by behavioral economics, related fields, and the developments in decision analysis, is best demonstrated by the many scientific journals which discuss the issue of decision making. Journals which deal with a behavioral approach to decision-making which were used in the present analysis include:

1. Behavioral Research Methods,
2. Behavioral Decision Making,
3. Behavioral Research in Accounting,
4. Decyzje
5. European Journal of Information Systems,
6. Information Seeking,
7. Harvard Business Review,
8. Harvard Business School: Working Knowledge,
9. IEEE Transactions on Systems, Man and Cybernetics,
10. Information Processing and Management,

11. Information Research,
12. Intelligent Systems,
13. Journal of the American Society for Information Science,
14. Journal of Behavioral Decision Research,
15. Journal of Behavioral Finance,
16. Journal of Economic Psychology,
17. Journal of Experimental Social Psychology,
18. Journal of Mathematical Psychology,
19. Journal of Management,
20. Journal of Marketing Research,
21. Journal of Usability,
22. Judgment and Decision Making,
23. Operational Research Proceedings,
24. Revue d'economie politique
25. Journal of Behavioral Finance,
26. Theory and Decision.

An analysis of the contents of these journals shows that: 1) problems of decision-making and behavioral economics are closely related; 2) the field of behavioral decision making is interdisciplinary, and stimulates the development of disciplines as economics, psychology, sociology, technical science, management science, political science; 3) in economic sciences, decision-making and behavioral problems first developed in microeconomics and within management science and marketing, and later passed into the areas of investment analysis, finances, accounting, macroeconomics and economic forecasting.

1.2.2. The decision as human behavior from the perspective of the axioms of game theory

Bearing in mind the approach of behavioral economics, we will now look at human behavior in the situation of preference of certain goods. We will refer to decisions of people when choosing a certain options (or alternatives) that are available for a player at a casino, lottery games or in other situations involving taking a risk. These behaviors were observed by J. von Neumann and O. Morgenstern (1947) and expressed in the form of six axioms, in a way which is typical for deductive sciences. The authors called their axiomatic system *Theory of Games and Economic Behaviors.* In the literature this system is also referred to as axioms of the classical utility theory.

Already the name suggests that the creators of game theory were strongly influenced by the inspirations of behavioral psychology and behavioral economics, and treated the behavior of people they observed in the casinos as *economic behaviors.* The intuitions from these behaviors were generalized and expressed in the form of axioms. Each of these axioms contains a specific aspect of behavior associated with the situation of a game of chance or other decision-making situation. Together, they form a systematic whole which allows to derive from them the theorems of the system called game theory, using the methods of deductive reasoning. In terms of methodology, these axioms are also an axiomatic definition of the concept of *rational decision.* To represent the axioms we will try to use the convention used in the literature.

Axiom A (1)

This axiom is called the *axiom of compatibility* or *axiom of consistency.* It concerns the preferential order of the set of data options, available to choose from in a decision situation. Symbolically, we may represent it as:

A (1) $$\bigcap_{x,y,z\in D} [(x > y) \vee (y > x) \vee (x \approx y)].$$

This formula reads as follows: for each of any two elements x and y belonging to the set of the decision options D (alternatives of action, strategies of action) in a given decision situation may occur only one of the following three possibilities: 1) the decision-maker prefers x more than y; or 2) prefers y more than x, or 3) equally prefers x and y, i.e. does not prefer one of these options over the other (he or she is indifferent towards them).

What insights does this axiom actually contain? The key issue is that in any decision-making situation, the decision maker analyzes only such set of possible actions whose elements (actions) are mutually compatible, and hence the set D is internally consistent. For example, if a consumer is in a situation of purchasing coffee in a shop, he or she stands in front of a shelf or a section where they are only various coffees. The consumer, as a rational decision maker, will not go to other shelves with products other than coffee, as it would cause confusion. Thus, axiom A (1) warns the rational decision maker of the initial chaos associated with the establishment of the set of alternatives in the decision situation *D*. He or she should include in this set only those elements which are compatible with each other, i.e. whose comparison and preferential ordering is possible. A violation of A (1) would mean a chaos of thoughts and an unnecessary loss of mental energy in a decision-making situation, which would not lead to an optimal decision.

Axiom A (2)

A (2) is called the *axiom of transitivity*. It says that the relation of preference (or rather, a weak preference, expressed by the symbol ≥) is a transitive relation in the set *D* of possible actions indicated by the decision maker for the given decision situation. The key idea of this axiom may be symbolically represented as:

$$\textbf{A (2)} \quad \bigcap_{x,y,z \in D} [(x \geq y) \wedge (y \geq z)] \Rightarrow (x \geq z).$$

This formula reads: for any three elements of the set *D* of possible actions related to the results of *x*, *y* and *z* respectively, one may say that if the decision maker favors (in the sense of weak preference) *x* over *y*, and simultaneously *y* over *z*, then when given a choice between *x* and *z*, one selects *x*. Intuitions contained in this axiom are treated in the literature as the basic postulate of rational behavior in a decision-making situation. It is namely about logic and consistency of the decision-maker in expressing his or her preferences regarding the choice of alternative actions.

The problem is, however, that in many decision situations people do not seem to behave in accordance with the requirements of axiom A (2). Why, then, does it happen that certain decision makers, despite the fact that from the pair of *x*, *y* they choose *x*, and from the pair of *y*, *z* they decide to choose *y*, but, when given a choice between *x* and *z* – still, they choose *z*, and not *x*, as predicted by A (2)? Are certain people so irrational in their decision-making? The answer is evident when we first determine what type of utility scale the decision makers use in considering the subsequent pairs of alternatives, as guided by A (2). If the decision maker uses the same utility scale in establishing preferences for the three subsequent pairs of alternatives, then he or she behaves consistently, according to the demands of A (2). The problem arises when, while considering the pair of *x*, *z*, the decision maker takes into account a new dimension in the utility scale, which was not taken into account while he or she compared the elements of pairs *x, y* and *y,* z. Then it may happen that, enriched by the new dimension of the utility scale, the decision maker quite reasonably chooses *z* from the pair of *x,* z, instead of *x,* as opposed to the situation of using consequently the same utility scale in the evaluation of the decision options. As already pointed out in the publications on multidimensional scaling, in more complex situations, decision-makers use a multidimensional utility functions. Therefore, for decision analysis of these situations one should first reconstruct the function that the decision maker uses to operate in the given situation, and only then may one check if it is used consequently, according to axiom A (2) (Biela 1992, 1995).

Axiom A (3)

In the literature A (3) is called the *axiom of reduction of compound lotteries*. Any risky activity, i.e., whose outcome is unsure, are called here "lotteries". To formulate this axiom, first we will accept the necessary assumptions and meanings of symbols. Let us assume that by lottery we understand the so-called simple lottery, i.e. one where an option to choose is not another lottery. We will represent this as *(x, p, y),* which means that the decision maker has two options: 1) to win *x* with the probability of *p* or 2) to obtain the outcome of *y* with the probability of *1-p.* Let us also assume the existence of a complex lottery, that is, where one of the options to choose from is a simple lottery. Such situation may be formally expressed as *[(x, p, y), q, y],* where the player may win either a lottery ticket (*x, p, y*) with the probability of *q* or obtain only *y* with the probability of *1-q.* With these assumptions, the idea of Axiom A (3) may be formalized as:

A (3) $$\bigcap_{x,y \in D} \sum_{p,q} [(x,p,y)q,y] \Leftrightarrow (x,p\,q,y).$$

The formula reads: for each of any two elements *x, y,* belonging to the set *D* of alternative actions, there are such two probabilities *p* and *q* that participating in the complex lottery we may obtain the same results (with the same probability) as in the simple lottery constructed in such way that the probabilities of these results are a product of the probabilities of the components of the complex lottery. To prove that, it is enough to calculate the probability of the results of *x* and of *y* in the complex lottery:

$p(x) = q(x)\, p(x) = p\, q;$

$p(y) = [(1\text{-}q)\, y]\, [(1\text{-}p)\, y] = 1\text{-}p\, q.$

Thus, since the two lotteries (the complex and the simple one) are related to the same results with the same probability, then, decision makers should be indifferent to participate in one lottery or the other. However, it appears that some people have an aversion to playing a complex lottery, while others on the contrary, prefer a more complex one. The degree of complexity of the lottery is for the latter group an additional dimension of attractiveness in participating in lotteries.

Axiom A (4)

This axiom is called the *axiom of continuity*. It excludes the possibility of existence of a decision option that would be infinitely better than other options. It may be formulated as follows:

A (4) $$\bigcap_{x,y,z \in D} (x > y > z) \Rightarrow \sum_{p} [y = (x, p, z)].$$

This formula reads: Let us assume that there is a preferential arrangement of any three decision options *x, y* and *z*, belonging to the set *D* of all alternatives of activity (the preferential arrangement is represented in the premise (antecedent) of the implication. If so, then it is possible to determine such probability acceptable for the decision maker, where it is indifferent to the decision maker whether he or she obtains the intermediate result *y* or chooses a lottery consisting of the most preferred result *x* (with the probability of p) and the least preferred result *z* (with the probability of *1-p*).

To explore the idea of this axiom, we will turn to an example. Let us imagine the decision situation of a producer of goods who is considering: 1) the possibility to sell goods on a market which is 300 km far, at the cost of *x,* 2) the possibility to sell these goods on the local market, at the price of *y,* however, twice as low as *x,* 3) and considering the risk of a road accident during transportation, which would involve the losses of *z,* including a fatal accident, given the woeful state of the roads. It happens that, for example, many agricultural producers, traders and wholesalers from the Lublin region, an agricultural area in Poland, every year travel to Silesian markets to sell their farm products. In accordance with A (4), they participate in a "lottery" of transporting goods from Lublin, using the not exceptionally safe roads leading to the region of Upper Silesia. However, the probability p of a lucky trip to the Silesian market is considered so high, and its complement, i.e. an accident is considered so low that they accept the risk of this lottery. We may give many similar examples where the decision maker takes the risk of various lotteries, as he or she has a sufficient sense of competence in mastering the decision situation.

Axiom A (5)

Axiom A (5) is referred to as the *axiom of substitution*. It concerns decision-making situations where the decision maker considers certain decision options as equivalent on the utility scale. The idea of this axiom may be represented in formal language as:

A (5) $$\bigcap_{x,y,z \in D} (x = y) \Rightarrow \sum_{p} [(x, p, z) = (y, p, z)].$$

Formula A (5) reads: for any three options *x, y* and *z* belonging to set *D* of possible actions, it is so that if the decision maker treats any two actions *x* and *y* within this set as equivalent (useful to the same degree), then he or she will treat any lotteries that contain these options (*x* and *y*), of any *p* and any other third option *z,* as equivalent. Equivalent decision options may thus be replaced by any lotteries which include these options.

Axiom A (6)

This axiom is defined as *the axiom of dominance*. It deals with actions whose results are totally/wholly/entirely sure and with activities of a lottery type. This idea may be formally represented as:

A (6) $$\bigcap_{x,y,z \in D} (x > y) \Rightarrow \sum_{p} [x > (x, p, y) > y].$$

The formula reads: for any two decision options belonging to set *D* of available activities it is so that if the decision maker prefers *x* over *y* (in the sense of a weak preference, i.e. prefers *x* at least as much as *y*), then necessarily he or she should prefer *x* over *y,* i.e. over an activity with a clearly worse result.

The regularities described in A (6) occur especially when the consequences of decisions concern money (e.g. money games). However, there exist counterexamples of this regularity, as in certain situations the behavior of decision makers do not meet A (6). Such counterexample may be the Russian roulette type of game, where participants clearly prefer the lottery of life and death over life itself and death itself. For obviously, a participant of Russian roulette may well remain alive by withdrawing from the game or may also kill him/herself alone, without participating in the deadly game.

Utility scale of decision-making activity

If axioms A (1) – A (6) are fulfilled, it may be shown that there exists a utility function *u* that assigns the consequences of the choosing *x, y,* z, respectively, the real numbers of *u (x), u (y), u (z)* – in the form of a Cartesian product $u\ (d_i,\ h_j)$ – such that

1. $x \geq y \Leftrightarrow (x) \geq u\ (y)$;
2. $u\ (x, p, y) \Leftrightarrow p\ u\ (x) + [(1\text{-}p)\ u\ (y)]$.

The first equivalence means that the utility of action *x* is greater than the utility of action *y* if and only if the decision maker really (and not hypothetically) prefers *x* over *y.* The second equivalence says that the utility of a lottery is defined as the sum of the utility of its results weighted by the probability of their occurrence. The fulfillment of both equations means that *u* is defined at an interval scale, i.e. one without a zero point and any interval units that are equal. If it is so, then any type of linear transformations like $au\ (x) + b$ (where $a > 0$) do not alter the properties of the scale.

However, such strong assumptions about the usefulness scale in a decision situation are not always met. In assessing the utility, not only ratio scales are applied (with zero point and equal intervals), but also interval scales (without point zero, but equal interval units) and ranking (ordinal) scales (where the points on the scale only retain an ordinal relationship). In the case of interval and ratio scales, the results of measuring utility may be added, which enables to determine their arithmetic mean and other statistics based on the product-moment (such as Pearson correlation *r*). When using the ranking (ordinal) scale, it is only possible to determine descriptive statistics such as the median or modal and calculate the correlations using the Spearman ρ coefficient. The type of measurement scale, however, is not an obstacle for decision-making analyses and for behavioral studies that use the methods of multidimensional scaling (Biela 1995, 2001).

Chapter 2

Optimality of the decision to invest in searching for new information

As Chapter 1 points out, determining the payoff matrix U by the decision maker enables him or her to formulate the decision problem. This comes down to posing a question like: Which of the possible actions from set D is optimal or satisfactory from the perspective of the given criterion of rationality? In any decision situation, the decision criterion identifies within the set D a subset of optimal (single or multiple) actions, i.e. the best in terms of this criterion.

In a dynamic decision situation one may also consider the problem of the decision to invest in finding new information in order to reduce the risk of the final decision. In this chapter we will focus on the problem of optimality of the decision in the search for new information. First, we will approach the situation of searching for new information as a communication model[11], including the associated problem of an investment decision. Next, the models of an optimal investment decision in search of new information will be presented based on the optimal decision criteria known in the theory of decision.

The present chapter will also investigate the relation between decision analysis and accounting as a branch of economic sciences. The problem of effectiveness of decisions related to investing in searching for new information enables to qualify these considerations into the area of managerial accounting, as investing in information concerns enriching the intellectual capital. That is because in the area of managerial accounting there is always the question to what extent one should invest in durable capital which undergo natural depreciation, that is, to enrich the durable assets and to what extent one should invest in gaining new knowledge that would provide a broader perspective in balancing economic activity.

2.1. The situation of seeking new information

In each situation where the decision maker considers at least a two-piece set of hypothetical states of the world, as events difficult to be predicted, he or she naturally updates the data on his or her situation. This trend leads to seeking new information which would

[11] The communication model used here bases on an adaptation of the commonly used models which originate from the Shannon-Weaver and the Roman Jakobson communication models.

allow him or her to reduce the risk and raise the optimality of the decision. This section focuses on seeking new information in the context of the communication model: the signal source – the decision maker, and then highlights the problem of an investment decision, related to the search for new information.

2.1.1. Searching for new information as a communication model: signal source – the decision maker

In the context of a dynamic decision situation, the communication model will be defined as: signal source – decision-maker. Let us suppose in a simplification that the information in the decision situation allows only to modify the probability distribution on the possible states of the world *H,* and the remaining elements from the definitional formula are fixed. Let us also assume that there is an object of information, which therefore enables the existence of the communication model; hence, this object of information is the very existence of a nonempty set of possible states of affairs $H = \{h_1,...,h_j,...,h_n\}$, where $n > 1$ in a given situation. Naturally, in the situation where this set is empty of or one-element, the "subject" of information does not exist.

2.1.2. Source signals in a dynamic decision situation

The source signal, i.e. the broadcasting system in situations of decision-making is a reality that informs the decision maker about its condition. For Abramson (1969), in this system one may distinguish two subsystems: the subsystem of providing information (the information source) and the subsystem encoding the information into signals (the encoder). If the broadcasting system allows the decision maker to directly perceive the information, then the encoding system is quite unnecessary, since it is inherent in the information system[12]. If, however, the source does not allow for direct perception of its state, then it is necessary to use a mediating coding system attached to the source. The system, then, translates the information about the state of the source into a code, that is, processes it into signals which are available for perception of the decision maker[13].

[12] For example, for a manager directly observing the market, encoder is not attached from the outside, but somehow stuck in the pattern of market behavior. Similarly, for a researcher directly observing reality coding system is part of that reality.

[13] For example, if the behavioral symptoms do not manifest themselves in a manner directly accessible perception, the manager uses analytical equipment, which acts as an encoder processor status signals available on the market for his perception. A similar function also serves as test equipment for a scientist, etc.

In decision situations, certain broadcasting systems are able to emit only one signal, while other ones – a sequence of signals. In the case of emitting a sequence of signals, their sources may be of a non-memory nature or of a Markov type, depending on the statistical relations between the emitted signals. In certain situations the decision maker may use only one signal source, while in other ones – more than one. In the literature, the first type of situations are referred to as simple or uniform, while the other type – as complex or heterogeneous (Kozielecki 1969a). In the latter situations, the decision maker may receive signals from all available sources, or only from selected ones, in a systematic or unsystematic manner. The decision maker may choose the information sources basing on rational thinking strategies or on the basis of random associations. Since in most heterogeneous situations the sources mostly emit signals of a varied informational value; thus, the decision maker faces a problem how to make a rational choice between these sources.

2.1.3. The decision maker as a receiver system – as a perceptual-transformational mental system

Communication models theory indicates that the receiving system includes a system of decoding (a decoder) and a system to receive information. The functioning of a decoding system, i.e. processing signals into information processing, implies the existence of: 1) a perceptual system (signal perception) and 2) a transformation system (processing signals into information).

The decision maker, as a component of the communication model, has two functions: of perception and of signal processing into information. These functions, although they remain in close interdependence, should be treated separately. It is thus possible to distinguish the system responsible for signal perception and the system transforming signals into information. Here, the output of the perceptual system is the input for the transformation system. Distinguishing these two systems obviously does not affect the fact that they constitute a single, integral functional structure, which will be called the perceptual-transformation system. Altogether, perceptual and transformational abilities play a significant role in the informational activities of the decision maker. Certain cognitive abilities are the determinants of this activity, such as the flexibility of the perceptual attitude, the encoding speed, creating classes, etc., as noted by Nosal (1974).

2.1.4. The communication channel

In dynamic decision situations the communication channel allows the flow of signals from the source to the decision maker. The properties of the communication channel largely determine the course and the final result of the informational activity. For an optimal course of action, it is important to properly adjust the structure and the functions of the information channel to the properties of the coding system and the transformation-perception system of the decision maker. Not always in a decision situation is it possible to select the information channel for the given encoder and decoder. In certain decision situations the communication channel is stable (i.e. it has a certain capacity and an unchanging probability of the so-called noise[14]), but there is a possibility to select the most suitable encoding and decoding systems in the communication process.

In the physical aspect, a communication channel is any environment that enables the flow of signals from a source to the decision maker. A mathematical description of the channel contains the following data: 1) a set of input signals, 2) a set of output signals, 3) a channel matrix, whose rows correspond to the given output signals, and elements of the rows are the probabilities of receiving the given signals at the channel output which correspond to the given inputs. Hence, each row of the matrix corresponds to one input of the channel, and each column – to one output. This property is based on obvious feature of the channel, in that if an input signal "enters" on one side, then a corresponding output signal "exits" on the other side (Abramson 1969). Introducing the concept of an information channel into decision analysis is useful e.g. because it allows to more precisely formulate certain issues related to the behavior of the decision maker in the conditions of the so-called noise or redundancy, etc.

2.1.5. The informational process and informational activity

The general diagram of the communication model of the "source signal – decision maker" may be represented as in Figure 2.1.

[14] In theory, the concept of information by all the noise meant distorting the proper flow of signals through a communications channel.

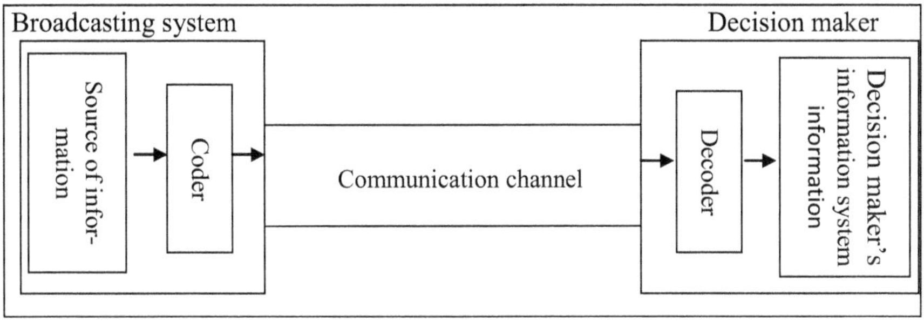

Figure 2. l. Communication model: source signal – decision maker[15]
Source: Own work, adapted form Abramson (1969)

Based on the proposed scheme in Figure 2.1., by process of information we will understand the flow of information in the communication model. The structure of thismodel lets us distinguish five phases in this process, which are the functions of the various elements of the system: 1) encoding information into a signal, 2) emitting the signal from the source, 3) signal flow through the communications channel , 4) signal reception, 5) signal processing into information. If the source emits not a single signal, but a signal sequence, then these phases are elements of new cycles. The number of the cycles depends here on the number of the possibly emitted signals and on the decision maker's decision regarding their purchase. A single cycle of the informational process will be called a flow of such information which may be sent by a single signal. Every single informational cycle begins with sending information about the state of the source by the means of a signal, and ends with receiving this information by the decision maker, i.e. by processing the signal into information.

Although a complete cycle of the informational process consists of five phases, we will focus on the last two, i.e. the reception (or rather, purchase and receiving the signal) and on processing it into the information about the state of things. These phases – as seen in Figure 2.1. – take place within the perception-transformation system of the decision maker (as opposed to the first three phases that take place outside the decision maker). Signal reception and processing it into information will be referred to as "informational activity", distinct from the "informational process", which covers all five phases, beginning with coding information into a signal, and finishing with the phase of processing the signal into information.

[15] In the numbering of graphs, tables and formulas there has been adopted the rule that the first number indicates the chapter number and the second - the number of a graph, table, or model in the particular chapter.

2.1.6. Reliable and unreliable information in a dynamic decision situation

Assuming that between the set of signals emitted from source $X = \{x_1, \ldots, x_i, \ldots, x_m\}$ and the set of possible states of the source $H = \{h_1, \ldots, h_j, \ldots, h_n\}$ there is a mutual one-to-one relationship, then each signal emitted from the source is assigned to exactly one state of the source – and vice versa. This dependence means that one may specify a deterministic law which defines the relationship between the state of the source and its emission of signals. Hence, one may conclude that the conditional probability of an emission of a specific signal with a given state of the source – is equal to one or zero:

$p(x_i/h_j) = 1$ or $p(x_i/h_j) = 0.$

Thus, the signal x_i will be emitted if and only if the source is in the state of h_j. If by $z(h_j)$ we mean that there is a state h_j, while by $z(x_i)$ we mean that signal x_i is being emitted – then the schemas of the encoding system may be represented as rules of reasoning (Biela, 1972, 1976) :

a) the encoding rules:

1. $z(h_j) \Leftrightarrow z(x_i)$
2. $z(h_j)$ (2.1) and

Therefore: $z(x_i)$

1. $z(h_j) \Leftrightarrow z(xi)$
2. $\sim z(h_j)$ (2.1')

Therefore: $\sim z(x_i)$

b) the decoding rules:

1. $z(h_j) \Leftrightarrow z(xi)$
2. $z(x_i)$ (2.2) and

Therefore: $z(h_j)$

1. $z(h_j) \Leftrightarrow z(xi)$
2. $\sim z(x_i)$ (2.2')

Therefore: $\sim z(h_j)$

Rules 2.1 and 2.1 'and 2.2 and 2.2' are patterns of reliable inference. Hence, information about the state of the source obtained though transforming signals by the decoding system will be called reliable. A similar explanation of reliable information was presented by Szaniawski (1971b), by referring this concept to a binary distribution of conditional probability. Reliable information is also referred to in literature as "categorical" (Kozielecki, 1969).

If in the given communication model the rules of encoding and decoding base on reliable patterns of inference, then the information emitted by this system is isomorphic with the information received by the decision maker, provided that no noises occurred.

Unfortunately, in many decision situations it is only possible to determine the conditional probabilities of the emission of signals related to the given the state of the source, satisfying the inequality:

$$0 < p(x_i/h_j) < 1,$$

which means that between the state of source and the emission of the signal there is only a probabilistic relationship. For a given situation, for a given set of signals $X = \{x_1, ..., x_i, ..., x_m\}$ and a given set of states of the source $H = \{h_1, ..., h_j, ..., h_n\}$, the distribution of the conditional probabilities of signals emitted at certain states of the source is represented as a matrix of probability distribution, where the sum of the probabilities in each column equals one, which means that they are probabilities of events which in a probabilistic sense form a complete system of events (see Table 2.1.)

Table 2.1 Distribution matrix of conditional probabilities of signals emitted by given states of the source

X \ H	h_1	h_2	...	h_n
x_1	$p(x_1 / h_1)$	$p(x_1 / h_2)$	...	$p(x_1 / h_n)$
x_2	$p(x_2 / h_1)$	$p(x_2 / h_2)$	...	$p(x_2 / h_n)$
⋮	⋮	⋮	⋮	⋮
x_m	$p(x_m / h_1)$	$p(x_m / h_2)$	...	$p(x_m / h_n)$

As indicated in Table 2.1, after receiving the signal x_i, the decision maker is not able to determine with certainty what the current state of affairs is. So in this decision situation, the transformation of the signal x_i into information about the set H may only be based on probabilistic inference rules. A commonly known scheme of probabilistic inference is the Bayesian theorem, which allows to determine the *a posteriori* probability distribution on the set H after receiving signal x_i, and, according to which the decision maker may only process signals into unreliable information, also known as "uncertain" (Kozielecki 1969, Szaniawski 1971b) or "probabilistic" (Pitz 1970). These terms will be used interchangeably.

2.2. The problem of decision related to investing in the search for new information.

The decision concerning an investment into searching for new information is related to the question: In terms of the economy, is it legitimate – and if so, to what extent – to invest into searching for new information in the situation of economic decisions? A wider context of this problem involves a possible methodology for analyzing the benefits and costs associated with searching for and acquiring new information in a particular decision situation. In the case of economic decisions such methodology seems to suggest accounting, and more precisely, the pragmatic theory of accounting, whose concept was introduced by Ronek (1995). He analyzes the relations between the costs of the inputs and the useful goods which are the effect of those expenditures (manufacturing, services), both at the macro- and the microeconomic level. Moreover, he asks about the reasons of the difficulties in determining the adequacy and comparability of costs and their effects, in terms of the procedures analyzing the activities that lead to these compliances. In his view, these reasons are a consequence of the assumptions in the methodology of accounting. The essence of these assumptions lies in the fact that neither the costs incurred nor production take place periodically and adequately to the accounting periods. He also pays much attention to the relation between the primary inputs and final inputs on the one hand, and the accounted costs on the other hand, with particular emphasis on the time factor in the cost accounting. The inputs/expenditures on strictly economic activity (production, services), involving the use of production factors are also distinguished from the inputs/expenditures that do not belong to the category of a cost (production loss). (Ronek 1995)

It should, however, be noted that the primary input, i.e. the collected economic resources, is a potential reality, which may be used during its actualization more or less optimally. Thus, according to Ronek, there is the problem of an optimal use of the existing production capacity, both at the macro scale, as well as at the scale of a single business. The novelty in this pragmatic approach to methodology is that its author points out that the present cost accounting still takes into account only the depreciation of economic resources (and therefore, the final inputs), while not taking into account the existence of primary inputs, that is, the accumulated results of the production process – and such approach to accounting does not support optimal management. What is more, he expresses the view that production costs should also reflect other figures derived from the primary inputs. For example, the investment of the primary inputs involves a great risk on the part of the business owner, so it would be reasonable to take it into account in the cost calculation, e.g. by interest on the primary inputs.

Following this path of thinking, the author shows if the investor involved the primary inputs into a given enterprise, then he or she resigned from using them elsewhere, perhaps more efficiently. Hence, there occur costs of this resignation or of lost potential gains. Ronek presented his methodological vision of commensurability of costs and effects in his market interpretation of the category/ies of costs – in a chart (see Diagram 6: Ronek 1995) – by introducing a new figure in the cost analysis, represented as *I*. This new cost category means that the cost accounting also includes the primary inputs which are not subject to depreciation/consumption.

In this pragmatic approach to accounting methodology I see the perspective of bringing the interdisciplinary approach, known as decision theory, closer to accounting as a discipline within economics. I will begin the interpretation of this relation with a statement that the primary inputs which are an accumulation of an economic potential at the macro- and microeconomic scale, should be updated by undertaking economic activities, i.e. economic decisions, on the global scale (macroeconomic decisions). An example here may be the decisions on restructuring concerning a specific region (e.g. the decision to organize the EURO 2012 championships and the related infrastructure, the decision to build a network of expressways in Poland, the restructuring of heavy industry in after the fall of communism). Adamus presented an analysis of the decision-making situation of Poland's joining the euro zone, in terms of the anticipated gains and losses associated with this situation (Adamus 2008a). Another example may refer to the scale of functioning of a business (microeconomic decisions) in terms of the decisions concerning the investments the company's investments, profile of production or services, the introduction of new products to facilitate the company's entry to new markets, etc.

The actualization of the economic potential is to take a series of economic decisions at both the macroeconomic level of the country or region, as well as at the managerial level in a company. The economic effects in this area rely on the best use of the accumulated economic resources which are the primary resource inputs. These, in turn, depend on how one makes decisions thanks to which economic resources are transformed into utility goods. Any economic decision in a market economy definitely involves risk, which in the approach by Ronek may undoubtedly be classified as the *I* factor/figure. These costs may be described as "the decision maker's risk costs". One may also speak about the investor's cost related to the input of resources into a given investment, instead of another one (perhaps more profitable). The creators of American pragmatism, when speaking about taking a given decision (as opposed to taking a different one), mention the grief about not taking the other decision (the one which was given up). In accounting, this grief may be expressed as the "cost of the lost benefit of a rejected option" in a decision situation.

To determine the relationship between decision analysis and the cost-gain analysis that have a financial result (profit or loss), I propose to compare the nature of the utility function u_{ij} of the payoff matrix U distribution (see Table 1.1.) with the financial result determined by analysis in accounting. The difference between these two categories is obvious: in accounting the financial result is determined based on existing financial documents (invoices, receipts) already issued in an accounting period that has passed, while the individual items u_{ij} in the payoff matrix are calculated as the expected financial result of a given activity d_i, assuming the future occurrence of a hypothetical state of the world h_j. The decision analyst does not carry out the cost-gain analysis based on existing financial documents, but on hypothetically assumed states that may lead to generating such documents. However, both in accounting and in decision analysis one establishes the financial result of economic activities: this is the similarity between the analysis in accounting and in decision analysis applied in economics.

After the general comparative analyses and the decision-oriented pragmatic interpretation of the accounting methodology by Ronek, we will focus on the initial problem of a decision to invest in searching for new information. The issue of such investment decision should obviously be treated in the broader context of decisions related to the question how to most effectively use the accumulated economic potential of the primary input? Finding new information by the decision maker may in many situations significantly improve the optimal use of the resources originating from the primary inputs. One should, then, analyse the economic profit of the costs of investing in searching for new information, in order to maximalize the economic effectivity of the primary inputs. The cost of obtaining such information would belong to the cost category I in the approach by Ronek.

What may be understood by the cost of obtaining new information in a decision situation related to the actualization of the economic resources accumulated in the initial input? This cost is generally composed of two elements: 1) the costs associated with investing in the infrastructure of the communication model: signal (data) source, where the decision maker secures for him/herself the future possibility of obtaining new information on the current economic situation, if necessary; 2) the decision maker's operational cost of obtaining the necessary data (signals) carrying new information about the current situation.

The previous analyses finally lead us to the stage when are able to answer the question when a decision to search for new information in a given macro- or microeconomic situation is economically optimal for a given decision maker. Such decision is economically optimal if after obtaining new information, and deducting the costs of obtaining this information, the value of the option chosen by the decision maker is, according to a given optimality criterion, higher than without this information. In this situation, only one issue must to be resolved: what is the determining "size" of difference between the values of the options available to the decision maker is worth undertaking the investment. The answer to this question is, however, a matter of more detailed investigation of economic decisions.

2.2.1. Criteria for optimal decisions related to investing in the search for new economic information

As pointed out in section 2.2, whether a decision about investing in searching new economic information is optimal, may be decided after determining the criterion of optimality of decision making. With this perspective, we will review the main criteria of optimality of decision that are known in literature on decision theory (Szaniawski 1971, 1971b). To carry out this review, we should first accept the definition of a dynamic economic decision situation as an ordered 5-tuple, discussed in Chapter 1:

$$\mathbf{SD = < D, H, \{p\ (h_{ij},)\ \}, u_{ij,}\ I >}$$

where:

D – is the set $\{d_{1,} \ldots.\ d_{i},.\ \ldots,\ d_{n}\ \}$ of decision options, i.e. actions available in a given decision situation;

H – is a collection of states of the world, independent from the decision maker, in the actual economic reality, $\{h_{1,\ldots,}\ h_{j}.\ \ldots, h_m\}$, whose occurrence will ultimately decide the outcome of the action d_i by the decision maker;

$\{p(h_j)\}$ – is the probability distribution on the set of hypothetical states of the economic reality *H,* determined on the basis of objective statistical data or estimated by experts;

u_{ij} – is the utility function determined by a Cartesian product of *D* x *H* in such way that each element d_i of set *D* is assigned a corresponding element from set h_j of set *H* – which may be expressed by the payoff matrix *U* (see Table 1.1);

I - a set of possible to obtain new business information in a given decision situation, $\{i_1, \ldots.,i_r\}$ simultaneously or sequentially.

As seen in the definition of *SD* as a data structure of an ordered 5-tuple, information *I* is the last element of this set. That is, new economic information about the decision situation may refer to any element of the definitional formula mentioned before it. The new information may thus refer to: 1) set *D* of actions available to the decision maker in the given situation, 2) set *H* of hypothetical states of this economic situation, 3) the probability distribution $\{p(h_j)\}$, that is, about the probability with which one may expect the hypothetical economic events, 4) the anticipated financial results of the given business activity d_i if one undertakes this activity and if event h_j occurs, 5) the system of searching for new information.

The relationships present when searching for information in a decision situation as an ordered 5-tuple may be schematically presented as seen on Figure 2.2:

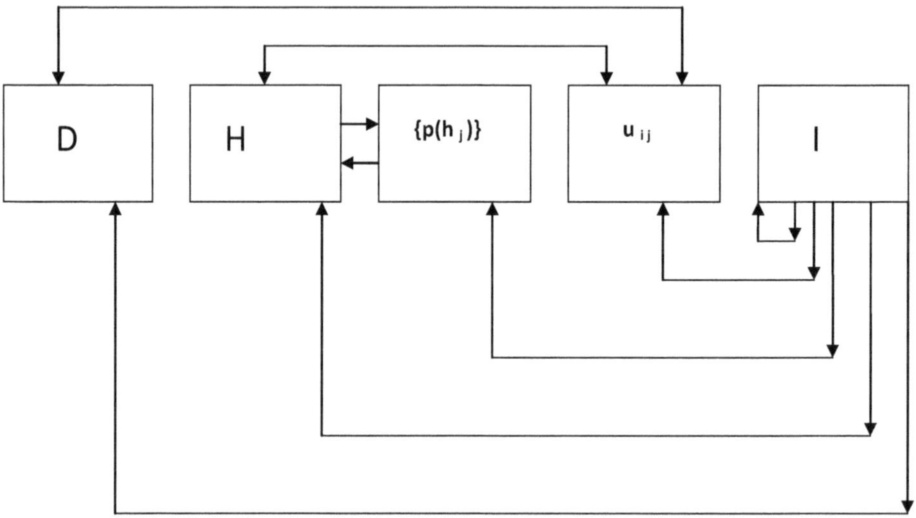

Figure 2.2. Scheme of relations present in information seeking in a dynamic decision situation.

As illustrated in the scheme, new information in a dynamic decision situation may refer to any item of the definitional ordered five. However, the decision maker (or a team of consultants, analysts or an IT system) must integrate this information in a way that allows him/her to eventually modify the utility functions u_{ij}, hence, to modify the structure of the payoff matrix *U*, which requires modifying the calculation of the Cartesian product *D* x *H*. The scheme also suggests that the relation occurring in information seeking may in this situation may be a reflexive one, i.e. the decision maker may obtain new information on the information system itself (e.g. its accuracy and reliability, the relevance of new sources of information, the availability of information processing, etc.) In further considerations we will refer to the scheme shown in Fig. 2.2 in order to relate it more to specific criteria of decision making.

2.2.2. The optimal decision related to investing in the purchase of new economic information, from the perspective of the extreme criteria

We will now consider now two simple optimality criteria, commonly known as maxmin and maxmax, originally formulated in game theory as a guideline helpful in the choice of strategy in a two-person zero-sum game, and then transferred to the field of decision theory (Szaniawski 1971b). These criteria may be called extreme due to the fact that they formalize the rationality of extreme attitudes in decision-makers who are either extreme pessimists (maxmin) or extreme optimists (maxmax) in decision making situations.

Maxmin criterion

We will begin with the *maxmin* criterion. For this purpose, we may represent the decision problem as a payoff matrix *U*, using Table 2.2

Table. 2.2. *A priori* payoff matrix *U* in a situation of economic decision making (in billion euro)

H / D	h_1	h_2	h_3
d_1	-1.8	4.3	0.5
d_2	2.5	2.7	3.0
d_3	1.7	-1.7	2.2
d_4	0.1	5.1	-1.5

This optimal action in the sense of the *maxmin* criterion is action d_i (from set *D)* that selects the greatest utility from among the minimal ones, from each action (row) available to the decision maker in the given situation. This criterion may be formally expressed as

$$d_i \text{ opt } \underset{i\ \ j}{\text{maxmin}} \leftrightarrow \max_i \min_j u_{ij} \quad (2.1),$$

where:

d_i *opt maxmin* – means the action which is optimal in the sense of the *maxmin* criterion;

$\max_i \min_j u_{ij}$ – is the maximum utility of action d_i from among the minimal utilities in each row of the payoff matrix.

In the sample situation of an economic decision which has the structure of the payoff matrix shown in Table 2.2, for action d_1 the minimum possible utility is -1.8 billion euro; the choice of d_2 implies the lowest utility of 2.5 billion euro; when choosing d_3 the minimum utility is -1.7 billion euro, while for d_4 the lowest possible utility is -1.5 billion euro. The maximal utility from among the minimum utilities in each of the four rows of the analyzed payoff matrix is u_{21} = 2.5 billion euro, which means that the optimal decision in the sense of criterion (2.1) in this situation is the choice of d_2.

When is it possible to say that the decision to purchase new information is optimal in the sense of the *maxmin* criterion? Let us suppose that on the basis of the obtained new data the decision maker was able to: 1) enhance set *D* with a new available activity option d_5, 2) apart from that, to simultaneously enhance set *H* with a new hypothetical economic state h_4, so far not taken into account, 3) and simultaneously also to modify the utility function u_{ij} as indicated in the new payoff matrix, which will be labeled as *U* * (see Table 2.3.). This matrix will be called *a posteriori* (i.e. after obtaining new information), in contrast to matrix *U*, which may be described as *a priori,* that is, the primary matrix.

Table 2.3. *A posteriori* payoff matrix (*U* *) after receiving new information.

D \ H	h_1	h_2	h_3	h_4
d_1	-1.8	4.5	0.6	1.2
d_2	2.5	3.0	3.1	-3.0
d_3	1.7	-2.2	2.2	4.7
d_4	3.0	3.2	2.8	3.3
d_5	0.5	2.1	2.1	3.1

The optimal activity after obtaining new information in the sense of the maxmin criterion is action d_4, whose utility is maximal among all minimal utilities of the activities. The purchase of new information is optimal in the sense of the *maxmin* criterion when the utility of the optimal activity (in the sense of this criterion) after obtaining this information and deducting the cost of obtaining it, is higher than the utility of the optimal activity (in the sense of the same *maxmin* criterion) without obtaining this information. This may be symbolically expressed as:

$$\text{maxmin } u^*_{ij} - c \geq \text{maxmin } u_{ij}$$

where: u^*_{ij} is the utility established in the U^* matrix *a posteriori,* while the other symbols are as before.

From the comparisons of the structure of the *a priori* matrix *U* with the structure of the a *posteriori* matrix U^* we may conclude that the decision to seek new information would be optimal in the sense of *maxmin.* However, the literature on decision theory (Szaniawski 1971a) raises an objection to the *maxmin,* mainly referring to two concerns: 1) it is an overly pessimistic criterion, as the decision maker assumes that undertaking each of the possible activities will lead him/her to the worst possible outcome, 2) if in the decision problem has a so-called saddle point (i.e., an element of the utility matrix which is also the smallest in its row and the largest in its column: such properties has the element in the second row and the first column of the *U* matrix), then, any information on this topic is worthless.

The first objection is obvious, yet, the *maxmin* criterion aims to be of help in the analysis of optimality of available activities for decision makers who view the world with a pessimistic approach, and their attitude is the result of their life experience, which is beyond discussion. Decision theory gives them a tool to be rational decision makers within their attitude to decision making.

The second objection is that if there is a saddle point in the payoff matrix, to the decision maker who uses this criterion seeking new information is worthless. This objection, however, would be justified only if the new information did not apply to set *D* or *H* (see the information diagram in Figure 2.2.). Because, as a result of obtaining this information, one expects that the matrix structure may change to the degree that the number of rows or columns may rise, so the existence of a saddle point does not make expecting the new information worthless. However, the problem is that the decision maker may certainly determine the structure of the *a posteriori* matrix U^* in an *ad hoc* way, i.e. only after obtaining the new information. Before obtaining this information, which is related incurring the relevant costs of investment, the decision maker may only be expecting this new payoff matrix. This is the situation in the example provided, where the *U* matrix is a 4x3-element and the U^* matrix is 5x4-element one.

Maxmax criterion

Considering the other criterion of an optimal decision, *maxmax*, one may formulate similar objections as to the *maxmin* criterion, the only difference being that the criteria refer to people who differ completely in that they represent extreme attitudes – of pessimism or optimism – in perceiving the decision situation. While the *maxmin* concerns excessive pessimists in attempting to predict a favorable outcome of their decision activities, the *maxmax* criterion refers to extreme optimists.

The *maxmax* criterion may be formulated as:

$$d_i \text{ opt } \underset{i \quad j}{\text{maxmax}} \leftrightarrow \underset{i \quad j}{\text{maxmax}}\ u_{ij} \qquad (2.2),$$

where:

d_i *opt maxmax* – means the action which is optimal in the sense of the *maxmax* criterion;

$\underset{i \quad j}{maxmax}\ u_{ij}$ – is the maximum utility of action d_i from among the maximal utilities in each row of the payoff matrix.

In the sample case of economic decision making with the structure of the payoff matrix shown in Table 2.2, for the activity d_1 the maximum utility is u_{12} = 4.3 billion euro; for d_2 the maximum utility is u_{12} = 3.0 billion euro, for d_3 the maximum utility is u_{33} = 2.2 billion euro, while for d_4 the maximum utility is u_{42} = 5.1 billion euro. According to criterion (2.2) the optimal alternative action in this situation is the choice of d_5.

We will now consider the optimal decision for the payoff matrix U^* shown in Table 2.3 in the light of the expectation of new information. For the d_1 activity the maximal utility is u_{12} = 4.5 billion euro; for d_2 the maximal utility is u_{23} = 3.1 billion euro; for d_3 the maximal utility is u_{34} = 4.7 billion euro; for d_4 the maximal utility is u_{44} = 3.3 billion euro, while for d_5 the maximal utility is u_{54} = 3.1 billion euro. The optimal decision activity in the sense of criterion (2.2), after receiving new information, would be to choose action d_3.

In order to answer the question whether the decision to invest in obtaining new information will be optimal in the sense of the *maxmax* criterion we may formulate the following normative condition:

$$\text{maxmax } u^*_{ij} - c \geq \text{maxmax } u_{ij},$$

where the sign symbols are the same as in the case of the *maxmin* criterion.

Savage Criterion (minimax)

The group of extreme criteria should also include the criterion introduced by Savage. This criterion does not use the concept of utility, but as the first analytical step it requires to transform the utility matrix established for the given decision situation into a loss matrix, also called a “matrix of grief”. This criterion is used by the decision makers who prefer to transform the basic business question *how much can I gain in this situation?* definitely and immediately into *how much can I lose in this situation?* With such mental attitude, the decision maker using use the Savage criterion transforms the utility matrix in Table 2.2. into a matrix of relative losses w_{ij}, defined as:

$$w_{ij} = \max_i u_{ij} - u_{ij}.$$

The relativity of losses here means that: from the maximum utility in each column of the payoff matrix one should deduct the utility of each subsequent row of this column. In this way, the utility matrix *U* from Table 2.2. becomes transformed into the matrix of losses, as in Table 2.4.

Table 2.4. The matrix of relative losses w_{ij} obtained from the transformation of the *U* payoff matrix into the *W* matrix of losses in a decision making situation.

H / D	h_1	h_2	h_3
d_1	4.3	0.8	2.5
d_2	0	2.4	0
d_3	0.8	6.8	0.8
d_4	2.4	0	4.5

After obtaining the matrix of losses in a given situation, using the Savage criterion, also known as the *minimax* criterion, requires: 1) to determine, in each row of the matrix, the maximal loss (max w_{ij}), and then 2) to determine in which of the rows the maximal loss is the smallest, i.e. *minmax* w_{ij}. The definition of the Savage criterion (*minmax*) may be represented as:

$$\mathbf{d_i \text{ opt Savage } \min_i \max_j \leftrightarrow \min_i \max_j w_{ij}} \qquad \mathbf{(2.3)},$$

where:

d_i *opt Savage (minmax)* – means the optimal activity in terms of the Savage (*minmax*) criterion;

$\max_i \max_j u_{ij}$ – is an activity d_i, where the loss w_{ij} is the lowest from among the maximal losses ($\max_j w_{ij}$) in each row of the matrix of losses.

According to this definition, analyzing the losses in Table 2.4., we may conclude that the optimal action in the assessed economic decision situation is d_2 resulting in lowest economic losses, as in $w(d_2) = 2.4$, while the remaining activities are much higher, because $w(d_1) = 4.3$, $w(d_3) = 6.8$, and $w(d_4) = 4.5$.

If, now, we consider the expectation on obtaining new information in this situation, then, by analogy, the U^* payoff matrix from Table 2.3 should, according to the Savage criterion, be converted into the W^* matrix of losses, as shown in Table 2.5.

Table 2.5. The structure of the W^* matrix of losses with the expected new information in a decision situation.

D \ H	h_1	h_2	h_3	h_4
d_1	4.8	0	3.5	3.5
d_2	0.5	1.5	0	7.7
d_3	1.3	6.7	0.9	0
d_4	0	1.3	0.3	1.4
d_5	2.5	6.6	1.0	1.6

An analysis of the structure of this matrix shows that the an optimal action in this decision situation, in terms of criterion (2.3), in the context of the expectation of new information, is action d_4, whose loss $w^*(d_4) = 1.4$ billion euro is the lowest among the maximal losses in each row of the loss matrix, as $w^*(d_1) = 4.8$ billion euro, $w^*(d_2) = 7.7$ billion euro, $w^*(d_3) = 6.7$ billion euro, and $w^*(d_5) = 6.6$ billion euro.

The purchase of new information in the analyzed decision situation will be optimal in the sense of the Savage criterion if the following condition is met:

$$\min_i \max_j w_{ij} \geq \min_i \max_j w^*_{ij} + c.$$

In the analyzed sample decision situation the above condition is fulfilled, as the optimal decision while expecting new information, taking into account the investment cost of obtaining this information ($c = 0.050$ billion euro), is associated with the loss of [$w^*(d_5) = 1.4$ billion euro] + ($c = 0.050$ billion euro) = 1.450 billion euro, which means a much smaller loss than in the case of the decision maker's optimal action without obtaining the new information. This loss amounts to $w(d_2) = 2.400$ billion euro. The pragmatic value of the expectation to obtain new information in this situation amounts to $[w^*(d_5) + c] - w(d_2) = 0.950$ billion euro. This means that if one decides to purchase the new information, then, the loss will fall to 0.950 billion euro, in accordance with the Savage criterion.

2.2.3. The optimal decision related to investing in the purchase of new economic information, from the perspective of criteria concerning the subjective weight

We have discussed the decision criteria formulated for use in the analysis of the behavior of decision makers manifesting an extremely pessimistic or an extremely optimistic attitude towards the anticipated events affecting the outcome of the decision. We will now consider the decision criteria which assume that the attitude of decision makers may be diagnosed on the scale of pessimism – optimism, and that one may use the result of this assessment (of optimism and pessimism) as a weight in calculating the utility of decision options. In our review we will consider three criteria: the criterion of Hurwicz, also referred to as the α criterion, the Laplace criterion and the β criterion.

The α criterion (Hurwicz criterion)

The originator of the criterion applying a weighting factor to assess the usefulness of alternative activities in decision making is Leonid Hurwicz – a Polish-American Nobel Prize winner of 2007 in economics – for the introduction of elements of decision analysis into economic analyses. This author proposed an empirical method to diagnose the decision maker's attitude to awaiting a more favorable vs. unfavorable outcome of an available action, called the attitude of pessimism – optimism, by determining the α coefficient for each individual decision maker. To determine this coefficient, Hurwicz proposes a diagnostic situation where the decision maker is given a choice of two activities with the following expected results: d_1 – the decision obtains 0 if an unfavorable event occurs, and if a favorable event occurs, he/she receives 1 billion euro; d_2 - the decision maker obtains a guaranteed x, regardless of what happens. This situation may be presented in a simple four-element payoff matrix (Table 2.6).

Table 2.6. Payoff matrix for an empirical diagnosis of the α coefficient in decision-makers, by Hurwicz.

H / D	h_1	h_2
d_1	0	1
d_2	X	X

The instructions for the hypothetical experimental game to test decision makers, shown in Table 2.6, are: *What would be your value of x so that you would assess d_1 to be as good as d_2, which means that you would be indifferent to choose d_1* or *d_2? That is: what would your x have to be?* From the equation: $u(d_1) = u(d_2)$ we may calculate that $\alpha = 1 - x$, by substituting the symbols with appropriate values from the payoff matrix in the equation (see Table 2.6).

The Hurwicz criterion requires to maximize the highest value from among the weighted sums of the minimal and maximal utility obtainable through the given action (for each row). The weighting factor here is α, which is all the greater, the more the decision maker counts with the worst possible outcome of his/her decision action. The greater a pessimist, the greater the α. Formally, the Hurwicz criterion may be expressed as:

$$\mathbf{d_i \ opt\ \alpha \quad \leftrightarrow \quad \max_i \ [\alpha \min_j u_{ij} + (1-\alpha) \max_j u_{ij}]} \qquad (2.4).$$

We will apply this formula (2.4) to determine which of the alternative actions, available to the decision maker in a situation of an economic decision with a payoff structure shown in Table 2.2, is optimal for the decision maker, whose α coefficient is α = 0.4. The results of the calculation for the given alternatives are:

$u(d_1)$ = 1.86 billion euro,

$u(d_2)$ = 2.80 billion euro,

$u(d_3)$ = 0.64 billion euro,

$u(d_4)$ = 2.46 billion euro.

The optimal action in the sense of the Hurwicz criterion in the analyzed decision situation is d_4.

We will now determine which action would be optimal, for the same decision maker, with the α coefficient = 0.4, in the sense of this criterion, while expecting to obtain new information which would change the payoff structure in the way indicated in Table 2.3. The corresponding results of the expected utility for the given activities are:

$u^*(d_1)$ = 1.98 billion euro,

$u^*(d_2) = 0.60$ billion euro,

$u^*(d_3) = 1.94$ billion euro,

$u^*(d_4) = 3.10$ billion euro,

$u^*(d_5) = 1.02$ billion euro.

The optimal action, after the possible new information, in the sense of criterion (2.4), is d_4. In the sense of the Hurwicz criterion, obtaining new information is an optimal decision if the following inequality is satisfied:

$$\max_i \left[\alpha \min_j u^*_{ij} + (1-\alpha) \max_j u^*_{ij}\right] - c \geq \max_i \left[\alpha \min_j u_{ij} + (1-\alpha) \max_j u_{ij}\right].$$

Assuming that the investment cost of purchasing new information in our decision situation is 0.050 billion euro, then, in the context of the results of analysis we may determine that the pragmatic value of the information in this situation is:

[$u^*(d_4) = 3.10$ billion euro - $c = 0.050$ billion euro] - [$u(d_4) = 2.46$ billion euro] = 3.05 euro billion – 2.46 billion euro = 0.59 billion euro.

This means that the decision to invest in the purchase of new information is economically favorable.

Please note that these calculations were performed for the decision maker whose α is 0.4. However, the α coefficient it is not always known for the given decision maker. In such situations, Lange (1971) proposes to considered $\alpha = 0.5$ as a balanced attitude toward the economic reality.

Laplace Criterion

Historically, the oldest of the optimality criteria is the criterion for decision-making by Laplace. He proposes to calculate the arithmetic average utility for different decision options and to maximize them. Hence:

$$\mathbf{d_i \text{ opt Laplace}} \leftrightarrow \max_i \sum_j u_{ij} \qquad \textbf{(2.5),}$$

where:

d_i *opt Laplace* – means the optimal decision action in terms of the Laplace criterion,

$\max_i \sum_j u_{ij}$ – is maximization the arithmetic average of the utility of the given d_i activity, considering all the utilities calculated in the row representing this activity in the payoff matrix.

The Laplace criterion implies that the decision maker has a very balanced tendency in the assessment of the events and never "leans" towards pessimism or optimism. However, a disadvantage of this criterion is that it treats all hypothetical events that determine the outcome of an action as of equal probabilities. Although this criterion simplifies the economic decision calculations, however, it oversimplifies and thus makes forecasting less efficient.

According to the Laplace criterion, the activities in the payoff matrix in the economic situation shown in Table 2.2 have the following utilities:

$u(d_1)$ = 1.050 billion euro,

$u(d_2)$ = 2.733 billion euro,

$u(d_3)$ = 0.733 billion euro,

$u(d_4)$ = 1.233 billion euro.

Comparing these results, it is visible that the optimal action in this situation, according to the (2.5) criterion, is d_2, with an average expected utility of $u(d_2)$ = 2.733 billion euro.

However, if we consider the expected utility after a potential search for new information that might transform the *a priori* U payoff matrix into the expected *a posteriori* U^* payoff matrix, then the average utilities of this matrix are as follows:

$u^*(d_1)$ = 1.125 billion euro,

$u^*(d_2)$ = 1.400 billion euro,

$u^*(d_3)$ = 1.600 billion euro,

$u^*(d_4)$ = 3.075 billion euro,

$u^*(d_5)$ = 0.900 billion euro.

Here, the optimal action in the sense of the Laplace criterion would be activity d_4 of the expected average utility of $u\ (d_4)$ = 3.075 billion euro.

Investing in new information is optimal in the sense of the Laplace criterion if the following inequality is valid:

$$\max_i \sum_j u^*_{ij} - c \geq \max_i \sum_j u_{ij}$$

In the case of the decision situation shown in Table 2.2, the optimal action is $u(d_2)$ = 2.733 billion euro, while for the modified structure of the expected payoff matrix after obtaining the new information – as presented in Table 2.3 –the optimal action would be $u^*(d_4)$ = 3.075 billion euro. If we knew the exact cost of obtaining new information, we would able to decide whether investing in the purchase of new information is in the given conditions an optimal step. Assuming that the cost of investing in the purchase of new information is the same as in the above criteria, i.e. c = 0.050 billion euro, the pragmatic value of the new information for criterion (2.5) may be determined as:

[$u^*(d_4)$ = 3.075 billion euro - c = 0.050 billion euro] – [$u(d_4)$ = 2,733 billion euro] = [3.025 billion euro] – [2.733 billion euro] = 0.342 billion euro.

From these calculations it follows that investing in the purchase of new information, in the analyzed decision situation, is optimal in the sense of criterion (2.5), and the pragmatic value of the information obtained is 0,342 billion euro.

The β criterion

The β criterion is a type of compromise between the *maxmin* and the Laplace criterion. It presupposes an evaluation of the utility of an action (in each row) using the weighted sum of the lowest utility and the average utility of this action (calculated as in the Laplace criterion). Analogically as with determining the level of α, an empirical determination of the β level by the decision maker is done by asking the decision maker to select a number which satisfies the condition 0 <β <1. This criterion may be formally represented as follows:

$$\mathbf{d_i \text{ opt } \beta \leftrightarrow \max_i [\beta \min_j u_{ij} + (1-\beta)\, 1/n \sum_j u_{ij}]} \qquad \textbf{(2.6),}$$

where:

d_i opt β – denotes an action which is optimal in the sense of the *β* criterion;

β – is an empirically determined weight of the individual decision maker's degree of pessimism in assessing adverse events;

$\min_j u_{ij}$ – is the minimal usefulness in the given row of the payoff matrix.

Let us determine, which one of the available activities *(d_1, ..., d_4)* in the payoff matrix in Table 2.2 is optimal in the sense of criterion β, where β = 0.7.

The results of these analyses may be presented as:

$u(d_1)$ = -0.260 billion euro,

$u(d_2)$ = 4.283 billion euro,

$u(d_3)$ = -0.457 billion euro,

$u(d_4)$ = 1.650 billion euro.

Thus, according to criterion β, an optimal action in the analysed sample situation action is d_2, whose utility is $u(d_2) = 4.283$ billion euro. And in the situation defined by the expected payoff matrix U^* (see Table 2.3), possibly after receiving new information, it is possible to determine the utility of the subsequent available activities as:

$u^*(d_1) = -0.135$ billion euro,

$u^*(d_2) = -0.700$ billion euro,

$u^*(d_3) = -0.060$ billion euro,

$u^*(d_4) = 5.035$ billion euro,

$u^*(d_5) = -0.570$ billion euro.

This means that, according to criterion (2.6), the optimal decision in this hypothetical situation would be activity d_4, whose utility is estimated as $u^*(d_4) = 5.035$ billion euro.

According to the β criterion, the decision to invest in the purchase of new information in this situation should meet the following condition:

$$\max_i \, [\beta \min_j u_{ij}^* + (1 - \beta)\, 1/n \sum_j u_{ij}^* - c] \geq [\beta \min_j u_{ij}^* + (1 - \beta)\, 1/n \sum_j u_{ij}],$$

which is satisfied in the analyzed sample situation, since $u^*(d_4) = 5.035$ billion euro, minus the cost of investing into searching for new information $c = 0.050$ billion euro, results is 4.985 billion euro. Thus, the pragmatic value of information obtained from this decision criterion for the analyzed case is 0.702 billion euro.

2.2.4. The optimal decision related to investing in the purchase of new economic information, from the perspective of expectational criteria

The criteria discussed above take into consideration the knowledge about the cognitive attitude of the decision maker regarding his or her pessimism or optimism related to the occurrence of favorable or unfavorable events in the decision situation. We will now discuss the criteria of optimality of decisions, which may be called the a family of expectational or probabilistic criteria. These include the following criteria: 1) the expected value criterion *(Expected Value - EV)*, 2) the subjectively expected value criterion *(subjective Expected Value - SEV)*, 3) the expected utility criterion *(Expected Utility - EU)*, 4) the subjectively expected utility criterion *(Subjective Expected Utility - SEU)*.

The common feature of the four above criteria is that the decision maker uses the probability distribution on set H of hypothetical economic states. The probabilities of each state are considered in the criteria as weights which allow to calculate the expectations related to the pragmatic outcomes of the given actions (decision options), in the form of weighted sums of assessments of these outcomes, measured on a scale of values (in the case of criteria: *EV* and *SEV)* or a scale of utility (in the case: *EU* and *SEU).* The concepts of *value* and *utility* are not synonymous even in the case of a seemingly obvious object, such as money, which is the basic means of economic turnover. It is an empirically confirmed fact that the utility of money is not a rectilinear function of the value of money itself (Mosteller and Nogee 1951).

In two of the four criteria, i.e., in EV and EU, the decision analyst uses the objective probability distribution of expected economic states, represented as $\{p(h_j)\}$, while in the two other criteria (SEV and SEU), he/she uses the subjective probability distribution, labeled as $\{\varphi(h_j)\}$. However, from the formal point of view, all four expectational criteria are of the same probabilistic nature. For this reason we will choose one criterion, the EV, to present the definition of an optimal action in the sense of the family of probabilistic criteria:

$$\mathbf{d_i\ opt\ EV} \leftrightarrow \max_i \sum_j \mathbf{p(h_j)\ u_{ij}} \qquad (2.7),$$

where:

d_i *opt EV* – means an action which is optimal in terms of the expected value criterion *(EV),*

$\max_i \sum_j p(h_j)\, v_{ij}$ – means the operation which maximizes the sum of the expected results of activity d_i, weighted by the probability.

According to the principle in (2.7), the payoff matrix in the analyzed decision situation should be complemented by the probability distribution on set *H.* We will assume that this distribution, treated as *a priori,* is as follows:

$$p(h_1) = 0.30;\ p(h_2) = 0.20;\ p(h_3) = 0.50.$$

We will treat these probabilities as the weight in determining the appropriate weighted sum in assessing the utility of the possible activities in terms of *EV in* Table 2.2. The results of these analyses are as follows:

$v(d_1) = 0.565$ billion euro,

$v(d_2) = 2.790$ billion euro,

$v(d_3) = 1.270$ billion euro,

$v(d_4) = 0.300$ billion euro.

The analysis shows that the optimal action is d_2 because in terms of *EV* the weighted sum of this activity is maximal.

In a dynamic decision situation the decision maker who uses the *EV* criterion or one of the other expectational criteria, wishes to obtain data that would enable him or her to update the original *a priori* probability distribution $\{p(h_j)\}$, that is, convert it to an *a posteriori* distribution $\{p(h_j/I\}$. In the case of the analyzed sample, obtaining new information resulted in extending set *D* with a new decision option d_5, and extending *H* with a new set of hypothetical economic state h_4. These elements were not included in the *a priori* payoff matrix in Table 2.2, and appeared only in the *a posteriori* payoff matrix in Table 2.3, after the decision maker received the new information *I*. In the analyzed example, the probability distribution of the new expanded set *H,* after obtaining new information by the decision maker, is as follows:

$$p\,(h_1/I) = 0.20,\ p\,(h_2/I) = 0.10,\ p\,(h_3/I) = 0.30,\ p\,(h_4/I) = 0.40.$$

After the decision maker obtained the new information, the according weighted sums of the utilities of the given decision options are as follows:

$v^*(d_1) = 0.760$ billion euro,

$v^*(d_2) = 1.610$ billion euro,

$v^*(d_3) = 2.660$ billion euro,

$v^*(d_4) = 3.080$ billion euro,

$v^*(d_5) = 1.759$ billion euro.

The above analyzes show that the optimal action in this situation is d_4, as its value is $v(d_4) =$ 3.080 billion euro.

Investing in the purchase of new information will be an optimal action, in terms of the *EV* criterion, if the following condition is met:

$$\max_i \sum_j p(h_j)\, v^*_{ij} - c \;\geq \max_i \sum_j p(h_j)\, v_{ij}$$

If in our sample situation the cost of purchasing new information is $c = 0.050$ billion euro, the value of the optimal decision before obtaining the expected new information *I* is $v\,(d_2) = 2.790$ billion euro, and the value of an optimal decision *a posteriori*, i.e. after obtaining the new expected information, as $v^*(d_4) = 3.080$ billion euro, then the above inequality is the following:

$$3.080 \text{ billion} - 0.050 \text{ billion} \geq 2.790 \text{ billion euro.}$$

The pragmatic value of the new information purchased in the sample decision situation, according to the *EV* criterion would amount to 0.240 billion euro.

2.2.5. Comparison of the decision criteria in the analysis of optimality in seeking new information

Having reviewed the decision criteria in terms of their suitability for resolving the problem of optimality of the decision to invest in finding new information in a given decision situation, we will compare these criteria using the sample dynamic decision situation, whose *a priori* conditions are presented in the U payoff matrix in Table 2.2, and the of *a posteriori* conditions (i.e., after the forecasted obtaining of the new information) are shown in the payoff matrix U * in Table 2.3. We also assume that the investment cost of purchasing the new information is in this case $c = 0.050$ billion euro.

The results of the comparison in Table 2.7 allow to conclude that except the *maxmax* criterion, all other decision criteria identified d_2 in the *a priori* payoff matrix as the optimal action. The same tendency occurred for the *a posteriori* payoff matrix, where all the decision criteria, except the *maxmax,* and the Hurwicz criterion (where the value of α is 0,40 which means that the decision maker is a little bit more pessimistic than optimistic), pointed to d_2 as the optimal action. For the *maxmax* criterion the purchase of new information is not an optimal decision in this situation, as the pragmatic value the new information is negative for this criterion. For the remaining criteria of optimality the pragmatic value of new information is positive. In the case of criteria which operate with utility, the pragmatic value of the new information ranges from 0.240 billion euro (for the *EU,EV,SEV* and *SEU* criteria) to 0.950 billion euro (for the Savage criterion).

The observed regularities clearly indicate that, in light of as many as 9 out of the 10 considered criteria for decision making, the purchase of new information is an optimal investment in this decision situation, resulting in visible and measurable benefits for the decision maker. Only extremely optimistic decision makers, who believe that the most favorable events will occur, will consider investing in new information in the decision situation as unnecessary and too costly. This attitude, however, in certain situations may lead to a failure in decision making and would not be recommended as rational. Operating with the other criteria of decision making is more rational and should be recommended, depending on the external conditions, information on the decision maker, the sources of information and about the probability of the events in the given decision situation.

A comparison of the ten analyzed optimality criteria – *maxmin, maxmax, minimax (*the Savage criterion), the α criterion (the Hurwicz criterion), the Laplace criterion, the β, *EV, EU, SEV* and the *SEU* criteria – is presented in Table 2.7.

Table 2.7 . Comparison of optimal actions according to the optimality criteria most commonly used in the literature (where: u_{ij} – utility of the action; v_{ij} – value of the action; w_{ij} – loss resulting from the action).

Decision criteria	Optimal decision and its utility/ loss/value in terms of *a priori* (in billion euro)	Optimal decision and its utility / loss (value) in terms of *a posteriori* (in billion euro)	Is the decision to purchase new information optimal?	Pragmatic value of the new information (in billion euro)
1. Maxmin criterion	$u(d_2)$=2.500	$u^*(d_4)$= 2.80	YES	0.250
2. Maxmax criterion	$u(d_5)$= 5.100	$u^*(d_3)$= 4.70	NO	-0.450
3. Savage Criterion	$w(d_2)$=2.400	$w^*(d_4)$=1.40	YES	0.95
4.Hurwicz criterion for $\alpha = 0.4$	$u(d_4)$= 2.4600	$u^*(d_4)$= 3.100	YES	0.590
5. Laplace criterion	$u(d_2)$= 2.733	$u^*(d_4)$= 3.075	YES	0.342
6.The β criterion for $\beta = 0.70$	$u(d_2)$= 4.283	$u^*(d_4)$= 5.035	YES	0.702
7. The EV criterion	$v(d_2)$= 2.790	$v^*(d_4)$= 3.080	YES	0.240
8. The EU criterion	$u(d_2)$= 2.790	$u^*(d_4)$= 3.080	YES	0.240
9. The SEV criterion	$v(d_2)$= 2.790	$v^*(d_4)$= 3.080	YES	0.240
10. The SEU criterion	$u(d_2)$= 2.790	$u^*(d_4)$= 3.080	YES	0.240

Chapter 3.

Behavioral methods of research into finding new information in a dynamic decision situation

Having looked at the decision situation from an economic approach (in Chapter 1) and the problem of optimality of the decision to invest in searching for new information (in Chapter 2), we will review the behavioral studies on human behavior in dynamic decision-making situations where there is a possibility to use the new information. These studies belong to the mainstream of behavioral economics, which we referred to in 1.2.1. and concern the decision situation as a dynamic stimulus situation which affects the decision maker.

The present chapter begins with a discussion of selected descriptive and normative models of searching for new information by the decision maker. These models are used within the mainstream research in behavioral economics. Next, we will see a new systematization of research situations within the stream of research on information processes in a dynamic decision situation. The review will present basic research on economic behavior, which might provide suggestions to be used directly or indirectly in the analysis of economic decision situations.

In the literature, the informational activity is called *information seeking*, *purchasing, gathering, reaching,* and *obtaining*. In reality, each of these terms refers to same thing, but emphasizes a different shade of the meaning, and certain authors use these terms interchangeably, but it seems that *informational activity* and *information processing* most adequately express the totality of information processes in a dynamic decision situation. Hence, the latter terms will generally be treated as basic ones in our further considerations. Another term used in the literature is *revision of opinion,* meaning the final result of information operations. The chapter will also present the experimental approaches to economic research, including the experiments by V. Smith, a Nobel Prize winner in Economics in 2002, who is known as a promoter of the experimental method in the economic sciences.

3.1. Selected descriptive and normative models in planning research on economic behavior in a situation of seeking new information

Although specific interest in research on behavioral economics started only in the 1950s, the number of publications in this field is relatively large. Created by the pioneer of research in this field, W. Edwards (1969), the bibliography of studies on decision making until 1968 includes about 1400 items. Not all of them directly refer to issues related to informational activities, but they are related. In the last four decades (i.e. from 1970 to 2010) the studies within decision analysis included such disciplines as economics, psychology, sociology, mathematics and information technology.

An important impulse in the development of research on informational activity was the creation of new scientific disciplines such as information theory, game theory and cybernetics, and the new theories within mathematical statistics, thanks to which we could use certain mathematical models in the planning of experimental research on the behavior of people in dynamic decision-making situations. Especially using mathematical models is a stimulator for the development of ever new trends of research within decision analysis.

The formal schemes, based on which most experiments are planned on the informational activity in dynamic decision situations, are mathematical models of game theory. The experiments often use the specific type of a decision-making model of a two-person game, called game with nature or against nature. In game theory, the *nature* means a player who is not interested in their winning or losing and behaves in a random way. But a human being playing with the *nature* understood in such way, is clearly interested in the possible win or loss[16].

Behavioral experiments often use schemas of the so-called game in the normal form, of a one-step type[17]. Typical schemas of games with the nature in the normal form assume the existence of at least two sets of possible actions of the decision maker: set $D = \{d_1, d_2, ..., d_i, ..., d_n\}$ and a set of at least two hypothetical states of nature, called states of things, i.e. set $H = \{h_1, h_2, ..., h_j, ..., h_m\}$. Carrying out a game with the nature in its normal form implies choosing one of the possible actions by the decision maker, with simultaneous the occurrence of one of the possible states of affairs. If the decision maker chooses action d_i while there occurs the state of affairs h_j, then the outcome of the game may be determined as v_{ij}, often called a

[16] A game with nature is mostly treated as a non-zero-sum game, because the trends of nature are not against the human being. In a typical experimental game, a real partner in the game is another person.

[17] In addition to games of a normal type, game theory also distinguishes an extensive game, also called a multi-step game, where a sequence of movements is performed by players in a specific order.

payoff in game theory. The game outcome is defined as utility u_{ij} – obtained by the decision maker when he or she selects action d_i and hypothesis h_j proves to be true.

In experimental decision-making game situations there is usually an *a priori* probability distribution on the set of possible states of affairs. The decision-making game participant is usually able to change this distribution by obtaining probabilistic information-bearing data about the state of things. The sub-disciplines of mathematics dealing with probability theory, provide a basis to construct models of the probability distribution changes in a dynamic decision situation. In the group of mathematical models the division into normative and descriptive models is still valid and proves to be useful (Kozielecki 1968). In the following sections we will review the commonly used mathematical models which allow to account for the behavior of the decision maker in a dynamic decision situation.

3.1.1. Normative models

Ideal models, also called normative models, have an essential heuristic function in scientific cognition and allow the development of new hypotheses about the behavior of humans under certain conditions. They also give the possibility to plan appropriate experimental situations which would enable to verify these hypotheses. We will review the normative mathematical models with regard to the following criteria: 1) the representativeness of the particular type of research problem, 2) the frequency of its use, 3) the prospects associated with using the model, 4) a relatively low degree of complexity of its formal shape. The overview of models will contain only a schematic description. A more extensive discussion of the models may be found in the cited literature.

Information theory models

As far as the kind of information possible to be obtained by the decision maker is concerned, the models may be grouped into those that allow to receive sure information and those where the decision maker receives probabilistic information. In the first group of models a particularly useful one is information theory (Shannon and Weaver 1949), whose axiomatic approach allows a quantitative measure of information as the difference between the successive states of uncertainty (vagueness, entropy):[18]

---

[18] Usually, after Shannon, the symbol H means uncertainty. In this book the symbol H means the degree of uncertainty which is defined in units of mostly bit: 1 bit of uncertainty is the situation when the system does not know what is the

$$I\,(H, X) = N\,(H)\text{-}N\,(H, X), \qquad (3.1),$$

where: $I\ (H,\ X)$ - the amount of information (measured in bits) which brings the average signal from set X about an event from the set H of possible events, $N(H)$ - unconditional uncertainty as to the occurrence of one of the events belonging to set H, $N(H,\ X)$ conditional uncertainty about the occurrence of one of the events belonging to set H after receiving one of the signals from set X.

The unconditional uncertainty, in turn, is determined by the formula:

$$N(H{=}{-}\Sigma p(h_j)log_2 p(h_j), \text{ where } h_j \in H \qquad (3.2),$$

and the conditional uncertainty is expressed, respectively, as:

$$N(H/X) = -\Sigma p(h_j/x)\ log_2\ p(h_j/x), \text{ where } x. \in X \qquad (3.3).$$

The first attempts to apply the normative model of information theory to experiments on the acquisition of reliable information in the U.S. were made by Hovland (1952), while in Europe they were made by Tichomirow and his colleagues (Tichomirow et al 1964). In the Polish literature the proposal to use the Shannon's quantitative measure to analyze the behavior of subjects in a situation of searching for reliable information may be found, among others, in Biela (1971, 1972).

The Bayesian model and its modifications

In situations with a supply of probabilistic information[19], the most well-known normative model, which also constitutes the basis for planning experimental studies, is the Bayesian model. This model defines the ideal – in a statistical sense – way of modifying the initial probability distribution on a set of hypotheses under the influence of new signals.

$$p(h_j / x_i) = \frac{p(h_j)p(x_i/h_j)}{\sum_{j=1}^{j=n} p(h_j)p(x_i / h_j)}, \qquad (3.4.)$$

This modification is a function of the *a priori* probabilities, which is reflected in the model[20]:

possibility of becoming one of two equally likely events .When ascertaining the occurrence of one event one can say that the arrangement was a bit of information. Measures of the binary are of course only in those cases where the base of the logarithm in formulas (3.1) (3.2) and (3 .3) is the number 2; the case of other bases will operate on the logarithm of the other metrics, such as decimals, etc.

19 Informational activity with an unreliable source of information is commonly referred to in literature as *Probabilistic Information Processing* (abbreviated PIP). Ways of understanding this term are described by G.F. Pitz (1970).

20 As we can see, formula (3.4) may be used to calculate the indeterminacy of formula (3.3), in which there is an *a posteriori* probability.

where: $p(h_j/x_i)$ – means the *a posteriori* probability of state h_j of the source after receiving the signal x_i; $p(h_j)$ – is the *a priori* probability of state h_j of the source, and $p(x_i/h_j)$ – means the conditional probability of an emission of signal x_i with the state h_j of the source.

A pioneer in the application of this formula in statistics was F. Ramsey (1931). This formula is justified only under the assumption of the so-called Bayesian statistics, where basic assumptions were formulated by R. Schlaifer (1959) are as follows: 1) the probability of the event is a structured opinion, 2) the inferences based on the data is nothing but a revision of that opinion in the context of the new message. W. Edwards, H. Lindman and L.J. Savage (1963) broadly discuss the role of Bayesian statistics in the analysis of decision-making.

One of the versions of the Bayesian model is its product formula of the initial probability and the ratio of conditional probabilities[21]:

$$\Omega_1 = \Omega_0 L, \tag{3.5}$$

where: Ω_1 – means the *a posteriori* probability, Ω_0 – means the *a priori* probability; L – means the ratio of the conditional probabilities. The product form of the Bayesian model is frequently used by decision analysts due to the greater efficiency of using the ratio of probabilities *(likelihood ratio).* Green and Sweets (1966), among others, who analyse the detection of signal, propose in their experiments to operate with only the ratio of the probabilities as a model for the revision of a probabilistic opinion, regardless of the *a priori* probability of the hypothesis.

In the case of two hypotheses, h_1 and h_2, to describe the situation with respect to the ratio of probabilities one should perform the following calculation:

$$L_{1,2} = \frac{p(x_i / h_1)}{p(x_i / h_2)} \tag{3.6}$$

If the number n of hypotheses is greater than 2, a full statistical characterization would require a calculation of n-1 relationships[22]. In the decision-making experiments (e.g. Pitz 1967, 1970), a modified logarithmic Bayesian model is also used (e.g. Pitz 1967, 1970 and Peterson, Schneider, Miller 1965):

$$\log\Omega_1 = \log\Omega_0 + \log L \tag{3.7}$$

[21] The products (formula 3.5) may be deduced from (3.4).

[22] For example, when $n = 4$, then one should calculate the probabilities of the three $L23 = \frac{L21}{L31}; L34 = \frac{L14}{L13}$. on is determined by three others, and when L_{12}, L_{13}, L_{14} are known, other values are:

Despite the criticism of the Bayesian rule by some authors, because of its normative nature (e.g. Wolf E. 1995; Smith 2004), this model is still used in behavioral decision studies (see Holt 2007), as its methodological advantages allow to determine to what extent and under what conditions it describes the behavior of decision makers, as well as how and when deviations from this model may be observed with real decision makers.

Integrative Models

An attempt to answer the question: How does one combine the information carried by the signals? – is made by the integrative models. Their systematization was presented by Stachowski (1973), who distinguished four basic types of integrative models, referring to: conjunction, alternative, lexicography and compensation. Although, as demonstrated by Coombs and Kao (1966), between the first two types of these models there is no mathematical difference, Stachowski points out that from the behavioral standpoint, these models are not identical. Regardless of their psycho-behavioral specificity, one must mention that a conjunction, in terms of formal logic, differs essentially from alternative. If one conjunctively integrates information, all signals – the compounds of the conjunction – must contain adequate information about the state of things, while in integration using alternatives it is sufficient that only one of the signals is a carrier of certain information.

The lexicographic model assumes first to order the signal characteristics of the stimuli in terms of their validity, and then requires a next selection because of the importance of the variables. This model, as not having a mathematical foundation, has not found wider application in decision-making experiments. Integrating information in a decision situation using a compensation model is based on mutual complementing of the dimensions of the stimuli carrying information. These models are based on the method of a multiple regression analysis and multivariable analysis. Models based on regression analysis were the basis of the Anderson's (1968) theory of integrating information, where information is described by two parameters: the value of the stimulus measured on a subjective scale of the decision maker and the weight of the stimulus. This model has the following form:

$$R = C + \sum_{i=0}^{i=n} w_i s_i, \qquad (3.8),$$

where: R - reaction force measured on a scale; C - a constant that specifies the beginning of any scale of the reaction, and $w_i s_i$ – denotes information after the obtained signal i.

The approach of behavioral economics is based on theories of learning, which assume that efficient economic behavior can be learned under the influence of adequate stimulation. It is therefore not surprising that learning models are widely used both in basic research on economic behavior and in practical application (e.g. in training and advising policy makers).

The basis of the models in the Bayesian situation is the assumption that the human learns to assess the *a priori* probability of events based on the data available in the given situation. It is understood that his behavior *(R)* is a function of the stimulus-signal *(X)* carrying the information and an intermediate variable *(0)*, thus: $R = f(x, 0)$.

According to Chlewiński (1972a), theories of learning allow to predict behavior in laboratory situations more accurately. Here he gives an example of the theory of sampling from the population of the stimuli-elements, formulated by Estes. The main terms of this theory are: stimulus, response, reinforcement and association, defined as axiomatic. Estes divides its main assumptions into two parts: 1) sampling from the population of stimuli-elements, and 2) the response to the stimuli.

1. Selection of stimuli items. Any perception of stimuli is a choice from set *N* of stimuli-elements, where the whole set of stimuli is divided as a dichotomy into two subsets: (a) the subset of efficient items in the sample, and (b) a subset of inefficient items outside the sample. The division criterion depends on the sampling scheme. The probability of receiving a specific element in the sample is a function of the number of choices or on the preceding events. If *Xn* denotes a series of stimuli, responses and reinforcing events that occurred to event *n-1* inclusive, then the probability of selecting item *i* within the sample in event *n* is a function of *Xn,* which is defined as *i(Xn)*. Thus, we may formulate the assumption that

$$\sum_{i=1}^{N} \sigma(\mathrm{x_n}) = 1 \qquad (3.9).$$

W.K. Estes originally assumed that all stimuli-elements have the same probability of getting into a sample of a fixed size. Later, however, it was assumed that the sample size may vary, and each element has its own probability of being drawn – which is fixed at the time of the experiment.

2. The second assumption concerns the pairing of each stimulus with only one response. In defining this reaction it is assumed that (a) only items from the current sample determine the reaction, and the stimuli that were not included in the sample do not affect this

reaction at all, (b) all elements of the stimulus in the sample have the same weight in determining reaction. The examples of mathematical models remaining in the mainstream of the general theory by Estes may be found in Chlewiński (1972b), who introduced a division into the following three groups of models: 1) conditioning and adaptation, 2) strategy selection, 3) the selection of hypotheses and conditioning.

Another learning process, based on mathematical models of information seeking behavior within the behavioral school, is a process of differentiating stimuli, whose analysis was used including linear discriminant functions.

Models of a *"random walk "*

Models known in literature as *general random walk models* are a distinct group of probabilistic models (Pitz 1970). Their assumption is that human being in an uncertain situation operates with two values on a scale of subjective beliefs, which are confidence and uncertainty. In this model a subjective probability of a continuum variable character is not accepted. Both subjective states in this model change stochastically depending on the type of stimuli selected in the sample. On the basis of the law governing the stochastic process, it is possible to determine the probability that, after drawing a stimulus, the decision maker will change his or her belief. The general idea of the *random walk* is illustrated in Figure 3.1, after Pitz (1970). The diagram in this figure shows that the decision maker operates only with two states of belief. This conviction, after receiving a signal does not change randomly, but probabilistically, as shown by the arrows in the figure: left or right, depending on the received signal.

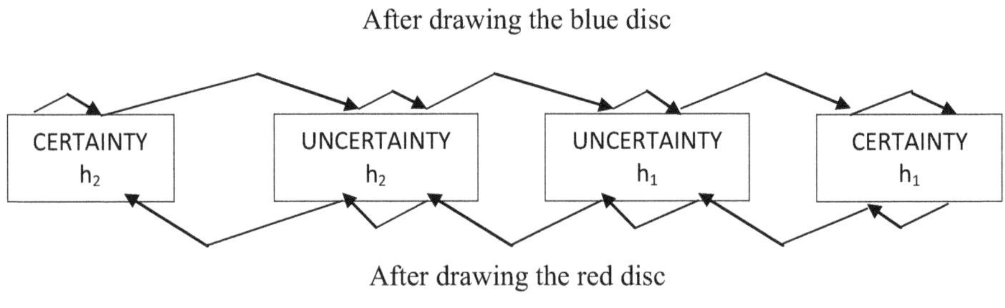

Figure 3.1. Scheme of the model of a *random walk* (after Pitz1970)

If the decision maker is certain about hypothesis h_1 after receiving a signal of a red disc, he/she "goes left" and maintains his/her assertion, or falls into a state of uncertainty as to the hypothesis. If the subject is uncertain as to hypothesis h_1, i.e. after drawing the blue disc he/she could "go right", but did not change the belief, or could "go ahead" and change it to the a belief which opposes the hypothesis. The transition from one state of belief to another depends on the probabilistic relationships between the decision maker's beliefs and the structure of the incentives.

This model gave the basis for the Markov models of learning and a model of signal detection, based on the assumption of three degrees of assertion, constructed by Kranz (1969).

Markov chain model

In decision analysis it is not always assumed (even approximately) that the random variables are statistically independent. Then it is convenient to use the Markov chain model in situations of gaining new information. This model is the basis for the theory of the Markov stochastic processes (Fisz 1967). This may is briefly described below.

We assume that a sequence of events is *n,* and that the result of each experiment is one and only one event from the set of possible states of affairs (as a set which is finite or countable, and its components constitute events which mutually exclude each other in pairs). We define that event h_I is the state h_j of the system. The symbol h_j^n will mean that the state was obtained in experiment n and h_j^0 will mean the initial state. By p_{ij}^n we will mean the conditional probability that, after the experiment *n,* event h_j, occurs if the system was in state h_i after the experiment of *n-1,* i.e.

$$p_{ij}^n = p(h_j^n / h_i^{n-1}) \quad (3.10).$$

A string of experimental results is related in a Markov chain if:

1) for *i, j, n* = 1, 2, 3, ... the following equalities are true:

$$p_{ij}^n = p(h_j^n / h_i^{n-1}) = p(h_j^n / h_i^{n-1}, \ldots, h_{i-2}^{n-2}, h_{i-1}^{n-1}, h_0^0 \quad (3.11)$$

2) for *i, j* =1, 2, 3 the probability p_{ij}^n does not depend on n, i.e.

$$p_{ij}^n = p_{ij} \ (n = 1,2, \ldots) \quad (3.12).$$

Thus, the probability of a transition from state h_i to state h_j depends only on h_i and does not depend on the earlier events. The Markov dynamic decision situation will need to be characterized by the so-called switch matrix, whose elements are the probability of transition from h_i to h_j.

In decision situations of a dynamic type, to study the informational activity, the Wald model is often used, which is a sequential decision making model, also called a statistical sequential quotient test (Wald 1947). It applies to the sequential procedure in the verification of a statistical hypothesis, where the sample size is not fixed in advance, and each drawn element may be associated with choosing one of the three decision options: 1) an adoption of the hypothesis, 2) a rejection of the hypothesis and accepting another one, 3) continuing the investigation, i.e., drawing a next item as a sample from the population.

For purposes of a description of this sequential test, we will assume that x is a random variable whose distribution depends on parameter Q. As in the experiments of decision making, the variable x is normally of a jump/step type function, $f(x,Q)$ will mean the function of the probability of this variable: $p = f(x,Q)$.

We will also assume that the value of parameter Q is not known and that there are two hypotheses specifying the value: 1) h_1 $(Q = Q_1)$, 2) h_2 $(Q = Q_2)$, where $Q_1 \neq Q$. Depending on the numbers: α and β, respectively, for the error of type I and II[23], figures A and B are determined, where $0 < B < 1 < A$. In the case of x, meaning the first observation, one should also accept the following symbols: $p_{21}=(x_1,Q_2)$, $p_{11}=(x_1, Q_1)$. In this context, the diagram showing the activity according to the sequential test has the form:

1. h_1 should be rejected in favor of h_2, if:

$$\frac{p21}{p11} \geq A. \qquad (3.13)$$

2. Hypothesis h_1, should be adopted when:

$$\frac{p21}{p11} \leq B \qquad (3.14)$$

3. Please continue the observation of x_2, if:

$$B < \frac{p21}{p1\,1} < A \qquad (3.15)$$

[23] In statistics type I of error is considered an error of rejecting the hypothesis h_1 if it is true. The probability of making this error is denoted by α. The error of type II is made if the hypothesis h_1 is accepted while it is false. Its probability is denoted by β. In statistics textbooks the so-called null hypothesis is defined as H_0, and the competitive hypothesis as H_1. In this book, the symbols h_1 and h_2 are used for the sake of uniformity of formal expressions.

If the inequality 3.15 is satisfied, the sequential procedure is repeated after further observations: $x_2,\ x_3,\ \ldots,\ x_n$ until the final decision is made. The conditions of making this decision, the way of calculating parameters A and B and other statistical issues associated with the sequential test are exhaustively discussed by Fisz (1967).

3.1.2. Descriptive models

In studies on the informational activities we may see two stages: 1) the sole use of normative models, 2) attempts to develop descriptive models. These stages represent the logical consequence of the experimental research methodology which involves deductive reasoning at the starting point of analysis, and induction in the later stages of the test procedure. The two types of models use different criteria. As far as the normative models are concerned, the basic requirement is the pragmatic criterion according to which one may only decide more or less their utility (in terms of its heuristic, systematizing or other value) for experimental studies. On the other hand, the descriptive models are evaluated in accordance to their adequacy of describing human behavior.

It is be difficult to comprehensively discuss all models of descriptive information operations used by theorists of decision. We will thus restrict our review to a few examples of models representing typical orientations in decision analysis.

Experimental research on decision indicates that there are very rare conditions in which normative models would describe the behavior of decision makers. We may specify three methods for constructing descriptive models of information operations: 1) by replacing certain variables in the models of objective normative values by subjective ones, 2) by introducing certain subjective parameters into normative models – identified in the analysis of the behavioral deviations from the models, 3) a combination of the two above methods.

One example of the first type of structure may be any attempt to replace the model of Bayesian objective probability – by a subjective one, usually calculated indirectly based on the choices made by the decision maker[24]. For example Edwards and Slovic (1965) in the normative version of the Bayesian model, substituted the ratio of objective probabilities with the ratio of subjective probabilities. Peterson, Schneider and Miller (1965), in turn, instead of

[24] The method of indirect measurement of subjective probability was introduced by F. Ramsey (1931).The exact description of some methods of measuring the probability can be found in T. Tyszka (1968, 1970). Comparison of factors, both direct and indirect measurement of the likelihood of simple and complex events (conjunctive, alternative, disjunctive) was carried out by Bujak (1974).

the logarithmic ratio of probabilities introduced a concept called *accuracy ratio,* which is expressed in the following form[25]:

$$AR = SLLR / BLLR \quad (3.16),$$

where:

$$SLLR = \frac{\psi(x_i / h_1)}{\psi(x_i / h_2)}; \qquad BLLR = \frac{p(x_i / h_1)}{p(x_i / h_2)}$$

where $\psi(x_i/h_1)$, $\psi(x_i/h_2)$- indicate the subjective conditional probability that signal x_i comes from a relevant source h_1 or h_2.

An example of another way of constructing models is a descriptive proposal by Phillips and Edwards (1966), which was created from formula (3.5) by supplementing it with a new empirical parameter[26]:

$$\tilde{\Omega}_1 = L^c \Omega_o \quad (3.17)$$

where $\tilde{\Omega}_1$ - *a posteriori* subjective probability of the decision maker; L, Ω_o - as previously (in formula 3.5); c is a function of b (i.e., the difference in the proportion of the red and blue circles in urns) for $b > 0.2$, while for $b < 0.2$ - c is a function of b and $(2r-n)$. The idea to introduce parameter c into the model occurred to the authors who analyzed one of the types of deviations from the normative Bayesian model that are defined in the literature as cognitive conservatism, which is based on underestimating the probabilities (Biela 2001). Another study used the decision making descriptive model as a modified log-linear form of the Bayesian model (Pitz 1970). This model was constructed by replacing the objective probabilities L ratio in the Bayesian model (3.7) by the subjective ratio λ and by introducing two new parameters: the weighting factor α and the random error factor ε. The descriptive model after these modifications is the following:

$$\log\Omega_n = \alpha \log \Omega_{n-1} + \log \lambda + \varepsilon. \quad (3.18)$$

In constructing descriptive models of the process of finding information in decision situations one often uses results based on theories of learning. An example of such approach is the Cooper and Johri's model of learning by doing (2002) or the model of experiential

[25] The symbols used in the text are those typically encountered in the literature. The individual elements indicate the first letters of the concept denoted: *SLLR* is short term: *Subjective Likefihood Logarithm Ratio* (log ratio of subjective probabilities); *BLLR* is short for: *Bayesian Logarithm Liketihood Ratio* (logarithm of the ratio of Bayesian probabilities), *AR is* short for: *Accuracy Ratio* (close ratio).

[26] Symbol *d* (the difference in English) is used most frequently in the literature to determine the difference in the proportion of spheres of two different colors of urns, *r* is the number of the red balls, and *n* is the total number of balls in the sample . In this work *d b* was replaced by *d b,* as the former one already has a different fixed meaning.

learning, suggesting differentiation of cognitive styles in information processes (Burchell, Kolb 2006).

A separate approach in constructing descriptive models of searching for information in situations of decision-making are simulation studies. Examples of such methodological approach may include modeling risky business decisions using the concept of bounded rationality by H. Simon (Chen, Hogg 2008) simulations of collective economic decisions based on expert data, taking into account the characteristics of an emotional decision situation and persuasive arguments (Marreiros et al 2010) and interactive model searching for information in complex decision situations, called PLATT (Kamphuis et al 2010).

3.2. Systematization of research on seeking for new information in decision situations

After reviewing the models for searching new information, we will try to systematize the study of behavioral situations based on these models. We first define the criteria for the systematization of these situations. As a criterion for systematization we understand a principle that would enable a logical division, classification, typology, clarification or even a rearrangement of certain elements of the test situation.

As for experiments on searching for formation, it would be difficult to extract a single criterion for the distribution of all situations and experimental techniques. It would always contain limited aspects, therefore, a categorization conducted on this basis would be incomplete and inadequate[27].

Before a systematic review of information seeking in decision situations, we should first of all mention the surveys carried out the literature in this field to date. The first systematic review of literature in this field, covering the period 1953-1968, was made by Edwards (1968). Biela (1976) conducted a meta-analysis of decision-making literature including a systematic position of research, techniques, and discussing the experimental results obtained synthetically by these studies. A large review of studies on the search for information was published by Case (2007). This review, however, covers a much wider range of literature than is necessary for the purposes of this monograph, as it also relates to research on aspects of searching for information outside decision situations. In our review, we will essentially follow the line designated by Edwards (1969) and Biela (1976), but also expand the scope with new experimental studies, particularly related to behavioral economics. The criterion for systematization accepted here is the object of experimental research and

[27] The most comprehensive review of the criteria for allocation of the decision situation was presented by Ekel (1970).

independent variables that are the subject to manipulation by researchers, such as: type of decision situation, the type of information source, the number of hypotheses, the probability of the initial hypotheses, the informativeness of signals, the number of available signals, the parameter of time, payment and cost of information, the type of instruction, the number of decision makers, how to measure the subjective probability, processes and factors that facilitate the search of information in the decision situation.

Type of decision-making situations

The main criterion for systematizing the studies on the search for information is the type of decision situation in which the decision maker is seeking information to reduce his/her uncertainty in this situation. We may consider a number of different criteria for the categorizing dynamic decision-making situations. One of the most fundamental issues is the analyzed period within the decision process, i.e. the pre-decision processes (e.g. Swani 1969, Kozielecki 1969), the exact time of decision-making (i.e. the act of choice, which is the essence of decision-making) or the time after the decision, called a post-decision process (Shani, Zeelenberg 2007, Shani, Tykocinski, Zeelenberg 2008).

The criteria for systematizing decision-making situations also include the conditions under which a decision is taken. This might be the objective or subjective conditions of rationality of the decision-making (Chen, Hogg 2008). Another criterion is the possibility or impossibility of making a so-called fuzzy decision (Tosi, Mero, Rizzo 2000). This concept is derived from the fuzzy set theory and indicates that the range of the sets is so vague that their elements may belong to more than one set at a time.

An important factor analyzed in situations of decision-making are emotions (Vohs et al 2007) and, more specifically, awareness of the emotional context in which the decision maker is looking for information (Mareiros et al 2010). For research on information seeking it the division of decision situations into static and dynamic ones is also important. A subset of the latter ones are situations of a sequential search for information (Berryman 2006, Hausman, L Age 2008).

Economic decisions

By economic decisions we understand such decision making situations whose content of decision, model of analysis and research results may be used in economic theory or practice.

Experimental studies of economic decisions began with an analysis of microeconomic systems (Smith 1982), managerial and consumer decisions (Tosi, Mero, Rizzo 2000; Scholtz, Wagner 2005). A formal model of research on decision making has also been used in analyses of strategic investment (Butler, Pike 1993), investment risk on the stock market (Ilard and Lipschitz 2006) and in studies on investment risk preferences (Felton et al 2003). Decision analysis was also used in the area of finance and accounting (Rockenbach 2004; Booker, Drake, Heitger 2007; Ricciardi 2008) and in financial market supervision (Adamus and Łasak 2010). Research on the capital market is methodologically advanced in terms of using experimental methods. Examples are Smith's experimental study on 72 market assets (Smith 2004).

Type of information sources

Due to the nature of the sources of information, experimental situations may be divided dichotomously into those where the decision maker may use qualitatively different sources of information (heterogeneous sources) and those where we are able to receive information from only one source (uniform source). Situations with a uniform source may be divided into: a) situations with a source of information which is reliable, categorical, certain, and b) situations with a source of information which is unreliable, uncertain, probabilistic. Experiments on the informational activity in situations a) and b) are two distinct types of research, based on different assumptions and experimental traditions. They have also developed independently and have different models of planning experiments.

The sources of information may also be categorized with regard to other criteria, such as the emission of signal series carrying information which is "consistent" or "incompatible" with the previously obtained information, or with regard to the degree of reliability of the information sources. Research on situations where the source emits a series of such signals includes experiments on the acquisition of concepts, carried out by Bruner and colleagues (1956) and Tichomirov and others (1964), i.e. experiment situations where decision makers may receive "yes" or "no" signals.

Less numerous experiments explored the informational activity in situations where decision makers have the opportunity to use more than one source signal. Examples are experiments conducted by Burrows and Okada (1973), who studied the informational activity in a situation with two signal sources: a semantic and a formal one. Hockey (1973) was interested in changes in the selection of warning signals emitted from multiple sources.

The number of hypotheses

As regards the third above criterion – the number of hypotheses in a decision situation – a classification of the experiments is relatively simple. Most studies were conducted on seeking information in situations of a choice between two alternatives. Experiments regarding this type of situation may be planned based on all mathematical models discussed above. It is for the situation of a choice between two-alternatives that most of the known regularities of informational activities in decision making have been found.

Initial probability of hypotheses

A systematization of experimental situations with regard to determining the probability distribution on the set of alternatives was given by Brichaček (1970). This author distinguishes: three types of situations: 1) situations where decision makers know the precise objective probability (in terms of the frequency of events, such as when you roll the dice, coin, etc.) when the subjective probability is exactly equal to the objective or if it differs only in certain extreme cases, 2) situations where the objective probability of events may be assessed only by an estimation (e.g. the expected exchange rate, the probability of a global crisis in the economy, and 3) situations where an objective determination of the likelihood of events is impossible (for example, forecasting if the following July will be sunny at the Baltic seaside, and therefore whether to accept a given marketing strategy). According to this author, most experiments focus on the study of informational activities in situations of the first kind, much fewer on testing the second type of situations, and examples of research situations of the third type include only experiments by such authors as Atkinson et al (1964), Jamison and Kozielecki (1968) and Kozielecki (1969). (Brichaček 1970).

Informativeness of signals and their precision of communication

In experimental situations an independent variable is also the informativeness of signals, called the diagnostic value of the signals (e.g. Snapper and Peterson 1971). If the emitted signals are independent events (i.e. the element is drawn "with returning"), their informativeness is only a function of the ratio of conditional probabilities. Examples of experiments where signal informativeness is an independent variable, i.e. where the proportions of white balls to black ones *(bag composition)* were changed include research by authors like Peterson and others (1968), Peterson and Swensson (1968), Vlek and Beintema (1967), Vlek and Van der Heijden (1967), Pitz et al (1969), Marks (1969) and Radzicki (1974).

Decision situations where the signals are not independent random events (the drawn element is not returned into the lot), the informativeness also depends on the sequence of signals. In assessing the informativeness decision makers take into account not only the conditional probability that the signal originates from a given source (data at the beginning of the experiment), but also learn to assess the conditional probability of an occurrence of a given signal in a sequence (Messick 1970) .

The number of available signals in the decision situation

With regard to the number of signals possible to be obtained – which is an independent variable – experiments are often dichotomously divided into situations of: 1) a limited range of signals, and 2) an unlimited range of signals. For example, Pitz (1968) and Goode (1962) conducted a comparative analysis of the behavior of decision makers in situations of limited and unlimited possibilities of purchasing signals.

Time as a variable in experiments

Using time as a parameter in classifying experimental situations we may distinguish those where the response time may be treated as a dependent variable, and thus acts as an indicator of progress in information, and situations where the timing is not at all taken into account. In the latter situations the measurement of time is not used as an indicator of the decision difficulties. The time parameter, measured as latency time, was a useful indicator of characterizing decisions in slightly more complex situations (see experiments by Audley 1964 and Gottsdanker 1969, Davis et al 1968, S. Streufert and S.G. Streufert 1968). It should be noted that in these experiments time was generally regarded as an indicator of difficult decisions and not of the informational activity process. Thus, the reaction time is regarded as a measurement of two different aspects of the dependent variable in these two groups of experiments. Yet another example of the response time as a dependent variable are experiments on decision making where the latency time before the decision was treated as a measure of the strength of the conflict faced by the decision maker in the situation of decision making (Diederich and Busenmeyer 2003).

The amount of payoff and the cost of information

Taking into account the size of the award/payoff, i.e. the structure of the payoff matrix and the cost of purchasing information, after Manze (1970), one may adopt a distinction of decision situations into ones where the payoff is determined from the beginning as established *explicite* and those where the payoff and cost of information are not stable.

Type of instruction as an independent variable

Taking into account the type of instruction in the experiments, most researchers do not take this factor into account as an experimental variable in decision making. The impact of the type of instruction on the behavior of decision makers in situations with probabilistic information was studied only by Pitz and Downing (1967). Unfortunately, this variable was not given more attention in decision making experiments, as the results of such research might shed a new light on the processes of searching for information in decision situations.

The number of decision makers in the decision situation

Considering the number of decision makers, experiments may be divided into typical studies on the informational activity in situations of individual decision makers (e.g. the classic experiments by Edwards, Phillips, Peterson and many other authors cited above), and experiments on group decision making (e.g. Wallach and Kogan 1967, Scodel, Ratoosh and Minas 1960, Davis, Hoppe and Hornseth 1968). There are also experiments where individual decisions were compared with group ones (such as by Middleton and Warren 1972, Chlewiński 1975). One should also mention group decision experiments in small groups (e.g. Driver and Hunsaker 1972, White and Davies 1996), and group decisions in social microstructures (Schotter 2008) and group decisions made under time pressure (Linkov et al 2008) and in the context of emotional involvement (Mareiros et al 2010).

Ways of measuring probability

Because of the way of measuring the probability we may divide experiments into such which used a direct measurement of subjective probability (i.e. a verbal assessment of this probability was asked of the decision makers), and those where the subjective probability was measured indirectly – on the basis of the choices considered. A description of both types of experimental situation may be found in the works b Martin and Gettys (1969) and Bujak (1972, 1974). Measuring the dependent variables in decision-making experiments one should also consider the methodological importance of research proposals based on multivariable and multi-criteria approach. Examples here include the – already regarded as classic – experiments by Anker and colleagues (1963).

The processes and factors that facilitate the search for information in a decision situation

Taking into account the processes and factors affecting the course of searching for information in decision-making situations, examples of the following experiments should be mentioned: experiments aimed to study the learning processes in these situations (Burchell and Kolb 2006), experiments testing information seeking (Cohen and Meudell 1968, Pitz 1969), research on the development of decision processes (Biela, Chlewiński, Walesa 1983) and experiments where information seeking is interpreted in terms of complex interactions (Connaway 2008).

Summary of the criteria

A synthetic comparison of the criteria used to systematize experimental situations in decision research is shown in Table 3.1, based on works by Biela (1976, 2001).

Table 3.1. Summary of the criteria used to systematize experiments on informational activity in decision situations

1. **Number of sources**	heterogeneous situation	unreliable source of information
	homogeneous situation	reliable source of information
2. **Number of hypotheses**	two-alternative-situation	
	three-alternative-situation	
	four-alternative-situation, etc.	
3. **Initial probability of hypotheses**	situations with a known objective probability	
	situations where it is possible to precisely assess the objective probability	
	situations where the objective probability is impossible to be determined	
4. **Informativeness of signals**	experiments treating the informativeness of signals as stable	
	experiments treating the informativeness of signals as varying	
5. **The number of available signals**	situations with a limited number of signals	
	situations with an unlimited number of signals	

6. **Time parameter**	situations where the timing is measured	
	situations where the timing does contribute anything to the description of informational activity	
7. **Type of instruction**	situations where the type of instruction is treated as a variable	
	situations where equal instruction is given to all participants	
8. **Number of decision makers**	situations of collective decision-making	small groups
		social microstructures
	individual decision-making situations	
	situations with a possibility of comparing the individual and group decision making	
9. **Ways to measure the probability**	situations where the probability of hypotheses is measured directly	
	situations where the probability of hypotheses is measured indirectly	
10. **Payoff matrix**	situations with a constant payoff matrix	
	situations with a variable payoff matrix	
11. **Type of decision situation**	pre-decision situations	static situations
		dynamic situations
	decision-making situations	
	post-decision situations	

The presented systematization indicates that the elements of individual divisions of the experimental situations are mutually related in various ways. Experiments may take into account various features of the decision situation. A more precise description of the research techniques in these situations is presented by Biela (2001). The following section will focus on discussing research techniques in situations with an unreliable source of information (probabilistic information) and the most common patterns of decision analysis in such situations.

3.3. Research techniques using an unreliable source of information and the most common patterns of decision analysis in such situations

Techniques and patterns of experiments examining the informational activity with an unreliable source of information may be divided into six groups:

1. laboratory techniques based on classical urn patterns *(urns-and-balls, bookbags-and-pockerchips)* or dice;
2. techniques based on typical patterns of psychophysical experiments concerning signal detection;
3. experimental techniques based on urn, dice schemas, etc., but applied in laboratory situations similar to natural conditions (e.g. simulation of the global market), which may be described as quasi-natural;
4. natural experiments;

5. simulation studies;
6. techniques based on urn or cube and psychophysical schemas, but applied to study problems related to human capital management, management components, brand equity and brand image.

3.3.1. Classic Techniques

Classical techniques of research on informational activity with an unreliable source of information include laboratory experiment procedures based on random event schemas, such as: drawing from an urn, throwing dice or coins, and a diagram of simple gambling games.

Urn schemes

In simple urn schemes the experimental situation is defined as follows: 1) there are two possible states of affairs: h_1 and h_2;, 2) there are two possible types of signals: x_1 and x_2. In decision games based on an urn scheme the decision maker is presented two urns with poker discs of red and blue. Each urn contains a different proportion of red discs to blue ones. The experimenter informs the decision maker on these proportions, hides the two urns, and the participant draws a sample of n discs. The task of the decision maker is to decide on the basis of a randomly selected sample, which urn the discs were drawn from. After seeing the sample, the participant may be required to verbally assess his or her belief as to the urn from which the discs were drawn, and then to make a final decision. Certain researchers do not require the participant to make his or her subjective verbal assessment of the probability, since the latter is defining with an indirect method.

The urn scheme has its numerous modifications, which generally relate to : a) the way the discs are drawn (in some experiments discs are drawn one by one, each time asking the participant to assess the probability of the hidden urn), b) the number of hypotheses (three or more urns are sometimes used).

Dicing schemes

The scheme of an experiment based on dicing may be explained using the example of the study of Pitz and Downing (1967). The experimenters presented the decision maker two dice: 1) cube K_1 with the letter B on three walls and the letter O on the other three, 2) cube K_2

with the letter B on four walls and the letter O on the other two. One of the dice was randomly chosen by the experimenter and thrown five times, and the participant was informed about each letter that was thrown. After five consecutive throws the decision maker had to determine which of the two dice was used.

A slightly different scheme based on dicing is provided, among others, by Green and Sweets (1966). The participants were presented three cubes: two ordinary dice with a number of points from 1 to 6, and a third dice with 3 points on three sides and the remaining three walls blank. The experimenter threw all cubes together, revealing only the total number of the points on all the dice (the respondents did not see the dice being thrown). The task of the game participants was to guess whether the result of the "unusual" cube was three or zero points.

3.3.2. Psychophysical schemes and signal detection

Dice schemes served as a model for decision analysis of the signal detection theory. Experiments of this kind are typical psychophysical procedures where the decision maker has a choice of two possible behaviors: 1) to decide that what he or she notices is a certain stimulus, or 2) to decide that what he or she notices is not the stimulus in question. Hence, the two hypothetical states of affairs in these experiments are: 1) the actual presence or 2) the actual absence of a stimulus-signal. The decision maker has to make a final decision to state the presence or absence of a signal. For such decision the operator-decision maker is given the information obtained through perception of sensory data within a specified time interval.

Using the dice or urn schema is convenient in that for these schemas it is relatively easy to develop mathematical models that may later be used for other experimental situations, such as detecting of signals within noise. In experiments on signal detection the ratio of the likelihood that the signal is emitted from a given source to a given critical value is often used as a model of behavior of decision makers. Reaching this critical value gives the operator-decision maker a possibility to resolve the decision problem in favor of the hypothesis about the actual presence of a signal within the background noise. A failure to reach the critical value results in adopting the opposite hypothesis, which means that only noise is perceived in the communication channel. An example of this type of experiment was indicated, among others, by Sweets, Tanner and Birdsall (1961). A slightly different model, rather closer to the general idea of a the random procedure *(random walk)* was used by Kranz (1969) in his experiments on signal detection.

Experimental decision games of a signal detection type may be used to analyze such economic situations as the identification of various types of market crises, financial crises or crises in the functioning of economic structures. The essence of decision analysis in such situations is to determine what constitutes a danger signal to ensure a safe operation of a particular economic system and how this signal may be recognized in the so-called noise (i.e. how to distinguish the signal of economic risk from the noise).

3.3.3. Laboratory experiments and the most frequent patterns of decision analysis

This section presents the conventional techniques of laboratory experiments on the search for probabilistic information in decision situations. In the context of these experimental techniques we will see the most commonly used patterns of decision analysis in these situations.

According to Manz (1970), laboratory experiments exploring the informational activity with an unreliable source of information are based mostly on two types of research. The first type of experiments mainly focus on studying the changes in the probability (*revision of probability type of experiments*) when new information is supplied. The other type of experiments are situations where the so-called research on delayed/deferred decision takes place (*information seeking in deferred-decision experiments*).

The criterion for distinguishing the two situations used by Manz is handling payoffs and costs of purchasing information, while in typical experiments on the revision of opinion, the authors did not use payoffs. The experiments on deferred decision are based on the payoff and the cost of purchasing information.

Experiments on changing a probabilistic opinion use the Bayesian model or its modification. The variables mostly taken into account in these experiments are: the number of signals, the initial probability, the conditional probability, the type of instruction, the structure of the payoff matrix, the cost of information, the way of expressing probability assessment of the events.

As for the size of the signal sample, the vast majority of authors (e.g. Phillips and Edwards 1966, Beach 1968, Du Charme 1969) examine the behavior of people who receive more than one signal. The authors who apply one-element signal sample are: Gettys and Manley (1968), Peterson and Swensson (1968). Experiments on multiple signals studied the impact of the relative signal frequency (*r/n*, where: *r* – number of signals of one type and *n* – total number of signals in the sample). Examples of such studies include experiments by authors such as Peterson and others (1965), Pitz (1967), Vlek (1965), Vlek and Van der Heijden (1967).

Another variable controlled in experiments is the initial probability of the hypothesis (Peterson, Schneider and Miller 1965, Phillips and Edwards 1966). The initial probability in experiments was only implicitly different and there was no certainty whether the subjects actually treated them as different. Therefore, other researchers determined the initial probability (e.g. Geller and Pitz 1968, Peterson and Ducharme 1967), or taught the respondents to determine the probability in a situation through an initial training, i.e. preparation phase of the experiment (e.g. Jungermann 1969, Biela, Chlewiński, Walesa 1983).

In many studies, the experimenters controlled the conditional probability as an experimental variable. In most experiments (e.g. Peterson et al 1968, Peterson and Swensson 1968, Vlek 1965, Pitz et al 1969, Manz 1968, 1969, De Swart 1972, Biela 1976), the conditional probabilities were constant for the given series of signals (e.g. the proportions of blue and green fields on roulette discs).

The cost of information or payoffs as an independent variable in experiments was studied, among others, by Pollack (1967). Pitz and Downing (1967) also took into consideration in their experiments the accuracy of the instructions as a variable: they used three variants of instructions informing the respondents more or less precisely about the decision situation which based on the dice schema. The first group of participants given minimal information which only allowed a rudimentary understanding of the experimental situation. The second group of respondents was additionally informed of the frequency distribution of the number of random letters in five consecutive throws of three dice (one of the cubes was "unusual"). The third group of subjects received instructions on how to most optimally use the rules to maximize winnings in the experiment.

Studies of seeking unreliable information used various ways to evaluate the *a posteriori* probability *(response mode):* 1) ratio, 2) percentage, 3) the probability ranging from 0.00 to 1.00. Experimenters who initiated considering this variable were Beach and others (1970), Martin and Gettys (1969).

As in experiments investigating the change of the belief the decision maker processes signals into probabilistic information, such experiments are often treated as a test of the probabilistic reasoning process, as in experiments by Phillips (1966), Phillips and others (1966), Phillips and Edwards 1966).

3.3.4. Experiments investigating the so-called deferred decision

A large group of laboratory experiments on the search for information entails research on situations of deferred decision-making. Experiments investigating deferred decisions include a fixed payoff matrix, and determine the cost of purchasing information, while the number of the acquired signals depends on the decision maker.

The formal theoretical base for these decisions is, among others, the sequential model elaborated by Wald (1947). The test procedures concerning deferred decisions refer to certain earlier experimental techniques which concerned judgments which change according to the new data successively flowing in *(expanded judgment)*. A typical example of this technique may be found in the experiments by Irvin and Smith (1956, 1957) which used 500 lettered cards with numbers (one number on each card). The set of numbers on the cards was determined by their mean and standard deviation. A card taken successively from the stack was given to the decision maker, who was required to make a decision: whether the average for a set of numbers on all cards is greater or less than zero. A correct answer won a sum of money. The decision maker had to pay an amount of money for each card shown to him or her.

In the literature (e.g. Goode 1962, Pitz 1968, Snapper and Peterson 1971) it is often stressed that experiments examining deferred decisions put the participant in a situation to determine the optimal point for stopping the information flow (called *optimal stopping tasks)*. In these situations the decision maker is required to: 1) determine the optimal criterion for allowing a final decision, 2) make a successive purchase of information to reach the critical point.

An example of a typical experiment examining the deferred decision on the basis of the Wald sequential model may be the procedure followed by Becker (1958). The study was conducted using laboratory apparatus equipped with two mechanical counters and a button, allowing the decision maker to change the number on one of the counters by one unit each time. Adding a unit on one of the counters was a function of a random variable. The experiment only defined the ratio of the added units for the two counters (1000 : 5000, 2000 : 4000, 3000 : 3000, 4000 : 2000, 5000 : 1000). Before each experimental series the participant was handed a card containing a description of the population (two, three, four, five – depending on the series) from which it was possible to draw. The task in Becker's experiment was to decide which population it was from. Each problem was repeated eight times in one series. The participants were acquainted only with the problem of decision-making and handling the equipment, but nothing was mentioned about the terms of finishing the informational activity. For a right decision the subjects received 5 points, and -5 points for a wrong one.

Another criterion for an optimal completion of informational activity, based on the Bayesian model, was suggested in their experiments by Snapper and Peterson (1971). Their situation was based on the urn schema. The task of the decision maker was to determine from which of the two populations (shown at the beginning) the experimenter had drawn a sample (the result of each drawing was revealed.) After receiving each signal, the decision-maker used a chart to assess the probability of drawing a ball from each population. It depended entirely on how much probabilistic information the signals carried. The sequence of signals in the experiment was administered according to the table of random numbers. The participants were informed about the accuracy of their decisions only at the end of the experiment.

A different type of experimental situations that require decision-makers to determine the optimum point of completion of the informational activity are experiments where the range of purchasing signals is limited in advance. For example, in experiments by Pitz (1968), the range of signals was a variable of three different values (5, 10 or 20 signals) in the three equivalent groups of decision makers.

3.3.5. Natural experiments, *quasi-natural* and simulated situations, searching for information in economic decisions

A separate type of experiments on searching for information is research on situations of economic decisions. In terms of the research techniques used and the type of research situations, we may specify three types of studies: 1) studies of economic behavior in natural situations (natural experiments), 2) studies in conditions called *quasi-natural* experiments, and 3) simulations of actual economic behavior.

Examples of natural experiments, are studies on decision making in situations of roulette games (Tokano et al 2010) in natural conditions of stockbrokers' work (Ilard and Lipschitz 2006) and in natural situations of consumer choices. Such situations are referred to in the literature as a natural decisions *(naturalistic decision making - NDM).*

Quasi-natural experiments are carried out within the framework of behavioral economics on problems of interest to microeconomics (Smith 1982). They came later into the area of the finance and accounting (Booker et al 2007) and developed their methodology also in experimental research on capital markets and trade (Williams et al 2000). Particularly valuable methodologically are experiments by Smith (2004) on over 72 markets of assets. The importance of *quasi-natural* experiments is that the experimenters are able to at least partially control the variables in natural conditions of economic situations, and the research results obtained in this way are likely to be included either directly to the practice of business, marketing, analysis and finances, as well as in economic theories.

The third group of studies represents the approach of simulation, which is aimed to the construct descriptive models of economic decisions. An example of a simulation approach to modeling may be risky economic decisions in the conditions of limited rationality (Chen and Hogg 2008). Mareiros et al (2010), in turn, developed a multifactorial model of economic group decision, taking into account the emotional characteristics of group members in the conditions of using persuasive argumentation. Komphuis et al (2010) built a simulation system called PLATT, which is a model of an interactive exploration of information in complex situations of an economic decision.

3.4. Research results on seeking new information desired in a dynamic decision situation

The state of research to date is not yet able to reconstruct a complete picture of the course of informational activity in situations of decision making. The results of the experiments and analyses, however, allow us to describe certain regularities in the behavior of decision makers seeking information in the conditions of uncertainty.

The overview of research on informational activity proposed in this chapter indicates typical results obtained in experiments and the main indicators of these patterns that may point to directions for further research in this area (theoretical aim), and to specific problem situations for analysis to focus on (applicative aim). First, we will discuss the general regularities of the process of finding information in a dynamic decision situation, and then we will focus on more detailed experimental results on informational activity with a source of reliable information, and then with unreliable, probabilistic information.

3.4.1. General rules concerning the informational process in a decision making situation

To begin the review of general rules of the informational process in a dynamic decision situation, we will look at the empirical generalizations as to when the process of searching for new information takes place, i.e. whether it is before the decision (pre-decision process), during the choice-making, or after the decision (post-decision processes).

Most of the behavioral regularities concerning the information seeking process were discovered during the pre-decision process. These regularities will be discussed in the present section. At the time of making a choice the decision maker generally does not seek new information anymore, but only takes into account the information resources already obtained. We will concentrate only on the general regularities of the pre-decision processes and on the search for information after the decision, i.e. post-decision processes.

General regularities of information seeking at the pre-decision stage

The main problem for the decision maker in a pre-decisional situation is its great uncertainty due to the lack of data that would allow to clarify and define the task in the situation. This state in the literature is referred to *an aversion to imprecision* (or *imprecision aversion).* The source of this aversion is the vagueness of probabilistic information, which is usually the only one available for the decision maker. Examples are studies by authors such as Gajos, Hayashi, Tallon and Vergnaud, from the economic academic center in Paris, who suggested an axiomatic model of decision making in conditions of uncertainty, where the decision maker has objective but imprecise information. These authors verified their model experimentally (Gajos et al 2008). Based on the results of their research one may say that in such conditions decision maker naturally develops a *need to find new information* (or *a need for information seeking)* to reduce the vagueness of the situation. Thus, as shown by Santos, Wei and Chan (2005), decision makers feel deep satisfaction from collecting information that reduces the vagueness in decision making. They do assess the utility of each information obtained in the pre-decision situation. Moreover, the acquired new information, according to Connaway (2008), gives a sense to both the decision situation and the decision itself.

Results of research on the informational processes in the pre-decision situation, have been recognized in the form of a synthetic theory of informational interaction, whose authors are Blandford and Attfield (2010). They assume that the situation of the decision maker itself is of an interactive nature, and he or she performs an *information journey* In the interactive process the decision maker undergoes further information stages: identifying information needs, finding information, interpretation and assessing the extent how much it is needed to achieve the goal, using this interpretation to make a choice in the given decision situation, and using it in his or her other activities.

Searching for new information in a post-decision situation

The stressful nature of the decision situation results from the very definition of this situation, as the decision maker's task is to choose only one option out of all possible alternatives. And just after the decision maker's selection of one option, which is always irrevocable – to some extent or totally – he or she experiences a sense of a post-decision regret. This regret concerns the decision option which was rejected. If the decision is made under the pressure of certain factors and contrary to the decision maker's beliefs, arises tension called cognitive dissonance (Festinger 1957). Researchers who interpret information seeking in a decision situation within the theory of cognitive dissonance include Y. Shani and Zeelenberg (2007). Other authors (Shani, Tykocinski, Zeelenberg 2008) similarly interpret the search for information about the possible negative consequences of the decision option which was rejected and was the object of the post-decision regret. Based on the results of their experiments, these authors argue that such knowledge is in this case less unpleasant than uncertainty and ignorance.

Learning to seek information in decision situations

A general conclusion that may be inferred from the results of many laboratory and *quasi-natural* experiments, as well as from analysis of the decision makers' behavior in natural conditions – is the *effect of learning* by the decision makers how to search for information in decision situations in order to make more accurate decisions. The learning curve in seeking new information effectively in decision situations, known from behavioral experiments on learning, is illustrated in Figure 3.2.

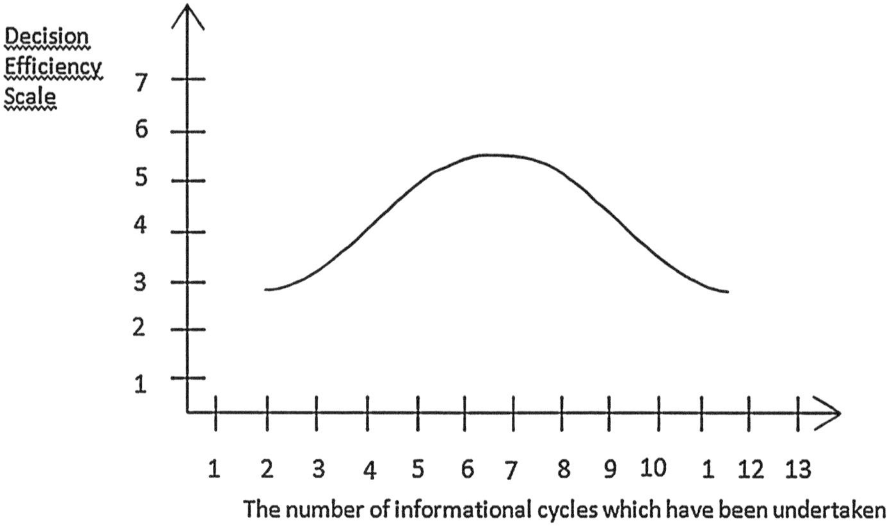

Figure 3.2. The relationship between the number of informational cycles undertaken and the effectiveness of decision

The graph in Figure 3.2. indicates that the cost of purchasing new information undertaken by the decision maker increases the effectiveness of the decision up to a certain level of costs, after which we observe *a plateau effect* in learning. According to the learning curve, after a period of a constant effectiveness of decisions, further investment in searching new information results in lowering of the effectiveness of the decision.

A new learning strategy concerning seeking information in decision situations was proposed by Newell (2004), who presented the results of experimental studies where decision makers had a choice of different data (information on the proportion of correct choices made using the data previously). The results indicate that in this experiment decision makers were much faster in learning to make accurate decisions based on data which was known to have been helpful in successful decisions.

Burchell and Kolb (2006) reported the results of their empirical research in the form of a theory of learning by experience. This theory concerns the search for information in a decision situation and is based on learning specific styles of information seeking. The authors distinguish four learning styles: a style of concrete learning *(feeling),* a style of conceptual abstraction *(thinking),* a style of active experience *(doing),* and a style of reflective observation *(watching).*

Emotions, information and decision

The behavior of a decision maker in decision situations is a result of not the informational processes, which are cognitive operations, but it also depends on emotions. Mareiros et al (2010), examining the awareness of the emotional context in group decisions where persuasive arguments were used, found out that decision makers who are aware of such context more effectively search for information, are faster and are more successful in decision making than decision makers who have no knowledge of the emotional context in such situations.

The emotional factor is also one that limits rational behavior in decision situations. An example analysis of such behavior is a study of the so-called big losses in casinos, carried out by Takano and others (2010). The analysis shows that these persons make desperate and irrational decisions in a completely impulsive way, which usually weakens their already bad situation.

3.4.2. Results of studies on the search for new reliable information

Based on our previous analysis we may state that in situations with a source of reliable information, the determinants of informational activities include such factors as: the number of hypotheses, the probability distribution on the set of hypotheses, the content of the hypotheses, the type of signals emitted from the source. The observed effects relate to the different stages of informational activity. The probability threshold and the preference of the content of the hypotheses are observed at the initial stages, while the effect of "negating" signals refers to the final stage of informational activity, i.e. processing signals into information.

Subjective threshold of an a priori *probability of hypotheses*

An important regularity of behavior in decision situations with a source of reliable information is the existence of the so-called probability threshold of hypotheses. This threshold is subjective and implies that the decision maker uses a given probabilistic criterion, allowing him or her to establish a set of hypotheses in the given decision situation. The probability threshold effect occurs only in situations where the decision maker does not accept the assumptions of an equal probability of hypotheses. This phenomenon was observed by Tichomirow and colleagues (1964), who gave the participants a long training on the *a priori* probability distribution of the hypotheses, and then observed in the experiment that to solve the decision problem the participants did not take into account claims whose probability does not reach a certain subjectively critical value. In these experiments, the subjective threshold for the *a priori* probabilities of the hypotheses was 0.05. In other experiments, this threshold might be of a different value, but this has not been studied thoroughly and requires further investigation.

The content of hypotheses

The effect observed in the experiments which assume an equal probability of hypotheses is the preference of the content of the hypotheses. It consists in the fact that respondents have a varying preference of abstract hypotheses which seemed to them equivalent and thus of equal probability (e.g. "two squares", "one figure in one frame", "a green circle"). Thus, it shows that the content of the hypotheses is a determinant of their subjective probability distribution. Therefore, the assumption of an equal *a priori* probability (Laplace rule) has proved to be not valid here. In fact, the experimental results show that the different contents of hypotheses are of a different "power to attract the decision maker's attention". This was observed in experiments by Bruner, Goodnow and Austin (1956), Chlewiński (1966) and Biela (1971), who stated that certain hypotheses were significantly more likely to be taken into account by the respondents than other ones, although none of the suggestions made by the experimenter recommended such choice. The hypotheses of a given content (e.g. "a black cross in the frames or three green figures") were statistically significantly more preferred than other ones (Biela 1971), which means that the subjects actually attributed to them a much higher *a priori* probability than to the other hypotheses.

Signal type

A discussion of the commonly observed regularities in experiments investigating the informational activity in situations with a source of reliable information should included the so-called effect of "denying" signals (Bruner et al 1956, Tichomirow 1964, Biela 1973a)[28]. By "denying" signals one means here a form of the verbal signal "no" or its equivalent (i.e. green light signals in the experiment by Tichomirow). The experiments show that decision

[28] The effect of "negative" signals was also achieved in certain experimental situations with a source of probabilistic information (e.g. Kozielecki 1965).

makers have more difficulty in processing this category of signals into reliable information than in processing signals of the "yes" category. In many persons the "no" signal causes a confusion caused by waiting for a signal which would "confirm" one's current direction of thinking. One's cognitive anticipation of the "yes" signal causes that the "no" signal is treated as "denying", which ultimately leads to such consequences as: 1) "undermining" the dynamics of the informational activity, 2) a failure to optimally process the received signal into information – or a redundant behavior.

Cognitive strategies

An analysis of the cyclic structure of the informational activity in experimental situations shows that in the search for data from a reliable source of information the decision makers are guided by certain rational rules, which organizes their behavior into a single sequential structure. These rules are defined in the literature as cognitive strategies or thinking strategies.

Research on cognitive strategies was developed within the psychology of thinking by Bruner and colleagues (1956). Their experiments enabled to distinguish four main strategies of thought: 1) a strategy of simultaneous investigation – involving a simultaneous consideration of all hypotheses, 2) a strategy of gradual testing – each hypothesis is successively tested separately, 3) a strategy of single focusing – where the decision maker considers the first designate of the concept as a kind of center, and further exploration is limited only to the selection of designates different from the focus by only one attribute, 4) a strategy of multiple (double or triple) focusing – which differs from latter by the fact that the decision maker selects designates which differ from the focus by two (double focus) or three attributes (triple focus). The strategy most commonly used by decision makers was of single focusing, the second most popular was the successive one, followed by multiple focusing, while the least operative strategy turned out to be simultaneous testing (Biela 1976).

Cohen and Meudell (1968) distinguished two types of thinking strategies in their experiments: 1) a strategy of a single element type (*element-type strategy*) – consisting of successive consideration of individual hypotheses based on a "belief in luck", 2) strategy to isolate a subset of hypotheses (*set-type strategy*) – where the search for the true hypothesis was carried out through planned testing of hypotheses from a certain subset. These experiments showed that: 1) older senior decision makers more often than younger people used the strategies allowing more data bits in each cycle of the informational activity, 2) they perceive the situation as a more organized structure and not merely a sum of its elements, which manifests itself in more frequently choosing the strategy of distinguishing a subset, 3) older makers are also more critical and cautious than their younger colleagues, which is also reflected in the fact that they do not generalize too quickly accidental success in their decision making.

Other aspects of the research strategy of searching for information in decision situations were of interest in by Newell (2004), who tested the effectiveness of the strategy choices considering the following features data available from the environment: 1) the ecological accuracy of the available data, 2) the discriminative power of the data, 3) "success" of the data, understood as a compliance of the proportion of random events with accurate previous decisions.

3.4.3. Cognitive fallacies (biases) arising from the limited rationality of the decision-maker

The use of so-called normative models (also known as ideal models) in experimental studies on the search for information, and the formulation of the concept of bounded rationality by Simon, resulted in several studies on how real decision makers actually get to know the reality of economic decisions. After all, no one expected actual decision makers as real people to behave in a manner literally consistent with the ideal models.

The regularity in the process of informational activity which is most frequently described and best known by experimenters is the phenomenon of *cognitive conservatism*[29], observed in situations with a source of probabilistic information, where the behavior of the participants is compared with the normative Bayesian model. Cognitive conservatism is observed when the decision maker overestimates the value of the following *a posteriori probability* of the hypothesis than is provided for the normative Bayesian model.

In the literature also exists a broader understanding of cognitive conservatism, considered as a general underestimation of objective probability. Using this interpretation, this concept may also refer to a situation where the participants do not receive signals successively, but estimate the probability events once[30].

---

[29] A term widely used in the literature for an underestimation of the probability of events, is "conservatism". Kozielecki (1969) introduced and spread the term "cognitive conservatism" as a more adequate one with respect to the observed phenomenon in diagnostic situations.

[30] The phenomenon of conservatism in such cases is discussed by Bujak (1972). Evaluation of simple events is, according to the author, more conservative than in the case of complex events. The literature (Kietliński 1972, Strojna 1974) also emphasizes that the result of assessing the likelihood of events (and hence, the degree of conservatism) in static decision-

The basis of the operational definitions of the concept of *cognitive conservatism* is provided by the descriptive models constructed by experimenters, which is a modification of the normative Bayesian model. An example of such definition is given by Peterson and Miller (1965), who introduced the notion of a close relationship (formula 3.16). Therefore, the operational definition of conservatism are all observed cases where the accuracy ratio is less than one. Thus, the smaller is the fraction of the value of this ratio, the greater is the degree of cognitive conservatism. On the other hand, Phillips and Edwards (1966) proposed an operational definition of cognitive conservatism based on a descriptive model they introduced (formula 3.18), which takes into account the parameter of a function of the difference between the two types of signals emitted by the source (sample). In 1968, Schum and Martin published the results of their research questioning the phenomenon of cognitive conservatism in decision making situations (Schum, Martin 1968). Their argumentations were of a methodological character dealing with experimental control of the assumed independent variables.

After clarifying the notion of *cognitive conservatism,* we may ask ourselves: what explains the nature of this phenomenon? Most authors explain the phenomenon of conservatism as an expression of a certain human attitude called "carefulness" (Manz 1979). In decision-making situations it may manifest itself either as an attempt to achieve a greater data resource than is required, just in case, or it may be expressed in a consequent "delay" in relation to the normative model. Phillips (1966) and Edwards (1968), outlining the concepts of the so-called *misaggregation* and *misperception,* explain that conservatism is caused by wasting of data by the decision makers, resulting in using an incomplete set of this data, which leads to an underestimated assessment of the probability of hypotheses in relation to the model.

The concept of *misperception,* in turn, draws attention to a slightly different moment of informational activity, namely, the perception of the emitted signals. According to Edwards (1968), the effect of conservatism is caused by errors in the reception of signals. They may either be due to the fact that the decision makers do not receive certain signals at all, or they identify them incorrectly. The essence of the phenomenon of conservatism is similarly

---

making situations, depends on whether the decision maker has an impact on the outcome of an event or not. If the decision maker's action has an effect on the event itself, then in certain cases he or she is willing to overestimate the probability of events in relation to the objective probability, and in other situations to underestimate this probability.

explained by Kozielecki (1969). Both authors refer this cognitive phenomenon to the concept of bounded rationality by Simon, who suggests that the main cause of cognitive conservatism is the limited human cognitive capacity, especially the limited capacity for processing signals into information (transformational hypothesis, see Kozielecki 1981).

Explaining the phenomenon of conservatism in terms of a prudential attitude, as well as analyzing it with regard to errors in the perception of signals and the scattering of data – assume human bounded rationality, and base on the assumption that the Bayesian model is the norm. With such assumption, any explanations boil down to finding answers to the following questions: 1) Why does the behavior of the experiment participants deviate from the model? and 2) What is the cause of these deviations? This problem may also be approached from a different perspective. One may simply say that the cause of conservatism is the fact that the human being uses different rules of processing signals into probabilistic information than is assumed in the Bayesian model. This way of thinking was followed by, among others, Marks and Clarkson (1973), stating that conservatism is a result of the respondents' using a different rule, much simpler than the Bayesian one. Stachowski (1974) holds a similar position and showed that the participants of experiments were generally guided by a rule of adding equal growths of probability, rather than using products, as predicted by the Bayesian model.

The way of explaining the nature of conservatism Phillips (1970) is also valuable for decision analysis. According to him, one should more seriously consider the fact that subjective probability is not possible to be expressed by characterizing states of the physical world, as it is a category of expressing confidence of a human being. In light of this fact, he argues, one should conclude that an attempt to explain conservatism as *misperception* or *misagregation* is a wrong approach to the problem. Since probability is a subjective category, there may be no erroneous perception of signals, and one may at most speak of a subjective recognition of reality. It may yet happen that two decision makers in the same conditions perceive the reality differently and assess the probability of events in a different way. Thus, the degree of conservatism is conditioned by subjective differences in the interpretation of the world, and not by erroneous perception. Decision analysts, as Phillips points out, should examine the impact of such variables as the nature of the signals, the type of situation, etc. to assess the subjective probability. It is unacceptable, however, to treat these variables as an objective basis for subjective evaluations. Decision makers are primarily human beings, resolving decision problems according to their own cognitive schemes.

In discussing the phenomenon of cognitive conservatism, Vlek and Van der Heijden (1970) postulated that the differentiation of weights of the particular stimuli, with a certain/given probability distribution in a multidimensional space, should be used as the basis for determining deviations from the discriminatory model. Differentiating the weight of the stimuli may, according to them, be the basis for distinguishing phenomena which are more basic than cognitive conservatism.

Literature also indicates other phenomena occurring in certain situations of searching for probabilistic information. One of them is the phenomenon of cognitive radicalism, which is the opposite of conservatism. About the behavior of the decision maker one may say that it is cognitively radical in terms of assessing probability if this assessment is higher than predicted by the Bayesian model. According to Kozielecki (1981), the phenomenon of radicalism is more typical for situations where the determination of objective probability is almost impossible. As indicated by Biela (1976), both conservatism and radicalism may become cognitive biases within the same situation of sequential search for probabilistic information: at the beginning cognitive conservatism prevails, while in the final phase of searching for information decision-makers behave more radically.

Determinants of conservatism

Studies on the phenomenon of cognitive conservatism consider the possibility of impact of the following variables on conservative behavior: 1) the *a priori* probability of hypotheses, 2) conditional probability, 3) the probability distribution of the signals in a sequence, 4) the way of expressing of probability of the events, 5) the payoff matrix, 6) group factors, 7) sex, 8) individual differences among the decision-makers (personality factors, cognitive and decision making styles), 9) cultural factors.

A priori *probability of the hypotheses*

The attempt to answering the question on the impact of the initial probability on the assessment of subjective probability did not bring uniform results. Peterson and Miller (1965) pointed out that a conservative assessment of the likelihood depends on the initial probability of the hypotheses. Other researchers, however, have not confirmed this factor (Phillips and Edwards 1966, Phillips et al 1966).

The findings discussed above, however, concerned experiments which studied the impact of the probability of hypotheses given at the beginning of the decision situation. In this context, we may ask: What is the impact of the *a priori* probability on the assessment of chances in sequential situations where the *a posteriori* probability of each informational cycle

k is also the *a priori* probability for cycle $k+1$? The phenomena observed in these situations are defined in the literature as sequential effects (Pitz 1965, Pitz and Downing 1967).

Analyzing the intensity of conservatism in the subsequent informational cycles, the following sequence effects were revealed: 1) the effects of the length of the sequence (the effect of short sequences, the effect of long sequences), 2) the effect of inertia, 3) the effect of priority. The effects of the length of the sequence show that the intensity of conservatism in assessing the probability of hypotheses depended on the length of the signal sequence. In situations where the respondents obtained a short sequences of signals, changes in the subjective probability were relatively high, which indicates a lower degree of intensity of cognitive conservatism (Pitz 1965, Pitz and Downing 1967). This phenomenon is defined as the effect of short sequences. On the other hand, in situations with long sequences, the reverse phenomenon was observed, indicating a slower increase in subjective probability and a greater intensity of conservatism. This phenomenon is referred to as the effect of long sequences.

An observation of the assessment of subjective probability after the subsequent signals showed that this assessment depends on: a) the decision maker's original belief as to the truth of the given hypothesis, b) the nature of the signals emitted in the sequence. The majority of respondents at the beginning of the experiment believe that the first hypothesis had more chances than the other one. This belief is formed either based on the *a priori probability* or under the influence of signals which "favor" one of the hypotheses at the beginning of the sequence, or due to certain factors of a purely subjective nature, which are difficult to be noted in the experiment. The experimenters found that if the decision maker has such belief regarding one of the hypotheses, he or she will find it very difficult to change it, even after receiving clear signals suggesting a greater probability of the other hypothesis. This phenomenon is referred to in literature as the *effect of inertia.* Another aspect of the same phenomenon is called the *precedence effect,* and may be observed when the decision maker increases his or her degree certainty regarding the favored hypothesis, even if the signals emitted sequentially indicate a greater chance of the opposite hypothesis. If, then, the received signals "confirm" the favored hypothesis, the decision maker tends to increase his or her original conviction rapidly. Intense conservatism is not observed, and in some respondents it hardly occurs. A more detailed discussion of the results of research on the sequential effects may be found in Biela (1976, 2001).

Many researchers were interested in the impact of the diagnostic value, or informativeness, of the data on the effect of conservatism. This variable may also be described as the diagnostic value of the data source. In the case of urn experiments, it was a structure of the urn (*bag composition*). Regardless of the terminology, the real factor determining the informativeness of signals is the conditional probability of the emission of certain signals from the source.

To Manz (1970), the not very precise handling of the informativeness of signals as an independent variable by many experimenters caused the discrepancy of the results. He proposed a different way of planning experiments, involving a combination of conditional probabilities with the emitted signals in such a way that the combination of conditional probabilities with the sequence of signals leads to a certain *a posteriori* probability provided by the normative model. In an experiment planned in such way, he obtained a confirmation that the diagnostic value of the source has an impact on the probability assessment and the associated effect of conservatism.

The probability of the sequence of signals

The impact of another variable on cognitive conservatism, the probability distribution of signals in the sequence, was studied, among others, by Phillips (1970). This variable is, according to him, one of the primary determinants of conservative behavior. He emphasizes that a more intense conservatism was observed only in situations based on the urn scheme (see experiments by Peterson and Miller 1965, Phillips and Edwards 1966, Beach 1966 and others) where the experimenters used essentially a binomial probability distribution on a set of signals sequentially emitted from the source. In order to predict what signal the source emits in cycle *k,* the decision maker would have to use this binominal distribution, which is deeply problematic. Phillips shows that decision makers have very little experience in dealing with this distribution and this is the cause of their conservative behavior.

In natural decision situations the decision maker has much more experience with a normal distribution of events rather than a binomial one, which is confirmed by experiments by DuCharme and Peterson (1968), where the source emitted signals sequentially, according to the principle of normal distribution[31]. In these experiments the degree of conservatism was very low.

Altogether, the analysis of the experiments clearly indicates a relationship between the intensity of the behavior of the conservative nature of the probability distribution of signals

[31] A normal distribution is illustrated by the so-called Gaussian bell-curve. Most of the abilities measured by psychometric tests have a normal distribution.

emitted from the source: conservatism is high in the case of a binomial distribution, and it is the low with in a normal distribution (Biela 1976).

Expression of the probability of events

For DuCharme (1969), the phenomenon of conservatism applies not only to the informational activity, but also to the nature of the scale used to measure the subjective probability. Indeed, the phenomenon of conservatism itself indicates that the scale used by the decision makers for a subjective assessment of the likelihood is different than the scale envisaged by the Bayesian model. This problem, however, raises another question: Is the decision maker's way of expressing the probability of events itself of an impact on the effect of conservatism?

Experiments in this field, in addition to expressing the probability of events using percentages[32] or a ratio/proportions, also use the method of assessing the probability from 0.0 to 1.0, for example by an interval of 0.1 or even 0.01. Experiments based on the theory of learning rather use the technique of operating with a ratio, while experiments inspired by decision theory the participants are asked to express the chance of the occurrence of certain states of affairs in the form of a probability (Vlek 1970). Comparing the results of experimental studies, we may conclude that the manner how decision makers express the probability is of no decisive influence on their level of cognitive conservatism.

The studies by Winkler (1967) and Staël von Holstein (1969) showed that even decision makers who were purposefully trained in the basics of statistics using certain techniques to express probability, behaved conservatively, especially after receiving the first signals. Thus, it appears that even the ease of using certain scales does not reduce the tendency of cognitive conservatism.

The group and decisions

The impact of the group on the decision situation was also the object of experimental research (Chlewiński 1975). The experiment plan intended to test the informational activity in situations of individual and group decision making[33]. An analysis of the empirical material

[32] It is worth mentioning that the diagram of errors in assessing percentage data is, according to the study by Nash), of a sinusoidal shape (see: Biela 1976).

[33] The members of the research team were: M. A. Gabiniewicz, H. E. Jasińska, M. Jaskulska, L. Langkammer, A. Szendzielorz.

allowed a conclusion that the group in which an individual participates has a significant impact on the course of this activity. After learning about the assessments of the probability by other group members, the individual participant is generally willing to modify his or her assessment in accordance with the dominant trend in the group. The most common type of change under the influence of the group was to modify the degree of assertion in evaluations, although "qualitatively" different types of changes were also observed, which was also reflected in the modification of the probability assessments. If most members of the group assessed the probability of the given hypothesis as higher, the individual member of the group who saw this was usually inclined to raise his or her assessment and thus reduce the degree of his or her cognitive conservatism. When the group assessed the probability as lower, a statistical member of the group followed the dominant trend and lowered his or her assessment. The results of these studies were generally confirmed by other researchers such as Rockenbach (2004), who found in his experiments that decision makers functioning in a group (group decision) are much more willing to take risks than when they make decisions individually.

An analysis of the cyclic structure of the informational activity in situations of individual and group decision making showed that individual decision makers bought many more signals than groups of decision makers. This also allows us to confirm the more general conclusion that the behavior of the individual decision maker is generally more conservative than the behavior of individuals in the group.

Experiments by Chlewiński (1975) revealed the phenomenon of social facilitation: in the experiment, groups were more effective in solving problems of decision making than individuals. It was also observed that the mere presence and cooperation of members significantly affected the efficiency of both signal processing and the final result of informational activity. The greatest intensity of cognitive conservatism found in the first four cycles of the information activities, and in the final cycles of seeking information the effect of conservatism was either reduced to a minimum, or even replaced by cognitive radicalism.

Payoff matrix

Based on the analysis of experimental results it is difficult to give a satisfactory answer to the question whether the assessment of the likelihood of events depends on the payoff matrix. The authors do not give a clear answer concerning this issue. Phillips and Edwards (1966) indicate that these evaluations depend on the given conditions of receiving the payoff. On the other hand, experiments by Winkler and Murphy (1968) and Staël von Holstein (1969) suggest that under differing conditions of payoff the assessment of the probability of events was constant.

From the experiments conducted by Chlewinski (1975) one may see that in situations of a three-alternative choice both individual decision makers as well as 5-person decision teams evaluated the likelihood of the same hypotheses differently for a matrix which assigned equal payoff for each hypothesis, as opposed to a matrix where the payoff differed. The results indicate that with an equal payoff the decision makers' behavior deviates less from the Bayesian model than in the case when the payoffs differed. In addition, the direction of deviation from the model differs in the two cases. Cognitive conservatism was more frequent with equal payoffs. In the case of differentiated payoffs occurred a tendency to assign higher probability to the hypothesis with the highest payoff. In these conditions, the degree of conservatism was much lower and cases of cognitive radicalism were even observed.

The use of normative models in experiments on searching for information in decision making situations (mainly based on the probability theory) led to the discovery of many cognitive deviations from these models, also called cognitive fallacies, biases or trends. In the previous part of this section we discussed cognitive conservatism and radicalism as a deviation from the Bayesian model. Now we will look at the following behavioral tendencies known in cognitive experiments on the search for information in decision making situations: conjunction fallacy, disjunction fallacy, the tendency to confirm the knowledge possessed, the effects of diversification, the tendency to overestimate the obtained information, the tendency of representativeness.

Conjunction fallacy and disjunction fallacy

In many decision situations there are often two (or more) random events in a conjunctive or disjunctive (alternative) relationship that allow to recognize the symptoms of the hypothetical state of affairs. The rules of probability predict that the probability of the conjunction of two independent events is a product of the probabilities of both of these events. The probability of a regular disjunction (also called an alternative), according to the normative model of probability theory, equals the sum of the probabilities of the single events which constitute this disjunction.

And how do decision makers behave assessing the conjunction and disjunction of events? Experiments by Kahneman and Tversky (1972, 1973) and by Tversky and Kahneman

(1982, 1983) show that the percentage of assessments of the likelihood of the conjunction that violates the normative rule of conjunction varies in 73% to 100% cases. Such behavior of decision makers is described as a *conjunction fallacy.* On the other hand, experiments carried out by Biela (1986) show that slightly less decision makers (66%) violated the probabilistic rule of conjunction. However, the predominant way of assessing the conjunction of events in these experiments was not a conjunction fallacy, where the probability of the conjunction is rated higher than the probability of one of its compounds. In his experiments Biela identified a more specific behavioral pattern related to the assessment of the likelihood of conjunctive events by the decision makers. The dominant deviation from the standard normative model was that the participants assigned the probability of the less likely compound of the conjunction to the conjunction event as a whole. This means that adding the other compound of the conjunction was virtually ignored when assessing the likelihood of the conjunction itself (*non-conjunction effect*).

A similar regularity was observed in the assessment of the likelihood of the regular disjunction (also called alternative) of two elementary events, where only 12.2% decision-makers proved to be consistent with the probabilistic normative model. Frequently (61.5%), decision makers in this case used the rule of ignorance in assessing the likelihood of the disjunction compounds, and the assessment of the probability of the disjunction itself was recognized as the probability of its less likely compound (Biela 1986).

The tendency to confirm the knowledge resources possessed

How to behave in a decision situation when the incoming information is incompatible with the information already obtained? Several experiments confirmed the tendency for seeking new information which would confirm the knowledge already possessed (Bruner et al 1956, Tichomirow et al 1964, Biela 1976). The regularity reported on the basis of the experiments by Łukaszewski (1971) may be defined as the *effects of leveling inconsistencies* or *contradictions.* They occur when the decision maker obtains data which is “incompatible” with the information system already created. With the increase in the degree of inconsistency, the trend observed in decision makers is to reduce this inconsistency, accompanied by a sense of uncertainty and fear. The following two behavioral regularities were observed in the decision makers: 1) a great inconsistence tends to cause changes in the incoming information, 2) a further increase in the inconsistency tends to partially or completely change system of processing signals into information.

Other trends observed in the cognitive process of searching for information in a decision situation

Having reviewed the cognitive trends, or biases, it also necessary to mention at least three new ones referred to in the literature: the *diversification effect, the tendency to overestimate new information* (*information overweight bias*) and the *overrepresentation fallacy.*

The diversification effect concerns the search for information in the situation of individual consumer choices or the characteristics of the entire consumption basket. From the experiments by Loewenstein (1995) we may learn that decision makers choose more consumer goods for future consumption than if they have make the choice immediately before the consumption. However, there was no research on the effect of diversification in situations other than consumer choices. It is not known so far to what extent these observations may also relate to situations beyond consumer decisions.

The effect of overestimating information is observed when the decision maker is strongly convinced of the truth of a given hypothesis (h_j) in the decision situation, and the signal received (x_i) provides information of an increasing likelihood of this hypothesis. Then occurs the possibility of an overestimation of signal processed into information in the decision situation. The overrepresentation fallacy concerns processing the signal into information on the basis of an ill-founded induction. It involves a too early generalization of the conclusion on the basis of insufficient evidence (Kahneman and Tversky 1972).

3.4.4. The problem of the number of informational cycles in the light of experimental studies

In situations which depend solely on the decision maker, when complete the transaction information, the number of informational cycles undertaken becomes a basic research problem. Any empirical regularity and behavioral effects detected experimentally are in a certain sense relativized to the number of informational cycles. An analysis of experimental results includes the following four aspects: 1) the stages of the formation of the probabilistic strategy, 2) the diagnostic value of the source and the number of cycles, 3) the effects of restricting the availability of information, 4) analyzing the decision maker's behavior with regard to the model by Wald.

Stages of creating a probabilistic strategy

Directly related to the problem of the number of informational cycles is the decision maker's possibility of using a criterion to judge when to finish the informational activity. What is actually meant by satisfying this criterion? The criterion indicator generally means that the decision maker achieves a certain critical level of conviction with regard to one of the hypotheses. What directs the decision maker to form his or her conviction in the given way? That is, how is his or her strategy of assessing probability shaped? This type of strategy should, of course, be distinguished from the cognitive strategies in situations with a source of reliable information which relate to the methods of searching for information, where a decision maker is essentially an active party in information seeking. In the strategies of assessing probability the decision maker refers to a situation where he or she only perceives signals and expresses the sense of probability of events on this basis.

In his analysis of experimental research, Manz (1970) distinguishes three stages in the developing a probability strategy of events: 1) in the first phase covering the first few cycles, decision makers pay attention to the dominant, feature of the random events (such as the color of the discs drawn); 2) in the second phase, usually in the middle of the sequence, the dominant feature of the random event is no longer the sole determinant of one's sense of probability, and the proportion of signals in the sample is also taken into account (e.g. the proportion of the red disc to the blue ones); 3) in the third stage of the development, the strategy of assessing the probability reaches the highest level of thinking in terms of proportions. The basis for determining the proportions is, according to Beach and others (1970), the first ten signals. Reaching the third phase allows the decision maker to determine the appropriate critical level, expressed in the belief that a given hypothesis is true. Hence, the final number of informational cycles depends primarily on the decision maker's achievement of the third stage in the development of strategies for assessing the probability of events.

The diagnostic value of the source of information and the number of cycles

The relationship between the number of cycles and the diagnostic value of the source of signals is defined in the literature as the effect of differentiation of the diagnostic value of the signal source (Green, Halbert and Minas 1964, Fried and Peterson 1969, Snapper and Peterson 1971). Research on determining the direction of the relationship between the number of informational cycles and the diagnostic value of the source of information was carried out, among others, by Snapper and Peterson (1971). Their conclusions from the experiments may be summarized as follows:

1. The number of informational cycles increases when the diagnostic value of the source decreases. The function of growth is a monotonic one.
2. The subjective criterion allowing to make a final decision is constant, i.e. independent of the diagnostic value of the source. This criterion requires the participant to buy more signals of a less diagnostic value to achieve the critical level of assertion.

3. Progressive lowering the diagnostic value of the source does not increase the number of cycles infinitely. The observed regularity may be defined as the *threshold effect of a low diagnostic value*. This means the growth is a function monotonically increasing only to a certain extent. With sources of a lower and lower diagnostic value the decision makers buy fewer and fewer signals. Empirically, it is possible to determine the threshold of a low diagnostic value of the source, beyond which the number of informational cycles decreases.

The problem of behavioral optimality in the search for probabilistic information may be considered from the perspective of normative models of rationality or a behavioral description of the regularity in the behavior of real decision makers in economic situations.

The previous chapters discussed the ideal models and rational criteria for determining the optimal decision making in a situation of investing in obtaining new information. Below is a summary of the most important results of research on the actual behavior of real decision makers in situations which were natural experiments, *quasi-natural* ones, laboratory and simulation studies described in previous sections of this chapter.

Although the research results on the optimality are not methodologically uniform, however, they allow a clear conclusion that decision makers generally do not use the normative-optimal criteria. The researchers differ only in the reported number of cases of deviations from the optimal criterion. Edwards and Slovic (1965) found an optimal behavior in as much as approximately 50% cases. Similar results were obtained by Becker (1958), Pruitt (1961) and Howell (1971). A much smaller percentage of optimal behavior was observed by Tversky and Edwards (1966). Pitz (1968), testing the three normative models (the Bayesian model, model of conduct random walk, the model of a fixed random sample), found that none of them is adequate to describe the behavior of decision makers in situations of a limited availability of information. The result of this study sheds some light on how ones operates with the subjective criterion for determining the number of informational cycles. These experiments may be treated as a simple model for many natural decision situations where the possibility of obtaining information is mostly restricted.

The regularities identified by Pitz (1968) may be called the *effects of limitations of the available information,* because in general they express the relationship between the behavior of the participant and the scope of the available information, and more specifically the relationship between the number of the signals possible to obtain and the number of actual informational cycles. The resulting effects of available information being limited may be described as follows:

1. Limiting the number of the signals possible to obtain significantly affects the number of informational cycles of the decision maker.
2. Reducing the number of signals does not affect the optimality of the behavior of decision makers.
3. With the possibility of purchasing a large number of signals the number of informational cycles is also higher than with the possibility to obtain a smaller number of signals.
4. If the received signals have the same characteristics (for example, the same color), then the decision makers are willing to undertake fewer cycles.
5. The descriptive model for the behavior of people in a dynamic decision situation is an empirical relationship between the critical value of criterion b^* (expressing the difference between two types of informative signals) and the number of informational cycles. To Pitz (1968), reaching the critical value of b^* would lead to the completion of informational activity making a final decision. The descriptive model by Pitz assumes that the critical value of b^* is not stable and decreases as the number of informational cycles increases.

Another regularity observed by Pitz, not related specifically to limiting the availability of information, is the weak *effect of the increased cost of buying signals.* According to the optimal model, an cost increase of the cost should cause a drop in the number of informational cycles necessary to make the final decision for all critical values. The actual study results show a weak impact of increasing the cost on the number of informational cycles undertaken (Pitz 1968).

Experimental studies of the first decade of the 21st century, attempted to answer the question: When does the decision maker consider that he or she has enough information and is able to make the final decision (Berryan 2006, Hausmann and Lage 2008)? These approaches, however, attempt to identify behavioral indicators to specify when actually the decision maker actually decides to finish the search for new information in the conditions of the possibility of a sequential investment in the informational process. For Hausmann and

Lage (2008), each decision maker has his or her individual threshold of seeking new information (*evidence-threshold*), which is expressed in its desired level of confidence in the available data (*Desired Level of Confidence - DLC*). This threshold is associated with the individual decision maker's level of aspiration.

Behavioral effects in sequential models

Based on the Wald's sequential model Becker (1958) conducted research that enabled him to determine – for each decision maker studied – a quotient criterion, i.e. the probability of a correct decision and its risks[34].

The analysis results showed that although the Wald's model does not describe the behavior of the decision maker adequately, it may be treated as a first approximation of the course of informational activity. Based on the results, curves of the best "hits" for the individual decision makers were determined. A comparison of the curves with the predictions derived from the Wald's model revealed a compatibility of the slopes of the empirical curves with the theoretical predictions by Becker which based on the Wald model, which allowed to conclude about the following regularities in the course of the informational activity:

1. Experimental tasks varied in being a challenge for the respondents in terms of the level of difficulty in decision making (on this basis, the decision tasks may be classified as "easier" and "more difficult"[35];
2. In "easier" situations certain categories of deviations from the Wald model appeared more frequently than in "difficult" situations. This regularity was not affected by the cost of purchasing the signals or the structure of the payoff matrix which defines the decision problem;
3. The risk level was significantly higher in "difficult" cases than in "easy" ones;
4. The probability of "hits" (correct responses) was essentially the same level in all decision problems;
5. The number of informational cycles proved to depend on the number of hypotheses in the decision situation;
6. The level of risk was independent from the number of alternatives;

[34] The method for calculating these rates is determined by the following formulas developed by G.M. Becker (see: Biela, 2001).

[35] An example of an "easy" problem was to determine whether the source of the changes registered on the counters was the population with a proportion of 3000:3000 or one of 1000:5000. An example of a "difficult" problem was to determine whether the source of population was the population of 3000:3000 or of 4000:2000 (see Becker 1958).

7. The decision makers revealed individual differences in the course of informational activity.

A relatively compact group of behavioral effects observed in the decision making experiments are so-called sequential results – obtained from tests involving a number of similar decision problems to be solved by the same people. Examples of typical experiments which revealed the sequential effects were ones by Pitz and Downing (1967), based on the dice schema. The general regularity observed by these researchers may be formulated as follows: decision makers expect a sequential dependence between the successive reactions. These expectations rely on the tendency to repeat the reactions which were previously not reinforced. This means that decision makers often chose to identify the random events which were previously the base of wrong decisions. This tendency is called the *negative effect of freshness* or the *effect the player's illusion.* A tendency to repeat decision sequences after reactions which were previously positively reinforced was, however, not observed.

An interesting regularity was found concerning the impact of the payoff matrix on the function of informational activity and the final decision (Biela 1976). The effects may be summarized in the following points:

1. Decision makers generally behave adequately to the probabilistic characteristics of the situation.
2. They have the greatest difficulty in deciding when the probabilistic properties of the stimuli do not provide an adequate basis for drawing conclusions.
3. In situations where, in their understanding, "probabilism fails" decision makers are guided by the principle of the maximum payoff.
4. Comparing the behavior of decision makers in a situation of a symmetric matrix with the situation of a maximum difference between the payoffs, clear divergence was observed in the behavior of the decision makers. In the case of the symmetric matrix the decision makers acted adequately to the probabilistic terms, while in the case of an asymmetric matrix they always preferred the action which would minimize the risk of a loss, where the profit had the same absolute value as the loss if the alternative was chosen.

In decision situations where subjects may obtain information from more than one source, the observed regularities are known as *the effect of noise* and *the parallelisml effect.* The effect of noise was described by Hockey (1973) in a situation where it was possible to use multiple sources of warning signals. It concerns the relationship between the phenomenon of noise in the communication channel and the decision to choose the source: an increase in the noise increases the tendency to make the final decision as to the signal source. The other regularity, known as the so-called parallelism effect, refers to the course of the informational activity in the situation of using two signal sources. It may be formulated as follows: in the case of parallel signals emitted from a semantic and formal source, the decision maker's reception is parallel indeed, but, according to Burrows and Okada (1973), a priority in the perception is given to the semantic signals.

In the case of signal perception of different modalities the *alternation effect* was discovered (Edward and Hold 1973), which consists in the fact that the subjects make more mistakes when they perceive alternating stimuli that differ in their modality and intensity. Decision makers also made more errors in conditions of auditory stimuli of alternating tones, rather than when they were exposed to the same tones.

The specificity of economic decisions

The authors who contributed to the area of economic decisions include E. Gaugler, who was a pioneer in this field in Europe. He developed an economic understanding of informational processes and decision making within company (Gaugler 1962), and later developed his conception of decision making in organization towards operational research and economic growth which involves an interdisciplinary cooperation between economists, psychologists and sociologists (Gaugler 1993). A broad spectrum of an operational approach to economic decision making is proposed by authors who publish their results in *The Operations Research Proceedings,* where, among others, the selected papers were prepared by Fleischmann, Borgwardt, Klein and Tuma (2008).

Another interdisciplinary contribution to an economic understanding of decision making was made by Kirsch (1988). His novelty was mainly in applying the conception of Lewin's field theory into a broader economic domain, and also in his concept of episodes in structuring one's decision making field, in micro-structures as well as in macro-structure realities.

A new direction of applying decision making approach in economic behavior was proposed by Ertelt and Ruppert (2011) who indicated the implications of decision analysis for vocational counseling. Particularly, they focused on the intentions of the heuristic theory of decision making and its possible application for career guidance.

A discussion of the results of experimental research on decisions will start with a comparative analysis of these decisions and the behavior of the same decision makers in situations of an economic and a task which concerned automobiles – both of a lottery type

(Wu, Delgado, Maloney 2009). The first conclusion from these experiments is to establish the fact that in the case of both types of situations the behavior of decision makers differs from the expectations resulting from the theory of expected utility (see the EU and SEU models). There were also no differences in the assessment of results by decision makers in both situations – the economic and the automobile one. However, differences were observed in assessing the likelihood of random events in both types of decision situations. In the case of the economic situations occurred a clear tendency to overestimate small probabilities of events, and simultaneously a tendency to underestimate large probabilities of economic events, while in the case of automobiles in the evaluation of probabilities the reverse trend was observed: the same decision makers underestimated unlikely events, and exaggerated the likelihood of the events with the greatest probability. These results may be regarded as expressing the behavioral specificity of decision makers in business situations.

In August 2004 the *Harvard Business School: Working Knowledge* published a duet-discussion on the results of experimental research on the exploration and evaluation of information in of finance and accounting (Gino 2004, Silverthorne 2004). They observe that if the decision maker pays for information, he or she has a tendency to overestimate its actual value. Paying for information causes the so-called *effect of the hidden cost of purchasing information,* which consists in the fact that it is assigned a greater weight in decision making than it actually follows from the objective possibility of reducing the uncertainty of the decision situation. One of the assumptions commonly adopted in normative models of decision making is that obtaining information is related to a cost, but unfortunately, these models do not take into account using information already obtained. The rational decision maker is looking for information up to the point where the marginal cost of obtaining additional information equals the marginal benefit from the decision. In standard models the decision maker rather ignores the information that does not raise the quality of his or her decisions. Experiments by Gino (2004) show that when the decision maker has paid for information, it is not so easy to ignore. This author gives two possible interpretations of this behavior of decision makers. The first interpretation is the cognitive tendency to indulge in the so-called mistake of sunk costs (*sunk cost fallacy*). It is based on taking into account one's investment to buy new information and not allowing it to be wasted nearly at all costs. The other interpretation of the observed regularity uses explanations inspired by cognitive dissonance, a mechanism which leads to the assimilation of new information into the system of knowledge already possessed.

The study by Gino (2004) and Silverthorne (2004) indicates that in finance and accounting, analysts and decision makers do not avoid cognitive tendencies and certain errors in decision making (e.g. *information overweight bias, sunk cost bias*). Other authors also draw attention to the behavioral regularity which determines the accuracy of estimating the costs of information and other cost items (Booker et al 2007, Fleischman et al 2008). We may, then, speak of a tendency to underestimate or reduce costs as a result of certain cognitive tendencies (*cognitive biases*).

Authors of experiments on investment point to other regularities which are important for behavioral economics. The research by Felton, Gibson and Sanbornatsu (2003) shows that the preference of investment risk depends on the level of optimism as a trait of individual decision makers. Holt (2007), however, focuses in his experiments on the investors' behavior in situations of irreversibility of investment decisions. He is interested in categorising the decision makers – investors – according to the types of investment decisions into ones that do it quickly and those who devote more time to such decisions. Experimental studies in economics are already included in textbooks which contain not only a generalization of the research results, but also the methodology these studies (e.g. one of the first textbooks in the USA, by Davis and Holt 1992). In his studies, Holt (2006) points to the possibility of using experimental research on the labor market, both for the formulation of the premises and practical recommendations for social policy on the labor market and to build theoretical foundations for behavioral work economics. The author also indicated the opportunities offered by the behavioral games in research on thesaurization at the macroeconomic level.

A conclusion concerning the experimental results of decision making situations, we will focus on their contribution into economic theories, exemplified by experiments carried out by Smith. This author first proposed a new methodology for empirical research in economics, based on the experimental method. Based on this methodology, he presented an economic theory of value (Smith 1976). This methodology was developed from microeconomic systems, which became the area of interest for experimental sciences (Smith 1982), and then extended to international trade, which was tested in a situation of a *quasi-natural* experiment (Williams et al 2000). Experimental studies by Smith contributed to the development of behavioral economics, not only in terms of methodology, but also made significant contributions to the development of economic theories themselves, as it was stressed when Smith was being awarded the Nobel Prize 2002 in the field of economic sciences.

3.4.5. Critical remarks concerning the research on the information-seeking activity in a dynamic decision situation

Two central questions will allow us to make a critical assessment of the research on informational activities in decision making situations: 1) Are the research problems formulated in the studies reasonably and accurately? 2) Are these problems satisfactorily addressed by the researchers?

Any evaluation of experimental research should always bear in mind their limitations stemming from the methodological specificities of the experiment itself. The experimenter must first limit him- or herself to the simultaneous manipulation of very small numbers of variables. There is also no possibility to fully learn about the impact of the tested factors on the given phenomenon.

The above restrictions also apply to experiments investigating the informational activities, but this is not yet a valid reason for negating the value of experimental research in this field. Our review of the research has shown that there is currently a multi-directionality, both as regards the application of mathematical models, as well as the techniques and experimental procedures. Experiments are planned on normative models, based essentially on the theory of probability and mathematical statistics, or they focus on constructing or verifying a descriptive model of a certain aspect of informational activity. We have seen how most studies may be divided into certain stages, based on the normative models, and into steps aimed at constructing a descriptive model.

As for the experimental situations, researchers were interested in informational activity both in terms of "pure" laboratory conditions (where the decision maker was given problems of a more artificial type, modeled on various lottery games), as well as in *quasi-natural* conditions. But in the late 1990s began to appear independent analyses of the various aspects of the decision-makers behavior in natural decision situations (e.g., stock market, casinos, consumer situations). The multiplicity of directions for using mathematical models and a variety of experimental procedures indicate the richness and multi-dimensionality of the decision analysis problems. This fact should be noted as a positive moment, pointing to the development of a new discipline of decision analysis. This multidirectionality is actually typical for contemporary trends in the development of science which progresses towards narrow-specialist research.

One should, however, ask a more general question: does this trend not involve certain risks? In the research on informational activities we may distinguish many orientations, following almost entirely separate paths. An example might be the stream of research on finding reliable information and experiments exploring human behavior with a flow if probabilistic information. To date, hardly any attempts to bring two lines of research together have been made. It is unquestionable that the informational activity has its specificity in situation with an unreliable source of information in comparison to situations with reliable information. However, this fact does not indicate that informational activity, in both situations should be considered as diametrically opposing. Many of regularities are, after all, common to the course of the informational activity, both in terms of the information flow (unreliable and reliable). The very nature of this activity is actually more evident when comparing the behavior of decision makers in both cases. A methodological cause of difficulties in integrating the different research orientations is, among others, the different conceptual apparatus used in describing the research results. This terminology is usually relativized to a given mathematical model which is the basis for designing the experiments. With a great number of models the terminology quickly becomes "specialist" when describing the results involving a very narrow class of behavior. In a very short time the specialized terminology is hermetically sealed within a very narrow circle of specialists.

In this context, the attempts of authors like Pitz, Shanteau and Anderson aiming to create theoretical basis for integrating experimental research on informational activity are particularly valuable. These authors, indicating the elements which are common to certain models, stress that when adopting certain conditions, these models may reducible to each other. This line of research on the theoretical foundations of integration should be continued, since its basic reason of existence is the fact that most models are to some extent based on the theory of probability.

Attention may also be drawn to the dangers associated with a very narrow-specialist approach to research on informational activity. This remark is particularly crucial in "pure" laboratory conditions. Many experimenters, wishing to maximally ensure the control of variables form the model and the possibility an adequate description of the behavior, puts the decision makers in situations which are not very similar to natural conditions. This creates a serious risk of a lack of relevance and justification of the research problems undertaken.

An invalid and unreasonably formulated research problem was, among others, the question of the universality of cognitive conservatism proposed in the first phase of research on this phenomenon. The irrelevance of this problem lies in the fact that it implied a false assumption of a binomial distribution of signals emitted from the source. Research by DuCharme and Peterson (1968) showed that the binomial distribution put the decision makers in a very unnatural situation. In turn Vlek (1965) drew attention to the unfounded problem of universality of cognitive conservatism, given the variable in the study which was not controlled in these experiments, i.e. the conditional probability. The study of various authors who took into account this variable showed that the problem of universality of conservatism is wrongly formulated.

Phillips (1970) also points to the inaccuracy and lack of reasonability of certain experimental problems by indicating the danger of "objectification" of subjective states. The matter is very basic, but also complicated: it is about the methodological status of experimental research. There are no "purely" experimental studies, because – as shown by logical analyses – empirical terms always include a theoretical component. The role of guiding the planning of an experiment is always played by a certain theory of reality.

In the experiments on information and decision are also applied mathematical models, which are something intermediate, at least at the point of departure, between theory and psychological reality. Certain researchers more or less consciously identify the "entity" of the model (in the philosophical sense) with reality itself, or with the theory of that reality. This is where the serious danger of "objectification" of subjective states begins, as the use of models requires the adoption of a number of assumptions about the behavior of the participants.

Unfortunately, many authors do not realize the need to treat the assumptions of the mathematical model only hypothetically. Moreover, in many experiments the authors do not realize certain assumptions which imply a model. Philips (1970) also notes that the insufficiently developed methodological sense makes certain researchers treat the probability assessment – expressing the decision maker's subjective probability – as a category of probabilistic relations which are typical for random events in the physical world. Issues raised in these "objectivizing" experiments are obviously invalid and unfounded.

Finally, a summary question may be asked: What is the present value of the results of research on informational activities? In assessing the value of these results, it should be emphasized that they must be viewed relative to the situation in which they were obtained, and to the model and its assumptions on which these situations are planned. Thus, there appears a problem: to what extent may the regularity revealed in the studies be extrapolated to a broader class of decision situation? A response to this question is not possible at the current state of research. One is only able to only point out that experimental situations in which certain effects were obtained may not always be comparable, hence, their representativeness for a broader class of decision situations is very problematic.

It a critical assessment of the state of research on information activities we may conclude that, like the phenomenon of cognitive conservatism – the other patterns of behavior studied in a dynamic decision-making situations will undergo further stages of development. Certain effects are sure to be substantiated by determining the extent of their occurrence, while other ones will be generalized into a wider class of situations.

We may also ask about the possibility of a practical application of the research results on information activity in the analysis of dynamic decision situation of an economic type. Such use is possible and requires a prior interpretation of economic events that constitute the interaction of the economic decision maker with the specific environmental conditions which create the legal and political environment of his or her economic behavior.

Chapter 4. Two new variants of the optimal probabilistic model of the sequential search for probabilistic information in a dynamic decision-making situation

In dynamic decision situations, the decision maker faces the problem how long to search for information in order to reduce the uncertainty of the situation. The issue to be resolved in these situations is the problem if it is worth to cover the additional investment costs associated with the purchase of new information. In a situation where there is a potential sequence of purchasing information, there is the problem of the choice when to stop the sequential investment, and when it pays to have it continued. The previous sections have presented various models of descriptive and normative behavior of the decision maker in such situations. Certain behavioral regularities in these situations have also been discussed. Moreover, we have examined the problem of an optimal decision about the purchase of new information in a dynamic decision situation.

In the present chapter we will focus on the experimental type of decision situations where there is a possibility to buy a sequence of information from a source that emits signals carrying probabilistic (unreliable) information when, from the perspective of economic optimality criteria, it is still worth investing in another new piece of information knowing that the investment would not bring sure and reliable information, but only a probabilistic one. I will present a proposal of an experimental game with a sequential search for new information in a decision making situation. It will be a situation based on the Bayesian model, where the decision maker may purchase new information in a sequential manner in order to make a more accurate final decision. The problem which arises is thus: when is the search for the new information still optimal with regard to the costs of its purchase (the cost of the investment effort associated with this purchase)? This chapter will present two variants of an optimal model for new information: a model of a sequential search for new probabilistic information and a combinatorial model for the search of new probabilistic information.

4.1. Experimental decision-making game as an empirical model for seeking new probabilistic information in dynamic decision-making situations

In this section we present an experimental decision making game about searching for new probabilistic information in a dynamic decision situation. First, we will describe the preparatory phase of the game, and then, the main part of the experiment alongside with the strategy of research and the experimental procedure. This experiment will be treated as an empirical model of a dynamic decision situation in where the decision maker has the option of a sequential search for new probabilistic information. This search is a sequential process of investment, because the decision maker must pay the cost of the new information.

4.1.1. Description of a decision-making experimental game: the preparatory phase

In the experiment, after a brief conversation in the pre-decision phase of the experiment, the decision maker was familiarized with the functioning of the roulette device, whose elements are schematically shown in Figure 4.1. The participant was then able to practice the guessing (the game objective) in order to understand the rules and task of the game. After the preparatory phase, four decision situations (Situation I, Situation II, Situation II, Situation IV), each with two discs to choose from, were carried out in the main part of the experiment. The roulette device consisted of a stand-base, on which it was possible to put discs with different proportions of fields in green and blue, and of a pointer that could be spun[36].

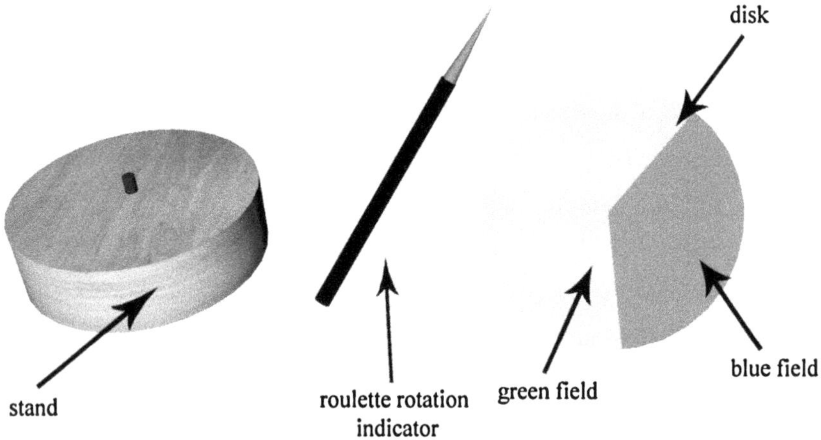

Figure 4.1. Elements of the roulette device used in the experiment

The decision maker spun the pointer of the device (as shown in Figure 4.2) and watched its movements and where it stopped. The trials with discs of varying proportions of colors in the preparatory phase aimed at teaching the decision maker how to properly assess the likelihood

[36] A description of this experiment is presented according to the version which carried for the first time by Biela in 1976. Choosing the colors we tried to avoid emotional preferences regarding the color itself; we generally managed to avoid this difficulty in the study.

of the pointer's stopping at a given color field. For example, if the decision maker spun the pointer over a disc where the blue field was twice as small as the green one, then he or she realized that the pointer was twice as likely to stop at a green field rather than a blue one.

After attempts to spin the pointer, the decision maker was informed that the device would be obscured with a screen, with a horizontal oblong hole through which the screw of the pointer was sticking out (for practical reasons, the screen actually had the shape of a box). The participant was explained that the roulette device would have one of the two already known discs, which he or she could also see in front of the screen, and the task would be to decide which one of them was inside.

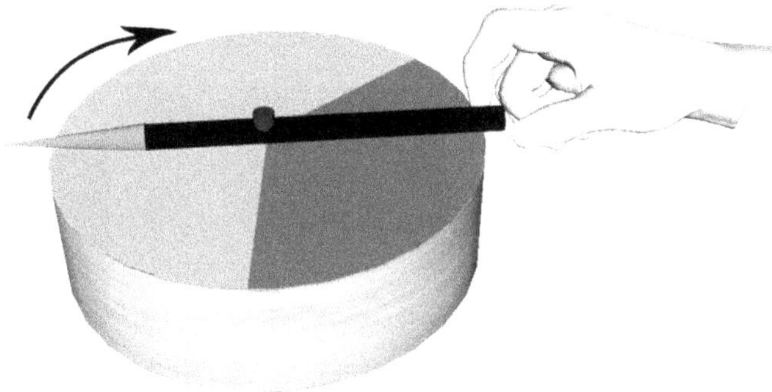

Figure 4.2. Putting the roulette pointer in motion in the preparatory phase of the experiment

Next, the experimenter explained to the decision maker that if he or she tried to guess which one of the two discs was hidden behind the screen, without any additional information, then in half of the cases he or she would guess correctly, and in half – incorrectly. In this way, the decision maker was *a priori* informed that the probability of the two discs being hidden behind the screen was equal and was $p = 0.50$. For a better understanding of this fact by the decision makers, two discs, with the same proportions of the fields as those behind the screen, were also placed in front of the screen (Figure 4.3a, 4.3b).

To visually illustrate the *a priori* and *a posteriori* probability, the decision maker was also shown a row of 100 probability markers (in the form of abacus beads) on a steel rod and explained that the markers reflected a forecasting which disc is hidden behind the screen. If someone guessed as many times as there were markers in a row, then half of the attempts might be successful, and half not. The experimenter illustrated this by sliding half of the markers towards the disc in front of the participant, and the other half towards the other disc (as in Figure 4.3.a).

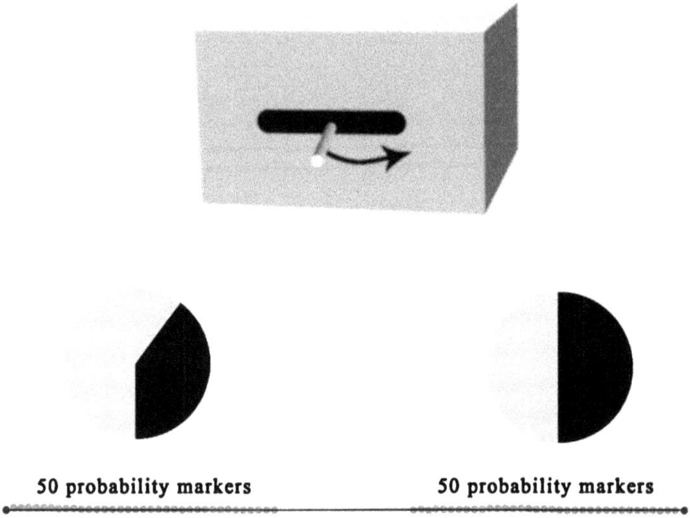

Figure 4.3.a. ***A priori*** **probability in the experiment illustrated by means of visual probability markers at the beginning of the experiment in Situation II of the experiment**

Hence, 50 probability beads on the right side of the bar meant a subjective probability of a correct guess if the indicated disc was on the right side, and 50 beads on the left side – indicated the probability of a wrong guess as to the hidden disc. This way, the participants were introduced into a dynamic decision situation of a closed type, where the *a priori* probability of hypotheses about the states of affairs equals $p(h_j) = 0.50$. The selection of such initial probability was also based on empirical arguments[37]. After spinning the roulette, the experimented informed the participant that the pointer stopped at the given color field (green or blue, accordingly). For example, in practicing Situation II (as shown in Figure 4.3b) if the pointer stopped at the given color field (e.g. green), the participants were informed that they may move a certain number of the probability markers (e.g. 7) towards the given disc (in this case, left). This exercise was repeated to teach the participants to express their assessment of probability.

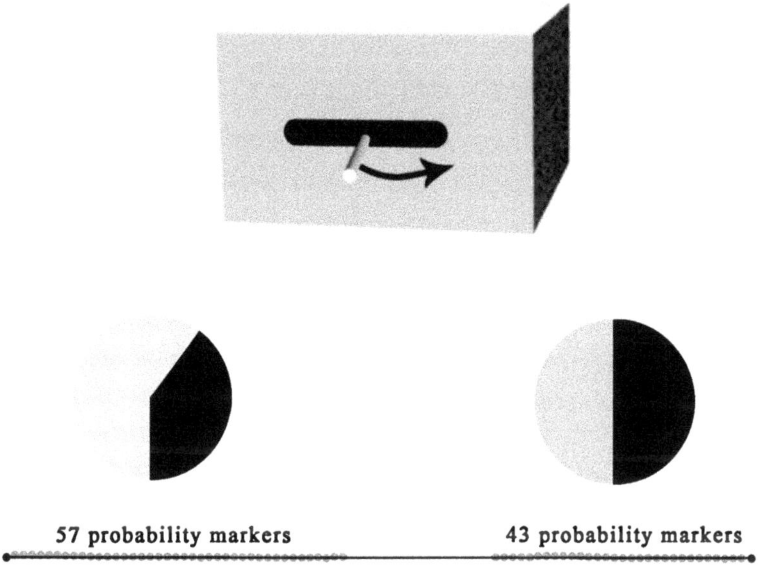

Figure 4.3.b. ***A posteriori*** **probability in the experiment illustrated by means of visual probability markers (57 and 43 beads on a rod) after obtaining the green signal** ***(z)*** **in the first informational cycle, as in Situation II of the experiment**

The last part of the preparation phase of the experiment was to inform the participants about the amount possible to be won, and the amount possible to be lost[38]. The decision

---

37 Another experiment, where the participant was to guess which of the two discs was hidden behind the screen, but without any additional information, showed that the participants estimated the probability of the hypotheses as close to the value of p(h) = 0.50 (Butrym 1973).

38 This experiment was preceded by a series of experimental situations in which participants judged the likelihood of simple and complex events, and made decisions regarding the amount of the bid in the game (see Walesa 1972). Before proceeding to this series of experiments, each participant received €3 in 10-cent coins. Thus, prior to the experiment

makers were also informed that for every signal they would be paying 10 cents[39], and that it is only up to them how many signals are bought. For a correct decision (proper identification) they would receive €2, while for a wrong one they would pay €6 (and have a debt with the experimenter, to be paid at the end of the experiment)[40]. The experimenter stressed that any mistake cost 60 times more than the purchase of one signal.

4.1.2. The key part of the experiment

After the preparatory phase, the key part of the experiment followed, which comprised four decision situations. In each situation, one out of two discs was hidden behind the screen. The proportions of the green field to the blue field on the discs in each situation of the experiment are shown in Table 4.1. The Table also presents the informative value of the obtained signals, expressed by the ratio of the proportions between the green and blue fields of the given two discs, as well as the correct answer as to which disc was hidden (the one on the right or the one on the left).

Table 4.l. The proportions of the green (z) and blue (n) area on the hidden discs used in the experiment in Situations I-IV

Situation No.	disc						ratio of green/blue proportions	correct answer
	right			left				
	z	n	z / n	z	n	z / n		
I	2/3	1/3	2:1	1/3	2/3	1:2	4	right
II	2/3	1/3	2:1	1/2	1/2	1:1	2	right
III	2/3	1/3	2:1	1/2	1/2	1:1	2	left
IV	2/3	1/3	2:1	3/4	1/4	3:1	0.66	left

In Table 4.1:

z – is the size of the green field on the disc;

n – is the size of the blue field on the disc;

z / n – is the relation of the green field to the blue one;

z / n (l) – is the relation of the green field to the blue one on the left disc;

---

regarding "decision making in situations with an unreliable source of information", the decision maker had the amount of money from €2 to €4, depending on the result of his or her performance in the previous situations.

[39] In the original experiments, Polish currency (zloty and grosz) was used.

[40] The experiment was designed to give the decision maker a chance to win some money in other series.

z / n (r) – is the relation of the green field to the blue one on the right disc.

The results in Table 4.1 indicate that in the subsequent cases, the smaller the differences in the proportions of the green and blue fields on the discs used, the smaller the informational value of the signal becomes. To make the experiment results comparable, a necessary simplification was that all participants heard the same sequence of signals – results of each roulette spin about the hidden disc – regardless of the actual results (however, this sequence of signals expressed the actual probability according to the random number generator. After the 12th and 15th spin, occurred a perfect match between the frequency of the appearance of a given signal and the conditional probability that the signal originates from the given disc. Biela (1976, 2001) presents sequences of signals in Situations from I to IV (*z* denotes the "green zone", while *n* – the "blue zone" on the x-axis) and the values of the Bayesian *a posteriori* probability after the successive signals (on the y-axis).

The experiment was designed so that in Situations I, II and III (each situation was a separate part of the experiment), to have a more clear picture of the probability as to the hidden disc, the decision maker could adjust the probability markers (physically move the beads) on the rod: after a green signal towards the disc with a larger green field, and after a blue signal towards the disc a larger field of blue. More significant differences between the proportions of blue or green fields on the two discs in Situation I facilitated a correct identification, because the signals allowed for larger changes in the value of the *a posteriori* probability (a higher informative value of the signals). However, the first three signals were in this situation "confusing". Although on the hidden disc 2/3 was blue and 1/3 was green, in the first three informational cycles the participants received signals informing them that the pointer stopped on the green field. In three following informational cycles, on the contrary, the signals indicated that the pointer stopped on the blue field. Hence, after the sixth cycle the *a posteriori* probability value – with an ideal modification of probability – was to reach the output value which was equal to the input, i.e. 50% (cf. Biela 2001: Figure 4.4). After the seventh informational cycle the decision makers received the green signal, and later from the eighth until the twelfth cycle they were receiving the same signals indicating that the pointer stopped on the blue field. The signal sequence in Situation I forced the decision makers to change the hypothesis, and thus helped to understand that the information the signals carry is only probabilistic (unreliable).

Situation IV was very difficult – although the signals exactly matched the random distribution (regularly every third signal was blue) – due to the small informative value of the signals. Here, the strategy of moving the probability markers on the rod towards the disc with a larger proportion of the green field (after the green signal) or towards the disc with a higher proportion of blue the blue one (after the blue signal) – would lead to an incorrect identification of the hidden disc.

4.1.3. The payoff matrix in the experiment and the method of testing

After each spin of the roulette pointer the decision makers paid 10 cents and performed an *a posteriori* probability estimation (by moving the probability markers on the rod towards the corresponding disc) as they wished. After each signal (giving the result of the spin: “green” or “blue”), the experimenter registered the estimation (how many probability markers were moved on the rod and in which direction) for each disc in the protocol card.

The participants decided alone how many signals to buy, how many probability markers to move and in which direction. In the main part of the study, the experimenter’s contact with the decision maker was limited to the display of the signals after each spin of the pointer, according to the standard distribution, and collecting the payments for the purchased signal. After the twelfth signal in all four experimental situations, the investigator asked the question: “Do you still wish to buy information?" If the decision makers agreed, the experimenter allowed them to buy three more signals, and then instructed them to identifuy the disc hidden behind the screen. For a correct guess the decision maker received a fixed reward (€2.00), and when an incorrect identification was made, he or she paid a fixed fine (-€6.00).

The study was conducted individually, strictly according to the instructions developed in the pilot studies[41]. The experiment took place without the presence of third parties.

4.2. Normative decision-making model of the sequential search for new probabilistic information

The preparatory phase of the informational activities in the experiment was limited to minimum. Such limitation was possible as the participant had initially been introduced into the decision situation of a set system: signal source – decision maker. The only necessary

[41] The pilot studies served to develop the preparatory and the basic part of the experiment . The instructions were modified several times, taking into account the criterion of their understandability by the participants.

condition for the participant to enter the decision situation with an unreliable source of information was to understand the instructions of the game.

The first version of the normative decision model of a sequential search for new probabilistic information was formulated by Biela (1976) for a psychological analysis of the informational process in a decision situation, focusing on the development of decision making and learning the optimal search for information by children and adolescents. In a further development of this model, its application was made for a probabilistic information search by managers in a dynamic decision situation (Biela 2001). The current application of this model is more general and refers to the behavioral aspect of finding probabilistic information in a dynamic decision situation. Such perspective of analysis is of interest not only to behavioral economics, but also other scientific disciplines belonging to the social and behavioral sciences.

4.2.1. The basic decision-making problem of the experimental game participant

To simplify our analysis of this experimental situation, we will be operating with a value function instead of a utility one. In this context, recalling the definition of the *DS* as a ordered triple (see: 1.1), for the purpose of a deductive systematization in the construction of a normative model, the decision situation in the experiment may be defined as:

$$SD \overset{df}{=} V = \langle D, H, v \rangle, \qquad (4.1)$$

where $D = \{d_1, d_2\}$ – is a two-piece set of actions; d_1 – is a guess that the disc hidden is disc 1; d_2 – is a guess that the disc hidden is disc 2; $H = \{h_1, h_2\}$ – is a two-piece set of states of affairs; h_1 – is a hypothesis of a hidden disc 1; h_2 – is a hypothesis of a hidden disc 2.

With a fixed value of the award (w = €2.00) and loss (s = - €6.00), the basic decision problem of the participant may be represented by a four-pole matrix V (see Table 4.2)

Table 4.2. Payoff matrix of the experimental game

D \ H	h_1	h_2
d_1	w	s
d_2	s	w

The decision situation in this experiment is a Bayesian one because the participant knows *a priori* the probability distribution on the set of hypotheses about the state of things: $p(h_1) = 0.50$, $p(h_2) = 0.50$. With a given distribution of the *a priori* of states of affairs, and the payoff matrix, the ideal decision maker may, in accordance with the *EV* criterion, determine the utility of the activities as the sum of the products of the value of the award w and the loss s multiplied by the probabilities of the given states of affairs:

$$\bigcap_i v(d_i\,; h_1, h_2) = wp(h_1) + sp(h_2)\,. \qquad (4.2)$$

Since matrix V in the experiment is symmetric, and the *a priori* probabilities are equal, the values of both activities d_i (where i = 1, 2), considering the results of the game, are the following:

$$\bigcap_i v(d_i; h_1, h_2) = (+1{,}00) + (-3{,}00)$$

As we may see, if the participants did not have the possibility to buy information about the state of things, it would be indifferent for them – in the sense of the *EV* criterion – what action to take action in the decision situation.

4.2.2. Posing the problem of the decision to start and continue the investment activity to find new probabilistic information

The participant of the decision making game has the possibility of a gradual flow of information in the experiment. We may thus say that he or she is in a dynamic decision situation, which may be defined as:

$$DSD^{df} = \langle D, H, v, I \rangle, \qquad (4.3)$$

where I is a one-element set ($I = \{1\}$), as the decision maker is only able to take one action, aiming to obtain a signal carrying information about the state of the source. The activity in the experiment is setting the roulette pointer (behind the screen) in a spinning motion. This operation will be referred to as *signiferent,* because it seeks to obtain signals z , or n from the source signals. In our experimental situation it is the preparatory phase, as this activity initiates the informational process, ultimately leading to a change of the probability distribution from an *a priori* to an *a posteriori* one.

Undertaking a signiferent activity is related to certain costs. In the experiment, the cost of the signiferent activity (putting the roulette pointer into motion) was c = €0.10. It is the investment cost to buy new probabilistic information in each informational cycle. Because in the experimental situation it is possible to undertake the signiferent activity many times, the informational activity was cyclic. In the subsequent experimental situations the decision maker was able to engage in up to 15 informational cycles.

Each cycle of informational activity – which consisted of a signal perception phase and a phase of processing the signal into information about the state of source – was preceded by an initial phase, called preparatory. At this stage the decision maker primarily considers the problem: *Is undertaking a signiferent activity in the given situation optimal, from the point of view of a given utility criterion?*

If the issue in question concerns the possibility of investing in the first informational cycle, we may call it a problem of *the decision to start.* If, then decision maker considers the value of undertaking a *following* cycle k (k>1), we may call it a *decision problem of continuing the information seeking.*

From a formal point of view, the decision to start may be considered such case of a decision to continue where k = 1. Psychologically speaking, however, there is a difference between these types of decisions. The function of the decision to start the activities is not only initiating the first cycle of information, but a certain attitude to "initiate" the whole informational process. A specific function of this decision is having a positive attitude which would facilitate the subsequent informational cycles. From the perspective of formal logic, the decision to start might be analogically interpreted as "the predecessor of the implication" for the decision to continue the information seeking in the informational process.

Regardless of the fact that these decision situations are psychologically different, in terms of their definition we will treat them both as:

$$SD_k \stackrel{df}{=} \langle D_{k-1}, Hv_{k-1} \rangle, \qquad (4.4)$$

Where: $D_{k-1} = \{d_{1(k-1)}, d_{2(k-1)}, d_{ik}\}$: $d_{1(k-1)}$ – is an adoption of hypothesis h_1 without initiating cycle k; $d_{2(k-1)}$ – is an adoption of hypothesis h_2 without initiating cycle k; d_{ik} – is an adoption of hypothesis k after possibly initiating cycle k (where i, j = 1,2); $H = \{h_1, h_2\}$; h_1 – is a hypothesis about hidden disc 1; h_2 – is a hypothesis about hidden disc 2; v_{k-1} – is the function of value determined on the Cartesian product of $D_{k-1} \times H$.

4.2.3 The value of unreliable information

To determine v_{k-1}, the decision maker must assess what value for problem SD_k may be provided by obtaining information in cycle k. By information about the state of the source (states of affairs) Szaniawski (1971b) understands an ordered pair:

$$R_H = \langle X, \{ p_H \} \rangle, \tag{4.5}$$

where: R_H – is the information on the state of the source, i.e., a set of states $H = \{h_1, h_2, ..., h_m\}$; $X = \{x_1, x_2, ..., x_m\}$ – is the set signals which may be obtained from the source; p_H – is a set of probability distributions on X indicated by the individual states of H.

The author defines the concept of pragmatic information in relation to the given decision problem. The value of information is seen as a possible way of using this information. Such a pragmatic interpretation, however, seems not to exclude the semantic aspect of information. On the contrary, the semantic criterion is one of the determinants of the pragmatic value of information, as it is not irrelevant to the decision problem if the decision maker, who must count with certain costs, is able to obtain information which is reliable or only unreliable. The pragmatic value of unreliable information for the given decision problem is different than the one of reliable information, with the same costs of purchase.

The pragmatic approach is also in line with the so-called Shannon's selective approach. There are three possible models of seeing the relationship between the pragmatic and the statistic/selective information: 1) treating Shannon's information as a specific case of pragmatic information, 2) a pragmatic interpretation of the Shannon's selective information, 3) an intermediate position, treating the two concepts as different aspects, reducible to each other when adopting certain assumptions.

An attempt to treat the quantitative Shannon approach to information as a special case of pragmatic information was made by Lissowski (1973). The basic assumption of his interpretation was treating the function of loss as a function of probability. A pragmatic interpretation of selective information also seems possible to be carried out. Such attempts would certainly have to assume, that measuring information is with reference to the specific decision problem. The bit measure would then be incorporated into the concept of information concerning the decision problem. The basis for such interpretation is given, among others, by. Hintikka (1968), who proposes a distinction between the measurement of information about unexpected events *(unexpectedness)* and the so-called actual information *(substantive)*. Although this author does not address the concept of information in the context of a decision situation, but he introduces the concept of an expected value of information, which seems to allow for such possibility.

The third proposal of approaching information is advocated, among others, by Szaniawski, who believes that both pragmatic and selective information in a similar manner depend on the two-dimensional nature of the probability distribution $p(x,s)$ = probability $\{X = x \wedge S = s\}$. This author limited the concept of pragmatic information to the so-called epistemic decision problem, defined by a utility matrix (Szaniawski 1974). To develop a model to assess the value of information for problem SD_k in the experimental situation it does not seem necessary to introduce the Shannon measurement. While using this measurement would be possible when analyzing the uncertainty of the decision maker, however, it would not bring any new elements to the pragmatic model for assessing information in the decision situation.

How may the decision maker assess the pragmatic value of the information possible to be obtained the informational cycle *k*? And further, how the decision maker will decide, according to the *EV* criterion (such is the basic criterion for the decision problem of the decision maker), whether or not to take a series of informational *k?*

To answer these questions, the decision maker needs to look at the point of departure, which is the relationship between the signals emitted from the source and the states of the source itself. Establishing this relationship will, among others, determine whether the information possible to obtain is reliable or not.

What is the source of the signals and how are signals emitted in the experimental situation described here? Signals that could be emitted in this situation were statistically independent, because the probability of the emission of a specific signal in a given information cycle did not depend on any signal emitted in previous cycles. Emission of signals may thus be interpreted as draw sample "with the phrase", and the signal source in our experiment will be interpreted as emitting signals " without memory" .

In each information cycle in this experiment, the decision maker may receive a green signal *(z)* or a blue one *(n)*. Signals may be emitted from a source that is in state h_1 – when it is hidden behind a screen disc 1, or in state h_2 – for the hidden disc 2. The probability of the origin of the signal from a given disc is defined by the conditional probability $p(x_i/h_j)$. For example, in case I, when hidden is one of the two discs: h_1 – with a proportion of green to blue of 1:2, or h_2 – with a proportion green to blue 2:1, the conditional probability of obtaining a blue signal, if hidden is disc h_1, is $p(n/h_1)$ = 0.66, while the probability of obtaining the blue signal from the hidden disc h_2, is $p(n/h_2)$ = 0.33. In the same situation, the conditional probability of obtaining a green signal with hidden disc 1 is $p(z/h_1)$ = 0.33, while with hidden disc 2 it amounts to $p(z/h_2)$ = 0.66.

Hence, in our case, the signals emitted from the source in the experimental situations do not contain reliable information about the state of things (i.e. the disc hidden behind the screen), and may only be processed into uncertain information, which a direct measure is the difference between the *a priori* probability of hidden disc 1 or 2, *a posteriori* probability (i.e., after receiving the green or blue signal), that is obtained under the Bayesian model.

As the informational activity in the course of this experimental situation is cyclical (sequential), and therefore the *a posteriori* probability of the hypotheses after receiving a signal in cycle k-1 becomes the *a priori* probability of the hypothesis before obtaining the signal in the next k information cycle. This is how the decision maker is able to modify the *a posteriori* probability distribution on the set of hypotheses about the state of things in the cycle k, depending on the sequence of signals obtained in the k-1 cycle, and the signal to be tested in cycle k.

We assume that e_{k-1} means a sequence of signals generated in the sequence of k-1 informational cycle. After a cycle of k-1, according to the Bayesian model, the *a priori* probability distribution on the set of hypotheses $H = \{h_1, h_2\}$, is transformed into the *a posteriori* distribution which may be determined as: $p(h_1/e_{k-1})$, $p(h_2/e_{k-1})$.

Operating with cash values may be considered to assess the value of $d_{1(k-1)}$ and $d_{2(k-1)}$, according to the *EV* criterion, as a sum of the product value of winning by the *a posteriori* probability of the corresponding hypothesis, and the product of the appropriate value of the loss by the *a posteriori* probability of the second hypothesis. The value of the award/winning and the value of the loss are, of course modified according to the cost of purchasing k-1 signals.

The values of $d_{1(k-1)}$ and $d_{2(k-1)}$ considering the possible states of affairs may be calculated as:

$$v\,(d_{1(k\text{-}1)}\,h_j) = [wp\,(h_1/\,e_{k\text{-}1}) + sp\,(h_2\,/\,e_{k\text{-}1})] - c\,(k\text{-}1), \qquad (4.6)$$

$$v\,(d_{2\,(k\text{-}1)}\,h_j) = [sp\,(h_1/\,e_{k\text{-}1}) + wp\,(h_2\,/\,e_{k\text{-}1})] - c\,(k\text{-}1), \qquad (4.7),$$

where c – cost of the signal – is constant in each cycle.

To assess the value of d_{ik} by the result of the game, according to the *EV* criterion, the decision maker must be familiar with the *a posteriori* hypothetical probability distribution on the set of possible hypotheses in cycle k. This distribution is not only a function of the *a priori* probability of the hypotheses before cycle k *(a posteriori probabilities* by cycle k-1 are *a priori,* before each k cycle), but also depends on the resulting signal in cycle k.

Before each cycle k of information seeking, the decision maker must consider the possibility of obtaining a green signal *(z)* with the conditional probability of $p(z/h_1)$ or $p(z/h_2)$ or a blue signal *(n)* with the conditional probability $p(n/h_1)$ or $p(n/h_2)$.

We assume that X_k is a random variable with values: z (cycle k to obtain a green signal) and n (cycle k to obtain a blue signal). To determine the probability distribution of this variable, one should calculate the average of the conditional probabilities of the *a posteriori* probability of hypotheses of cycle k - 1.

The probability of obtaining a green signal in the cycle k would therefore be:

$$p_k(z = p(z/h_1)p(h_1/e_{k-1}) + p(z/h_2)\, p(h_2/e_{k-1}) = \sum_j p(z/h_j)\, p(h_j/e_{k-1}). \qquad (4.8),$$

The probability of obtaining a blue signal in cycle k would, in turn, equal to:

$$p_k(n = p(n/h_1)p(h_1/e_{k-1}) + p(n/h_2)\, p(h_2/e_{k-1}) = \sum_j p(n/h_j)\, p(h_j/e_{k-1}). \qquad (4.9).$$

The conditional probabilities are constant in all cycles:

$$p\,(z/h_j) = \text{const. and } p(n/h_j) = \text{const.}$$

The hypothetical *a posteriori* probabilities change with each cycle, depending on the received signal. If in cycle k decision maker received a signal from the source, then the *a posteriori* probability distribution on set $H = \{h_1, h_2\}$ has been appropriately modified (symbol $\wedge$ denotes the conjunction of sequence e_{k-1} with signal z or n)[42]:

$$p\,(h_1/e_{k-1} \wedge z); \qquad p\,(h_2/e_{k-1} \wedge z).$$

In the case of the signal for n the *a posteriori* probability distribution would look like this:

$$p\,(h_1/e_{k-1} \wedge n); \qquad p\,(h_2/e_{k-1} \wedge n)$$

The way to use the information by the decision maker depends on making a choice in cycle k (i.e. d_{ik}) after the obtainable signal. This way, it is convenient for us to understand the way of using information, after K. Szaniawski (1971b), as a *function of decision* δ. Every decision is a function defined on a set of signals X_k and takes values from the set of possible actions: d_{1k} d_{2k} . The assignment of a set of signals to the elements of a set of actions by the

[42] These notations are perhaps difficult to read because of the uniqueness, but their value is for the accuracy and clarity. Each of the four introduced symbols shows that the *a posteriori* probability of the hypothesis is a function of sequence e_{k-1} and the type of signal obtained in cycle k.

decision function δ is understood in such way if the ideal decision maker obtains signal z or n in cycle k, then he or she takes an action due to be determined by δ the use of information.

In our experimental situation the set of all decision functions is a four-field one (2x2), as a player may receive two signals and point to one of the two discs possible to be hidden behind the screen. However, we may show that only one function from the set of 2x2 decisions is optimal in the sense of the *EV* criterion, which the decision maker uses. By δ^{k}_{opt} we mean the optimal decision function which assigns of signal n or z in cycle k an action that is optimal according to the *EV* criterion. This condition satisfies only the decision function, which allows us to us accept the hypothesis we are testing, if its *a posteriori* probability is the greatest when in cycle k the decision maker receives signal n, or the hypothesis whose *a posteriori* probability is the greatest after receiving signal z in cycle k. This condition may be summarized in a definition:

$$\delta^{k}_{opt}(e_k) \overset{df}{=} \begin{cases} d_{1(k)}, & \text{if } p(h_1/e_k) > 0.5, \\ d_{2(k)}, & \text{śli } p(h_2/e_k) > 0.5. \end{cases} \qquad (4.10).$$

Thus, $\delta^{k}_{opt}(s_k) = d_{ik}\ opt$,where $d_{ik}\ opt$ is the optimum performance in terms of *EV* designated by the function of an optimal decision. This definition does not cover the case where the *a posteriori* probabilities are equal. In that case the decision function prefers no action as they are indifferent in the sense of *EV*.

The sequence of signals s_k is known, however, only to the player in cycle k-1. The hypothetical *a posteriori* probabilities after cycle k may have one of two the following values:

$$p(h_1/e_k) = \begin{cases} p(h_1/e_{k-1} \wedge z) \\ p(h_1/e_{k-1} \wedge n) \end{cases} \qquad (4.11).$$

$$p(h_2/e_k) = \begin{cases} p(h_2/e_{k-1} \wedge z) \\ p(h_2/e_{k-1} \wedge n) \end{cases} \qquad (4.11').$$

According to definition (4.10) we may say that the decision maker takes action d_{ik} with the results of operations in the signiferent cycle k. He or she will take action d_{1k} if after receiving signal z the probability meets the inequality $p(h_1/e_{k-1} \wedge z) > p(h_2/e_{k-1} \wedge z)$ or if the probability of obtaining n signal meets the inequality $p(h_1/e_{k-1} \wedge n) > p(h_2/e_{k-1} \wedge n)$. The player takes action d_{2k}, if after receiving signal z the probability meets the inequality $p(h_2/e_{k-1} \wedge z) > p(h_1/e_{k-1} \wedge z)$ or if after receiving signal n he or she meets the inequality $p(h_2/e_{k-1} \wedge n) > p(h_1/e_{k-1} \wedge n)$. If, however, after receiving a signal, the *a posteriori* probabilities of both hypotheses are equal, then the optimal decision function determines the actions of d_{1k} and d_{2k} as indifferent in terms of *EV*.

The value of d_{1k} in obtaining the signal may therefore be determined in accordance with the criterion *EV* as:

$$v(d_{1k}, h_j) = wp(h_1/e_{k-1} \wedge z) + sp(h_2/e_{k-1} \wedge z), \quad (4.12)$$

where: $p(h1/ek\text{-}1 \wedge z) > p(h2/ek\text{-}1 \wedge z;$

or, if: $v(d1k,hj)=wp(h2/ek\text{-}1 \wedge z)+ sp(h1/ek\text{-}1 \wedge z)$ (4.12'),

when: $p(h_2/e_{k-1} \wedge z) > p(h_1/e_{k-1} \wedge z)$.

The conditions set out in models (4.12) and (4.12 ') stem directly from definition (4.10) and equalities (4.11) and (4.11') and means simply that the ideal decision maker will point to the hypothesis which is *a posteriori* more likely.

Also, the value of the d_{2k} probability after receiving signal n may be calculated according to the *EV* as:

$$v(d_{2k}, h_j) = sp(h_1/e_{k-1} \wedge n) + wp(h_2/e_{k-1} \wedge n), \quad (4.13)$$

where: $p(h_2/e_{k-1} \wedge n) > p(h_1/e_{k-1} \wedge n)$,

or: $v(d_{2k}, h_j) = sp(h_2/e_{k-1} \wedge n) + wp(h_1/e_{k-1} \wedge n)$, (4.13')

where: $p(h_1/e_{k-1} \wedge n) > p(h_2/e_{k-1} \wedge n)$.

The condition in formulas (4.13) and (4.13 ') should be understood as in (4.12) and (4.12').

With a given $p_k(z)$ in formula (4.8) and $p_k(n)$ in formula (4.9), the value of an optimal decision in cycle k may be calculated as an average of the maximum values of $v(d_{1k})$ and $v(d_{2k})$, minus the cost of buying the signal in cycle k:

$$v(d_{1k}, h_j)_{opt} = [v(d_{1k})\, p_k(z) + v(d_{2k})\, p_k(n)] - ck. \quad (4.14)$$

Using the terminology of Szaniawski (1974), we assume that $C_k(X, H, V)$ is the pragmatic value of information realizable in cycle k considering the fundamental problem of decision *(SD)* of an ideal decision maker who uses the *EV* criterion. The value of that information may be expressed as:

$$C_k(X, H, V) = v(d_k, h_j)_{opt} - max[v(d_{1(k-1)}, h_j), v(h_{2(k-1)}, h_j) \quad (4.15).$$

By $max\ v(d_{1(k-1)}, h_j), v(h_{2(k-1)}, h_j)$ we obviously understand the value of action maximizing that value without considering the information cycle *k*.

The decision maker's undertaking cycle *k* in an optimal way, should satisfy the inequality:

$$C_k (X, H, V) > 0 \qquad (4.16)$$

This condition appears clear, because no rational decision maker would undertake a cycle where the value of the information obtained would be negative. This would mean that the cost of cycle *k* exceeds the value of the information possible to be obtained[43].

The decision maker progresses according to the *EV* criterion decides to undertake cycle *k* if and only if the pragmatic value of the information possible to be obtained is greater than zero.

Knowing the value of the pragmatic information realizable in cycle *k,* the decision maker may therefore decide whether to undertake the first cycle (decision to start, where $k = 1$) and subsequent cycles (decision to continue, where $k>1$) of informational activities in the decision situation.

The equivalent figure of the pragmatic criterion of informational value expressed in formula (4.16) is a fulfillment of the following inequalities:

$$v(d_{ik}, h_j)_{opt} > v(d_{i(k-1)}, h_j) \qquad (4.17)\ .$$

The presented model of the evaluation of the sequential cycles of information, according to criterion *EV* assumes that the decision maker asks after each cycle k -1, whether to continue seeking information or not. This model will be referred to as the *model sequential simplel.*

It is also possible to develop such model that would enable to assess the usefulness of cycle *k* before undertaking any (first, second, etc.) information cycles. This model may be developed by using combinatorial accounting – the possible sequences of signals *k* [44]. The *combinatorial sequential model* requires from the decision maker quite complicated combinatorial calculations (with a larger number of signals) when calculating the *a posteriori* probabilities of hypotheses. This model may be more important in automated systems, programming and data processing.

[43] In experimental studies it has also been found that certain decision makers actually implement such cycles where the value of the obtainable information is negative.

[44] The combinatorial sequential model requires to consider the 2^{k-1} signal sequences in the calculation of $p_k(n)$ and $p_k(z)$.

4.2.4. The cognitive decision in processing signals into probabilistic information (transformational decision)

After deciding to continue, the decision maker implements the signiferent activity (puts into motion the roulette pointer), paying for the cost of the signal. After this preparation phase takes place the reception of the signal and the phase of signal processing into information about the state of things. In this experiment the phase of the reception only consisted in the perception of the visual-auditory green or blue signal.

The transition phase, i.e. the processing of the signal into information, consists of a change – influenced by the resulting signal – of the degree of certainty as to the disc hidden behind the screen.

Given the conditional probability that the signal source being state h_1 or h_2 and the *a priori* probability of the two hypotheses, we may conclude that for an ideal decision maker acting under the rules of the probability theory, the transformation phase is inference-based, according to the Bayesian rule. The result of this procedure is to modify the probability distribution on the set of states of affairs of a given signal according to the Bayesian model. The ideal decision maker after obtaining signal *k,* would not have any problems, in which direction and to what extent to change the belief as to the disc hidden behind the screen, or how to modify the probability distribution on the set of states of affairs.

The processing of the signals into probabilistic information is a cognitive activity, whose course is related to the decision concerning the establishment of a new probability distribution on the basis of the *a posteriori* probability obtained from the signal which may be regarded as a specific value of a random variable. If a person knew the rules of probability, the signal processing of information would then be a normal process of mathematical operations. There is even an approach which postulates treating the human brain as "intuitive statistics" (Peterson and Beach, 1966). This concept does not imply, however, that it is a probability system, but only uses a certain analogy. Essentially, a person having to solve a problem of cognition, which is signal processing of probabilistic information, is also facing the problem of decision making where a result of this decision is to transform the signal into information. Such decision may be briefly described as a *transformation decision.*

Based on the behavioral problems, transformation decisions in our experimental situation may be formulated in the following question: in what direction and how many probability markers (which indicate the degree of certainty) must the participant move after obtaining the signal?

In formal language this situation may be defined as:

$$SD_t = \langle Q, H, v^t \rangle$$

where $Q = q_1^l, q_2^l$; where : q_1^l - l the participant shifts probability markers towards disc 1, q_2^l - l markers move towards disc 2 (where l may take the value of 0 or a value from set L_1: {1, 2, ..., L} and L_2: {l, 2, ..., 100 - l}, where L is the number of the probability markers, e.g. of disc1, $H = \{h_1, h_2\}$, where: h_1 - hypothesis of hidden disc l, h_2 - hypothesis of hidden disc 2.

The equivalent figure of the decision problem SD_t is the matrix shown in Table 4.3.

Table 4.3. Payoff matrix V_t that defines the decision problem SD_t of transformation in the situation of experimental games

H / Q	h_1	h_2
q_1	$v^t(q_1^l, h_1)$	$v^t(q_1^l, h_2)$
q_2	$v^t(q_2^l, h_1)$	$v^t(q_2^l, h_2)$

The presented matrix is of course only a four-field V-diagram, because l is a variable receiving the value of the set L_1 and L_2. The $v^t(q_1^l, h_1)$ symbol is the value of the game where the decision maker has shifted a number of l markers towards disc 1 and this disc is actually hidden behind the screen; $v^t(q_1^l, h_2)$ represents the outcome of the game when the decision makers shifted l markers towards of disc 1, while disc 2 is actually hidden behind the screen.

Similarly, $v^t(q_2^l, h_1)$ designates the result of the game where the decision maker moved l probability markers towards disc 2, while actually disc 1 was hidden behind the screen, and $v^t(q_2^l, h_2)$ - the game result if the player moved l probability markers towards disc 2 and this disc was actually hidden behind the screen.

The actual number of rows in matrix V_t (i.e. the size of the set of actions Q) may be determined by aggregating the number of possible shifts towards disc 1 to the number of possible shifts towards disc 2 and taking into account the possibility of not shifting the probability markers in any direction: l + (100- l) + 1 = 101. Hence, if the player discharged all elements Q, matrix V_t would be of (101 x 2)-fields.

If SD_t is considered in isolation from SD and SD_k, the problem of the transformational decision may be interpreted as an epistemic decision problem, where $v^t(q_1^l, h_1)$ and $v^t(q_1^l, h_2)$ would have a unit value (i.e. be of value 1) and the remaining values would be zero. In this case the value of the activity would mean a cognitive satisfaction resulting from the subjective degree of compliance of the assessment with the objective state of affairs.

Such an interpretation is, however, not entirely accurate, because the transformational decision problem is entangled in the decision to continue informational operations in the decision situation. Therefore, the usefulness of the transformational decision must be viewed as an argument of value function which is a result of the game. Quite apart from any psychological factors, the optimal model of a transformational decision in the statistical sense should mean moving a number of probability markers, as defined by the Bayesian model.

The objective determinants of the transformational decision are: the output signal *n* or *z*; the conditional probability of its emission from the source which is in state h_1 or h_2,. *a priori* the probability of the hypotheses (as probability markers of disc 1 and 2 before the transformational decision has been taken). The function of the decision is to shift *l* probability markers towards one of the discs. The string of transformation decisions is an essential determinant of the transformation steps in a dynamic decision situation – the number and direction of moving the probability markers are essential factors for the decision maker: whether to continue the next cycle of information and take the final decision, i.e. to formulate a diagnosis as to the disc hidden behind the screen in the given experimental situation.

4.2.5. The scheme of decisions designating the informational activity

The above analysis enables to formulate a thesis that a model course of informational activities in situations of probabilistic information seeking, is *a string of decisions* in mutual relations. A diagram of these relations is shown in Figure 4.4.

As indicated by the diagram how a hypothetical decision making operates, the priority role is played by the block of the decision to start the operations. Its function is to undertake (or not) the first cycle of information, the first stage of the signiferent activity and shape a positive attitude of the decision-maker to facilitate the updating of cycles. In our scheme, these functions are illustrated by the two "exits" from the same block.

The relationships between the block initiating the first cycle of information are marked on the chart with a dotted line. The block of the decision to start serves as feedback to the block of transformation decision, meant to alter the *a priori* probability of the hypotheses into *a posterio*ri in the given situation. A behavioral expression of this decision is to shift a number of probability markers towards one or the other disc in the experiment.

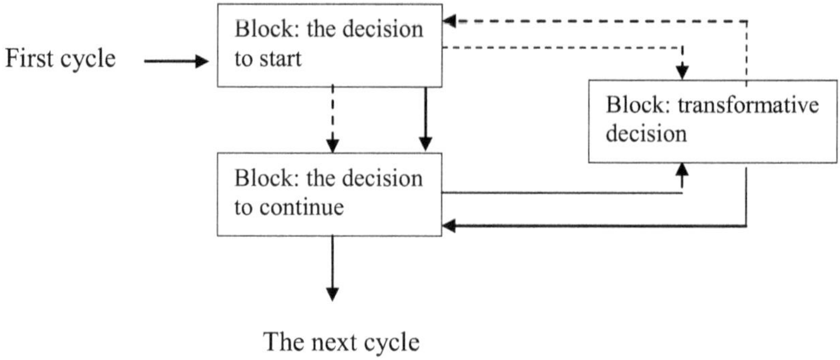

Figure 4.4. Schematic structure of decisions related to informational activities with an unreliable source of information

Before deciding to start any activity, the decision-maker must be aware of how to change the probability distribution on the set of hypotheses after receiving signal *z* or *n* in the first cycle. This function satisfies the block of transformation, which in Figure 4.4 is shown as a schematic feedback of the decision to start the operations.

In order to undertake the next cycle of information the decision maker must also be aware of the expected *a posteriori* probability distribution after signal *z* or *n* or in cycle *k*. On this basis, one may only assess the pragmatic value of this cycle. The transformation decision block plays a role of information evaluation in the expected next new informational cycle which may be undertaken by the decision maker. The decision making diagram in Figure 4.4 indicates the connection between the blocks actualizing the sequential information cycles – which is marked by the solid line.

The answer to the question what is the actual course of informational operations in a decision situation with a source of unreliable information requires to present the results of the experimental task. The decision making model of informational activity will serve as a reference point for analyzing the behavior of decision makers in the experiment.

The model may find wide application in the analysis of managerial decisions (Biela, 2001), where the decision maker has the ability to make investments aimed at providing information about the conditions in the market (e.g. based on data about the behavior of consumers, suppliers, competitors, capital market institutions). We may also indicate the scope of the application of this model for a sequential analysis in behavioral economics, including the analysis of macro economical decisions, where the decision maker, individual or group, has the opportunity to consider the issue of investing in the search for new information in a given situation (e.g. through an analysis of statistical data collected by the Central Statistical Office, EUROSTAT or other sources), which should be evaluated as the cost of investing in information.

4.3. Combinatorial model of decision-making concerning a purchase of probabilistic information

The model presented in the above section is a simple sequential model because after each cycle the decision maker asks whether to continue the search for information or not. It is also possible to develop a model that would enable to assess the usefulness of cycle *k* before undertaking any information cycle. In this section, this model will be presented. We will try to demonstrate the various properties that will help us to create creating the model.

The value of probabilities does not depend on the order of the sequence of signals

We will start our analysis from the Bayesian formula assuming, for example, that the decision maker received signal *z:*

$$p(h_1/z)=\frac{p(h_1)p(z/h_1)}{\sum_j p(h_1)p(z/h_j)} \tag{4.18}$$

Using this pattern, with an appropriate sequence of data signals, we may find a corresponding sequence probability $p(h_1/zz)$ and $p(h_1/n)$. Then, instead of hypothesis $p(h_1)$ and $p(h_2)$, we substitute them with the previously calculated $p(h_1/z)$. These models will look as follows:

$$p(h_1/zz)=\frac{p(h_1/z)p(z/h_1)}{\sum_j p(h_j/z)p(z/h_j)}$$

$$p(h_1/zn)=\frac{p(h_1/z)p(n/h_1)}{\sum_j p(h_j/z)p(n/h_j)}.$$

This shows that in order to find out the next *a posteriori* probability in the sequential simple model (i.e. step by step model) one know the earlier probabilities in previous sequence of informational cycles But there is another equivalent formula for counting these probabilities, with no need for further calculations. To determine the probability of disc 1 or 2 being hidden, the formula requires only the number of green and blue signals, and it is not necessary to know their sequence.

The following induction demonstrates the equivalence of these models. We therefore have to prove that:

$$p(h_1/e_{k-1} \wedge z) = p(\underbrace{h_1/znnznz...z}_{s-zi(k-s)-n}) = \frac{p(h_1)p(z/h_1)^s\, p(n/h_1)^{k-s}}{\sum_j p(h_j)p(z/h_j)^s} \tag{4.19}$$

To prove the above equivalence, we need to prove the following two implications:

1. $$p(\underbrace{h_1/znnznz...z}_{s-zi(k-s)-n}) \Rightarrow \frac{p(h_1)p(z/h_1)^s\, p(n/h_1)^{k-s}}{\sum_j p(h_j)p(z/h_j)^s}$$

2. $$\frac{p(h_1)p(z/h_1)^s\, p(n/h_1)^{k-s}}{\sum_j p(h_j)p(z/h_j)^s} \Rightarrow p(\underbrace{h_1/znnznz...z}_{s-zi(k-s)-n}) .$$

We first prove the first implication by means of mathematical induction.

Checking first for $k = 1$ we receive:

$$p(h_1/z) = \frac{p(h_1)p(z/h_1)}{\sum_j p(h_1)p(z/h_j)} .$$

We assume that for an r:

$$p(\underbrace{h_1/znnznz...z}_{s-zi(k-s)-n}) \Rightarrow \frac{p(h_1)p(z/h_1)^s\, p(n/h_1)^{k-s}}{\sum_j p(h_j)p(z/h_j)^s} .$$

We prove that for $r+1$:

$$p(\underbrace{h_1/znnznz...zz}_{s+1-zi(r-s)-n}) = \frac{p(h_1)p(z/h_1)^{s+1}\, p(n/h_1)^{r-s}}{\sum_j p(h_j)p(z/h_j)^{s+1}} .$$

This statement may also be formulated as:

$$p(\underbrace{h_1/znnznz...z \wedge z}_{s-zi(r-s)-n}) .$$

The first part of the formula we have taken as an assumption. Using Bayes' formula (4.15) we may state that:

$$p(\underbrace{h_1/znnznz...zz}_{s+1-zi(r-s)-n}) = \frac{p(\underbrace{h\ /znnznz...z}_{s-zi(r-s)-n})p(z/h_1)}{\sum_j p(h_j)p(z/h_j)^s + \sum_j p(h_j) * p(\underbrace{h_1/znnznz...zz}_{s+1-zi(r-s)-n})} \tag{4.20}$$

Substituting the numerator of our inductive assumption, and grouping the sum in the denominator, we receive our thesis. The r selected was arbitrary, so by mathematical induction we may define our probabilistic expectations. It is a very important achievement, because it allows much faster, easier and cheaper decision making.

In order to demonstrate the equivalence of the formula (3.16) is still required to prove the implication:

$$\frac{p(h_1)p(z/h_1)^s\, p(n/h_1)^{k-s}}{\sum_j p(h_j)p(z/h_j)^s} \Rightarrow p(\underbrace{h_1/znnznz...z}_{s-zi(k-s)-n}) \quad .$$

The proof will be carried out by mathematical induction.

For $k = 1$ we obtain the Bayes' formula:

$$\frac{p(h_1)p(z/h_1)}{\sum_j p(h_j)p(z/h_j)} = p(h_1/z) \quad .$$

The first part of the inductive proof is met. We assume that for any r, the following implication is true:

$$\frac{p(h_1)p(z/h_1)^s\, p(n/h_1)^{r-s}}{\sum_j p(h_1)p(z/h_j)^s} \Rightarrow p(\underbrace{h\ /znnznz...z}_{s-zi(r-s)-n}) \quad .$$

We may prove that it is also true for $r+1$.

If it is determined for $r+1$, we may obtain the following expression:

$$\frac{p(h_1)p(z/h_1)^s + 1p(n/h_1)^{r+1-s}}{\sum_j p(h_j)p(z/h_j)^s + 1} \Rightarrow p(\underbrace{h_1/znnznz...z}_{s-zi(r+1-s)-n}) \quad .$$

This expression may also be formulated as:

$$\frac{p(h_1)p(z/h_1)^s\, p(n/h_1)^{r-s} * p(z/h_1) * p(n/h_1)}{\sum_j p(h_j)p(z/h_j)^s + p(h_j)p(z/h_j)^{s+1}} \Rightarrow p(\underbrace{h_1/znnznz...z}_{s-zi(r-s)-n}) \quad .$$

Using the inductive assumption and the Bayes' formula (4.15) after appropriate grouping of the above formulas we receive the thesis. Hence, by mathematical induction, the implication proves to be true. As has been proven for two implications, we may conclude that the equivalence of these two formulas is shown to be proved.

The next step is to define the inequality which will determine whether it is more profitable to buy information or to make the final decision. Therefore, let us consider a cycle where there are green signals r and blue signals r-s. We will calculate the number of possible combinations of the green and blue signals:

$$S = \sum_{s=0}^{r} C_r^s = \frac{r!}{s!*(r-s)!}\quad .$$

For example, for $r = 6$ we receive:

$$S = \frac{6!}{0!6!} + \frac{6!}{1!5!} + \frac{6!}{2!4!} + \frac{6!}{3!3!} + \frac{6!}{4!2!} + \frac{6!}{5!1!} + \frac{6!}{6!0!} = 1+6+15+20+15+6+1 = 64\quad .$$

Knowing the number of all possible combinations, we may calculate the probability of occurrence of a given combination. This will allow us to determine the *a priori* probabilities $p(h_1/e_{k-1})$ and $p\,(h_2/e_{k-1})$ as:

$$p(h_1/e_{k-1}) = \sum_{s=0}^{k-1} \frac{C_{k-1}^s}{S} * \frac{p(h_1)p(z/h_1)^s\, p(n/h_1)^{k-s-1}}{\sum_j p(h_j)p(z/h_j)^s}\quad .$$

where in the sequence: s - times occurs the signal green and k-s-1 - times it is blue, and:

$$p(h_2/e_{k-1}) = \sum_{s=0}^{k-1} \frac{C_{k-1}^s}{S} + \frac{p(h_2)p(z/h_2)^s * p(n/h_2)^{k-s-1}}{\sum_j p(h_j)p(z/h_j)^s}\quad ,$$

where: s - times it occurs the signal green and k-s-1 – times it is blue.

Having the given *a priori* probability, we may define the value of d_k according to the *EV* criterion as:

$$v(d_{1k}, h_j) = w * p(h_1/e_{k-1} \wedge z) + s * p(h_2/e_{k-1} \wedge z),$$

when $p(h_1/e_{k-1} \wedge z) > p(h_2/e_{k-1} \wedge z),$

or $v(d_{2k}, h_j) = w * p(h_2/e_{k-1} \wedge z) + s * p(h_1/e_{k-1} \wedge z),$

when $p(h_2/e_{k-1} \wedge z) > p(h_1/e_{k-1} \wedge z)\cdot$

The same applies to the blue signal:

$$v(d_{1k}, h_j) = w * p(h_1/e_{k-1} \wedge n) + s * p(h_2/e_{k-1}^n),$$

when $p(h_1/e_{k-1} \wedge n) > p(h_2/e_{k-1} \wedge n),$

or $v(d_{2k}, h_j) = w * p(h_2/e_{k-1} \wedge n) + s * p(h_1/e_{k-1} \wedge n),$

when

$$p(h_2/e_{k-1} \wedge n) > p(h_1/e_{k-1} \wedge n) \cdot$$

Analogically as in the sequential model we may define the value of the optimal decision:

$$v(d_{ik}, h_j)_{opt} = [v(d_{1k})p * k(z) + v(d_{2k})p_k(n)] - c\,.$$

The cost of purchasing information in this case is much smaller, because we need only information about the last signal.

In order to initiate cycle *k* by the decision maker, the following inequality requires to be fulfilled:

$$v(d_i k, h_j)_{opt} > v(d_{i(k-1)}, h_j).$$

4.4. Application of the combinatorial model of decision-making concerning a purchase of probabilistic information

The combinatorial decision making model of purchasing probabilistic information may be used in various fields of behavioral sciences including psychology, sociology and economics. This paragraph will present an example of its application in the field of microeconomics, where this model[45] may be used.

Suppose that a cosmetic company intends to sell more of its cream *K* for women. In order to check if there is demand for greater production, pilot studies were conducted among a thousand randomly selected women in the city. Each of the women received the following brief description of the new product.

Night Cream. Intensely moisturizes and nourishes the skin. It stimulates the production process of components that improve its firmness and elasticity. It helps to get rid of small wrinkles. Improves skin tone. Price: €75 per 50ml.

After a description of the cream, each woman received a short questionnaire to complete. The most important question was whether she would buy this cream. In addition, she was asked to justify why she would not decide to buy the product (if that was the case), and she was finally asked to mark her age.

To be able to use the sequential model, we will go through the following four stages:

---

[45] The combinatorial purchase decision making model of probabilistic information presented in 4.3 and its empirical exemplification presented in 4.4 has been developed by E. Micał (2008) in the framework of a decision analysis seminar at the Institute of Economics and Management at the Catholic University of Lublin, under the supervision of the author of this monograph .

1. Determining the market segmentation according to the selected criteria and determining the conditional probabilities for each segment.

After the analysis of 1000 responses, three groups of women were identified, depending on the willingness to buy the product. We managed to identify three age groups that were characteristic in the number of positive and negative answers regarding the purchase of the cream.

The first group (called the youngest group) comprised of 312 people. It included women between 20 to 27 years old. Only 15% of them were willing to buy the cream. Those who would not buy it (85%) argued that it no need yet for them for such a cosmetic

The second group (middle-aged) were women aged 28 to 50. This group consisted of 360 women. In this group, 40% women wanted to buy the cream, while more than half (60%) were against the purchase.

The third group (the older group) were women over 50 years old. The group consisted of 328 women. Here the proportions of willingness were most encouraging to increase production, since 75% women in this age group were willing to buy the cream. Only 25% of women refused to purchase it, and argued that it was because of their attachment to another product because of using a medicinal cream.

A representative group of 1000 people revealed the distribution of the different age groups and their willingness to purchase the cosmetic product, as illustrated in Figure 4.5.

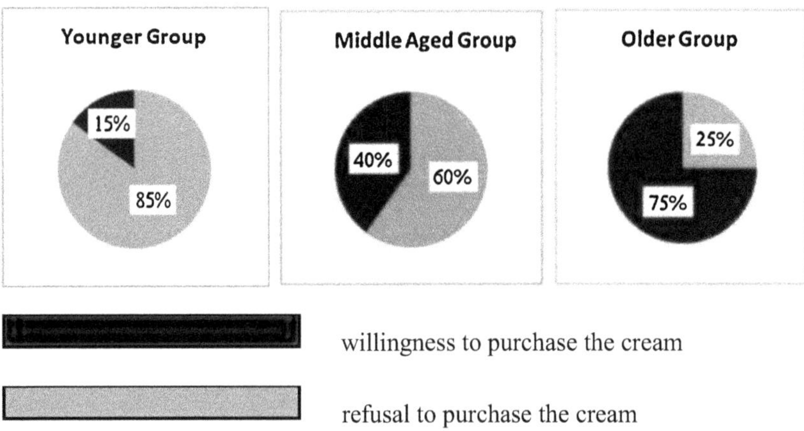

Figure 4.5. Distribution of women willing and refusing to purchase the cream in the different age groups

2. Defining the a posteriori probabilities of the individual segments in the market.

Based on the data of Central Statistical Office for 2006 we may determine the number of women in each segment. For the purpose of this study were used data for the municipality of Głogów Małopolski in 2006[46].

The smallest group of women is the younger group (called g_1), which represents only 21% women aged over 20. The middle-aged (g_2) and older groups (g_3) are equally big and constitute 39.5% women in the age range tested.

Therefore:

$p(g_1) = 0.21$, $p(g_2) = 0.395$, $p(g_3) = 0.395$.

3. Presenting the decision situation.

The company produces 100 000 jars of cream per month. It is intending to significantly increase their production so that production would amount 300 000 per month. The company sells the cream for €75 per a 50ml jar. The fixed monthly costs is nearly €1.8 million. The cost per unit of production (i.e. per jar) is €53. The company had to bear the cost of marketing research, estimated at €100 000 per month for the younger age group. The middle-aged group requires more sophisticated marketing efforts, therefore the marketing cost is higher and amounts to €500 000. The most expensive marketing campaign is in the third group, as it requires to adapt tools which are specific for this group and high professionalism. The cost for the third group is €1 000 000. The number of women who could possibly buy the cream in a given month is 640 000. Taking into account the conditional probabilities illustrated in Figure 4.5, the number of women willing to buy the cream among the younger age group is 0.15 × 640 000 = 96 000, for the middle-aged group it is 256 000, while for the older group it is up to 480 000.

With the above data we may count the possible gains with the production of 100 000 units per month and 300 000 units per month for each group.

The situation for Group g_1

For group g_1 and production N_1 = 100 000 the company would receive the following financial results:

Revenue g_1 : 96 000 × €75 = €7 200 000.

Cost for g_1 :100 000 × €53 + €1 800 000 + €100 000 = €7 200 000.

[46] www.stat.gov.pl

Therefore, for the younger age group the volume of production $N_1 = 100\ 000$ does not generate any losses, but does not provide a profit.

If the company increased production from 100,000 units to 300,000 per month, its revenue in the younger group would not change, because still only 96 000 women would be interested in buying the cream, but at a significantly changed cost.

With a production of $N_2 = 300\ 000$ the distribution of income and costs for the younger age group is as follows:

Income g_1: 96 000 × €75 = €7 200 000.

Cost for g_1: 300 000 × €53 + €1 800 000 + €100 000 = €17 800 000 .

The calculated loss with such large production is:

€17 800 000 - €7 200 000 = €10 600 000 .

This shows that the company would suffer a great loss from increasing production for in the first group.

The situation for Group g_2

A different situation is for the second group (middle-aged).

For the production of $N_1 = 100\ 000$ the demand is greater than the amount produced in the cream. Thus, all cream is sold. The income and costs for this group are as follows:

Income g_2 100 000 × €75 = €7 500 000.

Cost for g_2 100 000 × €53 + €1 800 000 €100 000 + = €7 200 000 .

Thus, the company gains from the production of €300 000, but they do not use the entire capacity of the market.

Let us now examine the increased production of $N_3 = 300\ 000$ units.

Revenues g_2 256 000 × €75 = €19 200 000.

Cost for g_2 300 000 × €53 € + €1 800 000 + €100 000 € = €17 800 000.

Revenue – cost = €19 200 000 – €18 200 000 = €1 000 000. Thus, we may see that in this group an increase of sales would pay off.

The situation for Group g_3

For the group of older women the situation is the following:.

For the production of $N_1 = 100\ 000$:

Income g_3: 100 000 × €75 = €7 500 000.

The cost for g_3: 100 000 × €53 + €1 800 000 + €100 000 = €7 200 000.

At this level of production the losses are €600 000. Only 21% satisfy the demand in this group.

However, it is quite a different situation in the production of $N_2 = 300\ 000$ units.

Revenues g_3: 300 000 × €1975 = €22 500 000.

Cost for g_3: 300 000 × €53 + €1 800 000 + €100 000 = €17 800 000.

Revenue - cost = €22 500 000 - €18 700 000 = €3 800 000.

This shows that that for the group of older women it is highly profitable to increase production. The financial results for each group and various production valumes are presented in Table 4.4.

Table 4.4. Payoffs in the situation of a managerial decision to increase production for the market

	g_1	g_2	g_3
N_1 = 100 000	0	- 100 000	- 600 000
N_2 = 300 000	-10 600	1 000 000	3 800 000

Analyzing Table 4.4, one may notice that if the market was advantageous for the first group (the youngest), it would not make sense to increase the production, because even at production N_1 = 100.000, the demand is less than the supply. If the company increased production, they would only receive losses. If the second group was in favor, one would be able to venture an increase in production, although it would not bring radically more profits. However, if the market is advantageous for the third group, the increase in production would be a good option and significantly increase the profits.

It is easy to see that the key to success is the correct estimation of the distribution of various groups in the market. If we know which group has the market advantage, we will be able to choose the right strategy. The problem lies in the fact that the market is very dynamic, constantly changing and we may not rely on the information from two years before (while such information is published by the Central Statistical Office), because it is not adequate and may be confusing. We also may not ask women directly about their age, because it is regarded as impolite, and the response – if any – may be unreliable. In this case, in estimating the market conditions it may be helpful to use the model of sequential decision making purchase of probabilistic information. In this model, based on the information about whether the majority of respondents would buy the product or not, we will be able to find the distribution of the individual segments.

In order to find the distribution of the groups, in other words to define the *a priori* probability, we need to find the *a posteriori* probabilities, the conditional probabilities and to purchase the signal. Based on previous studies the conditional probabilities and the *a posteriori* probabilities were determined. In that case it was only needed to buy the signal.

For this purpose, we must first determine how many women do not buy cosmetics in general. The research results show that 10% women do not buy cosmetics other than soap and shampoo. The remaining 90% visit the store from time to time.

In order to check whether the majority of women would buy the produced cream *K* or not buy it, special discount flyers were made, and the price of the leaflets was 10 cents. Any woman who came to the store with a leaflet, would 5% discount on the cream. On a given day a hostess counted the women who were interested in buying the cream and took a leaflet, and the clients of this store who did not. It was found that the majority of women, as many as 58% were not interested in buying the cream, and only 42% paid 10 cents and received a discount flyer. The price of 10 cents was introduced in order to authenticate the desire to buy.

Taking into account the data about purchasing cosmetics and the results of the experiment, we may determine the percentage of women who are willing to purchase this cream, and the percentage of those who do not need it.

The desire to buy the cream is denoted by n, and by z – no need to buy it. Based on the above data we may determine z and n : n = 42% out of all 90% of the women who buy cosmetics.

Thus, $n = 0.42 \times 0.9 = 0.378$.

By contrast, z = 58% to 90% + 10% who do not buy cosmetics.

Thus, $z = 0.58 \times 0.9 + 0.1 = 0.522 + 0.1 = 0.622$.

Because signal z is more valuable, we may assume that signal z was received. In the context of the model, we may say state:

n - the desire to purchase the cream,

z - no desire to purchase the cream,

g_1 - younger age group,

g_2 - middle-aged group,

g_3 - the older group.

On the basis of the calculations by the Central Statistical Office we may state that:

$p(g_1)=0.21$, $p(g_2)=0.395$, $p(g_3)=0.395$.

In turn, on the basis of the first empirical marketing research carried out, we may determine the conditional probabilities as follows:

$$p(n/g_1) = 0.15; \qquad p(z/g_1) = 0.85.$$

$p(n/g_2)= 0.4;$ $p(z/g_2)= 0.6.$

$p(n/g_3)= 0.75;$ $p(z/g_3)= 0.25.$

It is very important to estimate the cost of information. The company produced 1.000 leaflets, where there they managed to distribute 168 of them (the shop was visited by 400 people that day). Each discount leaflet cost €3.75 – the sum of the discount. Ten cents covered the cost of printing. The hostess who conducted the calculations received €100.

Thus, the total cost of information was: €3.75 per 168 sheets + €100. Therefore, the total cost of information was €730.

We have all the data to the model and need only to substitute the Bayesian model.

$$\frac{p(h_1)p(z/h_1)}{\sum_j p(h_j)p(z/h_j)} = p(h_1/z).$$

Thus, in our case:

$$p(g_1/z)=\frac{p(g_1)p(z/g_1)}{\sum_i p(g_i)\,p(z/g_i)}=\frac{0.21 \times 0.85}{0.21\times 0.85+0.395\times 0.6+0.395\times 0.25}=0.42$$

$$p(g_2/z)=\frac{p(g_2)p(z/g_2)}{\sum_i p(g_i)\,p(z/g_i)}=\frac{0.395\times 0.6}{0.21\times 0.85+0.395\times 0.6+0.395\times 0.25}=0.557$$

$$p(g_3/z)=\frac{p(g_3)p(z/g_3)}{\sum_i p(g_i)\,p(z/g_i)}=\frac{0.395\times 0.25}{0.21\times 0.85+0.395\times 0.6+0.395\times 0.25}=0.023$$

New probability has been established, different than the one of the Central Statistical Office. The cost of obtaining the statistical data is €730. For such set we may calculate the probabilities of costs and revenues for the production of 100 000 and 300 000 units.

We may first calculate the number of people in each group on the market.

For the first group it is:

$$0.42 \times 640\,000 = 268\,800;$$

For the second group it is:

$$0.557 \times 640\,000 = 356\,480;$$

for the third group is:

$$0.023 \times 640\,000 = 14\,720.$$

From the first group g_1, only 15% would buy the cream, which gives:

$0.15 \times 268\,800 = 40\,320$ people.

From the second group g_2 40% of women were willing to buy the cream, so the number of people in this group is of $0.40 \times 356\,480 = 142\,592$.

By contrast, from the third g_3 group, 75% were willing to buy, so the number of women in this group is: $0.75 \times 14\,720 = 11\,040$.

Adding all the three numbers, we receive the demand. Thus, the number of women who would buy the cream is $40\,320 + 142\,592 + 11\,040 = 193\,952$.

With **a production of N_1** $= 100\,000$, the revenue and cost are as follows:

Revenues: $100\,000 \times €75 = €7\,500\,000$;

Cost: $100\,000 \times €53 + €1\,800\,000 + €730 + (0.42 \times 100\,000 + 0.557 \times 50\,0000 + 0.023 \times 1\,000\,000) = 7\,100\,730 + 343\,500 = €7\,444\,230$.

Therefore, our profit is € 55 770.

However, with **a production of N_2** $= 300\,000$ units, the costs and revenues are as follows:

Revenue: $193952 \times 75 = €14\,546\,400$;

Cost: $300\,000 \times €53 + €1\,800\,000 + €730 + (0.42 \times 100\,000 + 0.557 \times 500\,000 + 0.023 \times 1\,000\,000) = €17\,700\,730 + €343\,500 = €18\,044\,230$.

Balancing the revenues and costs, the company obtained a substantial loss of €3 497 830.

Here we may see that the increase in production is not profitable. It should remain at a lower level. Of course, the above analysis should be repeated as often as possible, because the more it is carried out, the more reliable the results are and our decision is more valid economically. However, in the subsequent analysis, the *a posteriori* probabilities from the last analysis should be treated as *a priori* for the next ones .

Chapter 5.

A proposal to integrate the concepts of *information, decision, mass* and *energy:* a behavioral approach [47]

The present chapter, whose topic is within, but simultaneously also beyond the scope of the above economic decision analyses, is an introduction to a new, interdisciplinary approach to the concepts of *information, decision, mass*, and *energy*, which belong to quite distinct theoretical frameworks, but seem to have a significant number of aspects in common. I will present the behavioral approach as a way to integrate these concepts so that the outcome may be also applicable to analyses of economic decisions. The result of this integration will be a formula of *information* as a function of *decision, mass*, and *energy*. These four concepts will retain their original meanings, as they are in decision theory and physics, respectively. However, they will gain a behavioral interpretation, i.e. as *informational activity*, *decision making behavior, active mass*, and *actualized energy*, respectively. Thus, the behavioral approach will lead us to formulating the equation of information, where *information* is a change of an *energy mass* understood as a physical transfer behavior from one position/location/state into another one in a well defined certain space. Our analysis will be inspired by the Aristotle's conception of *act* and *potency*, and the notions of *theoretical* and *observational terms*, introduced by R. Carnap (1930) and advanced by a representative of the Polish school of logic – Przełęcki (1955, 1961). The present proposal may prove to be useful within the behavioral approach to economic sciences. However, the proposal is in its initial stage of development, and its concrete implications for the analysis of economic decision making need to be developed in cooperation with representatives of behavioral economics and/or behavioral accounting.

In the history of science, first in the times of classical physics by Newton, and then in the developments by Einstein, known as the relativity theory, the concepts of *mass* and *energy* were integrated into a coherent conceptual whole. The concepts of *information* and *decision* originate from other theoretical traditions. Although intuitively one may sense an organic relation between the concepts of *information* and *decision*, the belief about their duality is spread in scientific literature. This pair of concepts has become the base of information

[47] This chapter is an adaptation of the paper presented by the author at the International Conference: *The Man and his Decisions*, which was held at the Catholic University of Lublin, 17-18 November 2009,(see Biela, A. (2009), Conception of information, mass and energy: In the direction of an integrated approach, in: K.A. Klosinski, A. Biela, Man and his Decisions (Eds.) Lublin: Wydawnictwo KUL.

theory, also called statistical theory of communication systems, and the base of decision theory. The other pair of concepts, *mass* and *energy,* alongside with ones like *time* and *velocity,* have become the basic canonical concepts of contemporary physics. The concepts of *mass* and *energy* evolve independently in two different disciplines, i.e. computer science and physics. Within computer sciences (also called information technology) themselves developed parallel two relatively independent specializations: *hardware* and *software.* To simplify, the first of these specializations deals with matter and energy of information-carrying signals, their transport and processing, while the other one with controlling the informational processes in electronic systems.

The concept of information formulated by the Polish logician, philosopher and theorist of decision, Szaniawski (1971), is based on different premises. His concept is founded on elements of game theory, classical utility theory and the theory of rational decision. The main thesis of this concept indicates that one may speak of a pragmatic value of information only in the context of information utility to solve a given decision problem.

Considering the main points of the pragmatic conception of information, we may state that information is always related to a given decision problem, i.e. the decision situation where there is the possibility of carrying out a balance of gains and losses resulting from the given action alternatives, that is, decision options (Biela 1976). Strictly speaking, we mean carrying out the anticipated balances, according to the conventions of decision theory, in the form an $n \times z$ -element payoff matrix, where n indicates its rows corresponding to the decision options, and z is the number of hypothetical states of nature, more or less favorable for the decision maker.

The purpose of the present analysis is to identify the possibility of linking the concept of *information* in terms of decision theory with the concept of *energy* in modern physics. To achieve this goal, we will first examine the status of *energy* in physics, and then in the same way the concept of *information* in information theory and decision theory. This perspective will allow us to notice the relationship of the concept of *energy* in physics with a new look at the concept of *information* originating from decision theory. This new interpretation of *information* will allow to interpret *mass* as energy remaining in a state of potentiality.

The theoretical perspective which will serve to bind these concepts will be the integrative approach based on the methodology of behavioral sciences, which include behavioral economics, psychology within the neo-behaviorist framework, as well as natural sciences that study physical phenomena in terms of reactions to stimuli.

5.1. The concepts of *mass* and *energy* in physics

The concepts of *mass* and *energy,* alongside with the concepts of *time* and *space,* serve to conceptualize the basic notions in physics. In the physical sense, mass is the resistance that bodies have at any changes in velocity or direction of motion. In his work, *Philosophiea Naturalis Principia Mathematica* (first ed. 1687), Newton describes mass as *quantitas materiae* (*mensura eiusdem orta ex illius densitate et magnitudine*). Since his time it is assumed that bodies are able to move without an internal force. If a body ceases to move, it is solely a result of the forces that inhibit the movement, such as friction or air resistance. This kind of behavior of the body is expressed in the principle of inertia. In physics, mass is considered to be an attribute of matter called inertia or resistance of the body against forces which try to change its speed (Mazierski 1969).

There is also the so-called energetic way of defining the mass of a body. Each state of motion of a material body is related to a notion called kinetic energy. At the same velocity v of a given material body, the kinetic energy E_k of the given body depends only on its mass m:

$$E_k=mv^2/2 \qquad (5.1).$$

Thus, mass may be regarded as a reservoir of potential kinetic energy of a material body as a whole or an isolated particle of matter.

If electrons are to be an object of a physical analysis, one may demonstrate experimentally that the velocity of electrons increases their mass. The closer their speed to the speed of light, the greater their mass. Through theoretical analyses and experimental research, Einstein (1961) formulated the following relationship:

$$m = m_o / 1 - v^2/c^2 \qquad (5.2),$$

where:

m – is the mass of the particle of matter in motion,

m_o – is the mass of the particle of matter at rest,

v – is the velocity of the particle of matter,

c – is the speed of light.

If we assume that the electron has a velocity which is close to the speed of light, and is forced to pass through a difference in potential by giving new energy to matter, then the work put into it will not be used to increase the velocity, but to increase the mass of the electron. In the context of these assumptions and the relationships expressed in formula (5.2), Einstein concluded that the relationship between mass, energy and velocity of the electron may be described as

$$m = m_o + m_o v^2/2c^2 \qquad (5.3),$$

or as

$$m - m_o = 1/c^2(m_o v^2/2) \qquad (5.4).$$

Formulas (5.3) and (5.4) show that the increase in the electron's mass is equal to the kinetic energy given to it: $E_k = mv^2/2$, divided by c^2. The energy is thus equivalent to the mass of a body or the mass of an isolated part of matter. However, strictly speaking, the weight gain is equivalent only to a part of the total energy of the body, namely the kinetic energy, while the entire body weight is equivalent to its total energy – which Einstein (1961) expressed in the formula:

$$m = E/c^2 \qquad (5.5),$$

which implies that

$$E = mc^2 \qquad (5.6).$$

Formulas (5.5) and (5.6) enable to interpret the mass of a body or its isolated particle in a manner which is analogous to kinetic energy: mass is the potential total energy of a material body or its part. This energy may be brought to a concrete actualization from its potential state, which requires the use of certain means, hence, it implies an input which would actualize the state of energetic potentiality of the given material system, called mass. The problem is, however: in what direction to carry out the intended update of the given material-energetic system? At this point emerges the need of information in order to direct the actualization of the potential system of energy.

From the viewpoint of behavioral sciences, the motion of bodies in physics may be interpreted as the behavior of these bodies that is their response to stimuli from the physical environment.

5.2. The notion of *information* by Shannon and Weaver and by Szaniawski.

In order to carry out a comparative analysis of the conceptions of information proposed by Shannon and Weaver and by Szaniawski, we will first focus on the concept of infomation in information theory, and then the concept of pragmatic information by Szaniawski. Both conceptions of information are related to decision making. Although they propose distinct perspectives on analyzing and measuring information, we will try to see that they are mutually compatible, and each of them is a particular case of the other.

5.2.1. *Information* in information theory

The creators of the statistical theory of communication systems, also known as information theory, presented their theory on the model of a deductive system, where theorems are derived from a set of accepted axioms, using the rules of deductive reasoning (Shannon and Weaver 1949). The significance of the basic terms in this theory – which include *information, entropy, signal, noise, communication channel, encoder, decoder* – lies in the context of the axioms and theorems of the whole deductive system constituting this theory. Undoubtedly, *entropy* and *information* may be regarded as the basic terms within it.

Initially, the concept of *entropy* was used solely in thermodynamics. An entropy of a given system in thermodynamics is considered a function of the likelihood of adopting a specified location by this system. The second law of thermodynamics shows, in this understanding of entropy, the tendency to approach the states with the highest degree of probability. Specifically, in thermodynamics one speaks of says entropy of e.g. gas in a closed space, regarding its state of diffusion.

The basis for determining the entropy of a system in thermodynamics is the formula originally described by Boltzmann. This formula was modified by the creators of information theory and presented as follows:

$$H = -\sum_j p(h_j) \log p(h_j) \qquad (5.7),$$

where:

H – means the entropy of the system;

$p(h_j)$ – means the probability of adopting a specific location h_j by the system.

Shannon, adapting the term *entropy* into his theory, did not change the general principles of its mathematical determination. However in information theory the concept of *entropy* has a more general range than in thermodynamics. Information theory is the general theory of systems of communication, although itself it is a result of a generalization of mathematical analysis of certain issues from wired communication. Thus, its basic concepts include a wide range of all known communication models.

The central concept of information theory is, nevertheless, *information.* The key idea of refers not as much the physical nature of information, but rather a measure which is a difference between the state of entropy prior to the experience (i.e. prior to obtaining the given signal x_i) and after the experience (i.e. after the given signal x_i), which is expressed by formulas (5.8) - (5.10) accordingly:

$$I = H(h_j) - H(h_j/x_i) \quad (5.8),$$

where:

I – is the measure of the information obtained (in bits);

$H(h_j)$ – is the state of entropy of the given model regarding the adoption of location h_j put before obtaining the new signal x_i;

$H(h_j/x_i)$ – is the state of entropy of the given model regarding the adoption of location h_j after obtaining the new signal x_i.

To express the state of entropy, the authors of information theory also use bits, and determine it as indicated in (5.9) and (5.10), respectively:

$$H(h_j) = - \sum_j p(h_j) \log_2 p(h_j) \quad (5.9),$$

$$H(h_j/x_i) = - \sum_j p(h_j/x_i) \log_2 p(h_j/x_i) \quad (5.10),$$

where the symbols are like in formulas (5.7) and (5.8).

In cases where the positions of h_j of the model are equally probable, formulas (5.9) and (5.10) take the simplified form of (5.11) and (5.12), respectively:

$$H(h_j) = - \log_2 p(h_j) \quad (5.11),$$

$$H(h_j/x_i) = - \log_2 p(h_j/x_i) \quad (5.12).$$

Certain models of (5.7) – (5.12) were already presented in Chapter 3 as (3.1) – (3.3) in the inference and formal deductive reasoning, but for the sake of this chapter, they are repeated here in the convention of the present analysis. The sense of *information,* determined basing on formulas (5.8) – (5.12) is referred to as *selective information,* whose function is to reduce the degree of uncertainty of the model. This term must be distinguished from the term *signal.* While by *information* we understand a factor which reduces the uncertainty about the state of affairs, whose quantitative measure is determined by the Shannon and Weaver's axioms (1949), *signal* is a material medium of information.

Reactions of the scientific community to the terminological proposals of Shannon and Weaver were at first very diverse. According to Broglie (1966), by *information* the creators of information theory meant negative entropy, by analogy to thermodynamics. Cherry (1966) expressed a regret that a mathematical concept was called *information* at all. Despite these reservations, the concept of information in information theory may be called *quantitative information (binary)* or *selective,* as it dichotomously divides the sets of considered hypotheses into two parts: a set of hypotheses which are excluded from further analysis (whose probability is zero) and a set of hypotheses which are not excluded (whose probabilities of occurrence is treated as equal, following the LaPlace rule). Information that equals 1 bit is obtained both when the set of hypotheses under consideration is reduced from 32 to 16, and when the resulting signal allows to reduce the initial set of 8 hypotheses to 4 or from 2 hypotheses to 1 (Biela 1971).

Among the authors who dealt with the analysis of informational processes one may, unfortunately, observe a certain methodological confusion, caused by the fact that the term *information* is used in different senses. Most frequently, the quantitative sense of given to *information* by the creators of the information theory is not distinguished from the semantic meaning, where by *information* one understands a message, i.e. a content which one uses to inform. Another misunderstanding is the use of the term *information* interchangeably with the term *signal,* which denotes its material carrier, or the term *data*, whose relational meaning was precisely determined by Coombs in his theory of data (Coombs 1964).

5.2.2. The pragmatic value of information

The conception of the pragmatic value of information by Szaniawski (1971) assumes that the value of information for the decision maker depends on two factors: the decision problem and the nature of information. In his approach, information I_H is defined in the context of the decision problem, expressed as an ordered triple (see 1.1.):

$$SD = \langle A, H, u \rangle \qquad (5.13),$$

where:

SD – is the decision situation where the decision maker has to choose one of the options;

$A = \{a_1, a_2, a_3,\dots, a_n\}$ – is the set of possible actions in a given situation (decision options, alternative activities);

$H = \{h_1, h_2, h_3,\dots, h_z\}$ – is the set of possible states of affairs, that is, hypothetical states of the world where the decision maker knows that there occurs exactly one of the h_j states, but does not know which one;

u - is the a utility function defined on the Cartesian product of sets *A* and *H.*

Assuming that the sets A and H are finite, the form of decision the problem, equivalent to (5.13), is the utility matrix U. To simplify, we will also assume that all information concerning the decision problem refers to set H. By evaluating the mere fact of obtaining an answer to the question which of the hypothetical states of the world is the real state of affairs, the decision maker decides whether he or she will seek information, considering the necessary costs in advance.

In his approach, Szaniawski uses the conceptual apparatus derived from Wald's (1950) theory of decision functions. By the X set Szaniawski understands the set of answers to the question which of the hypothetical states of the world is real – the elements of this set are thus the answers: $X = \{x_1, x_2, \ldots, x_r\}$. The relationship between set X, and H has a probabilistic distribution $\{p_H\}$. Information about set H Szaniawski treats as an ordered pair:

$$I_H = \langle X, \{p_H\} \rangle \qquad (5.14).$$

The way to use information I_H is that undertaking an activity depends on the response to the question generated by X. The response is a function of decision d, which assigns an action to each response. Each decision function defined on set X, takes its values from set A:

$$d\,(x) = a \qquad (5.15),$$

which means that if the decision maker receives the response x, then he or she takes action a dependent on the way the information will be used by d. The set of all d decision functions, leading from X to A, is designated as D.

Obtaining information is thus related to incurring a non-negative cost c, measured by the same unit of utility which one operates in the given decision situation. This cost should be, according to Szaniawski, deducted from the utility of any effect received thanks to the response x – based on the decision function d. Thus, one may calculate the utility of an action achieved with d when the state of affairs h_j occurs and the cost of information is c:

$$u_c\,(d, h_j) \;=\; \sum_{x\epsilon X} [u(d(x), h_j) - c]\; p_{hj}\,(x) = \sum_{x\epsilon X} u(d(x), h_j\,) x p_{hj}\,(x) - c \qquad (5.16),$$

where:

$u_c(d,h_j)$ – is the utility of the activity achieved through d, if the h_j state of affairs occurs, with the c cost of information.

The statement (5.16) is based on an average of utility considering the possible answers form set X, assuming that the h_j state occurs. The value of information, in the context of (5.13) – (5.16), thus depends on the c cost of obtaining it in the SD decision situation, where the decision maker operates with established decision criteria in determining the utility of the given A activities considering the H hypothetical states of the world. This "value", in terms of the given decision criterion, we will call *the highest cost of information c, at which in set A there is an optimal element (in terms of this criterion) of set A∪D* (Szaniawski 1971, p.330).

Szaniawski determined the pragmatic value of information for the problem of decision, based on the following criteria: *maxmin*, Savage, Hurwicz, Laplace, β criterion, and the EV criterion. Based on the Szaniawski's concept of information, Biela (1976) developed a model of a sequential search of probabilistic information for the EV decision criterion, assuming that the decision maker uses the Bayesian model for processing signals into information, i.e. modifying the initial *a priori* probability distribution on set *H* of hypothetical states of the world into an *a posteriori* distribution, that is, after receiving the x_i signal form the source of probabilistic information. The concept of information by Szaniawski may also be called behavioral, since it determines the value of information in terms of its usefulness for the decision maker's behavior in a dynamic decision situation.

5.2.3. The relationship between the Shannon's and the Szaniawski's concepts of *information*

A comparative analysis of *information* as proposed by Shannon and by Szaniawski was carried out by Biela (1976), and indicates that there are three ways to see the relationship between *selective (quantitative) information* and *pragmatic information:* 1) treating *information* in the Shannon sense as a particular case of *information* in the Szaniawski sense, 2) a *pragmatic* interpretation of *information* in the Shannon sense, 3) an intermediate position, treating both concepts as different aspects which are reducible to each other if certain assumptions are made.

G. Lissowski (2003) interpreted the quantitative information by Shannon as a special case of Szaniawski's pragmatic information. The basic idea of this interpretation is to treat the loss function as a function of probability. It is also possible to interpret the pragmatic information as a kind of selective-quantitative information, assuming that the set of the considered loss events, in each step of the sequential search for information, is dichotomously split into two subsets, where one subset is a conjunction of hypotheses with a probability equal to zero, while the hypotheses in the other subset (with non-zero probability) are treated, in accordance with the Laplace rule, as equally probable.

In the interpretation of pragmatic information as a kind of selective information, we must assume that the measurement of information refers to a specific decision problem. The /bit measure would then be incorporated into the concept of *information value* with reference to the decision problem. The basis for this interpretation is given by Hintikka (1968), who proposes to distinguish between measuring information about unexpected events *(unexpectedness)* and the main events *(substantive).* Although this author does not relate the concept of *information* to the decision situation, but his concept of the *expected value of information* seems to allow such possibility.

Szaniawski himself is in favor of the third position from the above ones. He believes that both pragmatic and selective information in a similar way depend on the nature of the two-dimensional probability distribution, i.e. $p(x_i/h_j)$ = *probability of* $\{X = x_i \cap H = h_j\}$.The notion of *pragmatic information* Szaniawski (1974) limited to the so-called epistemic decision problem, defined by a utility matrix equal to 1 of the following general type:

A \ H	h_1	h_2
a_1	1	0
a_2	0	1

Both the concept of *information* in information theory and the *pragmatic* concept of *information* by Szaniawski have their behavioral provenance in the sense that they are refer to *information behavior* in decision-making situations. This behavior is a search for information, signal processing into information, making decisions about buying a specific information, etc. Hence, we will try to consider whether the behavioral analysis of decision making would be an appropriate arena for an integration of the concepts of *energy* and *information*, which – so far – have been developing within two independent streams. In these deliberations, a helpful concept will be *information* understood as energy, whose philosophical origins go back to the Aristotle's concept of *motion*.

5.3. The concept *of information* understood as *energy*

The question that we are going to focus on is: to what extent is it possible to combine the physical concepts of *mass* and *energy* with the concept of *information?* We tried to point out that both of the existing concepts of information – the one in information theory, as well as the pragmatic approach to information, based on decision theory – actually do not correspond with the attributes of the physical realities defined by the terms of *mass* and *energy*. Hence, is the dualism of the physical concepts of *mass* and *energy* on the one hand, and of the concept of *information,* on the other hand, conceptually incompatible? To answer this question, it is suggested to follow a path of thoughts which has its origins in the Aristotle's concept of motion, and more precisely, in his energy conception of being, where being as a such is understood as an energy. From this perspective, we will take a look at the meaning of the concepts of *mass* and *energy* in modern physics, and in this context we may reflect whether an informational implementation of mass and energy may potentially be useful for physics, and – if so – how this implementation might be of a heuristic, systematizing or systemically creative value, for physics as such, and for disciplines related to decision theory (such as economics and psychology).

5.4. The concepts of *act* and *potency*, and their usefulness in science

Aristotle developed the concept of *kinêsis,* which gave rise to the concept of *kinetic energy* (E_k), used by both classical and modern physics. In his treatise *Physics,* the concept of *motion* (*kinêsis*) is defined as *act of being which is in potency, if it is in potency (Phys III 1, 201a 10-12)*, what may be expressed in other words as the fulfillment of what exists potentially, insofar as it exists. However, understanding all Aristotle's physics and its concept of *motion* is possible only in the context of his entire philosophical system, which is the theory of being, where the fundament is the theory of *act* and *potency* (also called *potentiality*) (Aristotle 1990a, 1990b, 1993). According to Krąpiec (1963, 1973), basing on Aristotle's theory of being, motion as a feature is present in all categories of existence and shows that becoming a being consists of two correlative factors: the *act* and the *potency* (Lat. *actus et potentia). Motion* is to be understood as an actualization (immediate or successive) of the potentiality, while the being which results from the change consists of the *act* and *potency*, because the very being that has become, is existing.

The concept of *act* and *potency* in Aristotle's theory of being is closely related to his concept of *matter* and *form*. It is thanks to the form that Aristotle explains the pluralism of the physical world. The form is a constitutive element of existence, including the existence of physical phenomena, and is interpreted as an *act*. According to Tatarkiewicz (1990), for Aristotle, form is both the force acting intentionally, as well as and it is the cause of an individual being. Because the nature of the form is action, Aristotle called it *energy* (Gr. *energeia,* Lat. *actus).* This feature of the form made Aristotle the first one in the history of philosophy to create the concept of an *energy being* (Glencoe, 1990). It is expressed in the fact that the form is an essential component of being, and hence energy, activity, and action are the very essence of being. If the form that actualizes the being of the physical reality is energy, then, what is the matter of a physical body or a physical phenomenon? Matter is the potency (Gr. *dynamis),* potentiality, or the disposition of the force which actualizes the physical entity. Aristotle's concept of *potency* was based on the inner experience of strength, which he objectified, applied to material phenomena, and introduced into the inventory of philosophical concepts.

Using the concepts of *energy* and *potential,* and their parallel pair of *form* and *matter,* Aristotle explained both the process of becoming, as well as the products of this process, constituting the physical reality which is the object of sensory observation. His observations of nature were most accurate with regard to biology (e.g. in the field of zoology, physiology, embryology, botany). Many of his observations (e.g. classification of species) still retain their value. Less fortunate were the applications of the theory of being by Aristotle for other natural sciences, such as the mechanics or astronomy. For example, the natural motion of bodies like the falling of a stone, and the rising of smoke, Aristotle explained it as their deliberate proceeding to the place of the given body's proper nature. He also attributed almost magical properties to circular motion. We do not know why centrifugal motion is, in his view, natural, and centripetal movement is to be unnatural (see Aristotle, 1990a: Mech. *849a.* Moreover, Aristotle accepted a false assumption that distance - as being only a relation (and thus belong to the category of features, and therefore not a substance) – cannot act and thereby change the force of the natural desire of a moving body (Glencoe, 1990).

Similarly, in astronomy Aristotle inappropriately applied his theory of *act* and *potency*, and *motion*, basing, unfortunately, on too superficial observations and apparent movements of the heavenly bodies, also being too heavily influenced by his cosmology. He strongly rejected the geocentric view proclaimed by Eutolycus of Pitane, a Greek astronomer contemporary to him, and returned to the system of Eudoxus of Cnidus. It was not until several centuries later that Copernicus made what Kuhn (1962) calls a scientific revolution, which gave rise of a new way of thinking in astronomy.

However, despite the obvious failures in applying his theory of motion based on the concept of act and potency to mechanics and astronomy, Aristotle's conception is extraordinarily useful in contemporary science, which distinguishes strictly potential states (i.e. possibilities), also called potentialities, and the path of transition from *potency* to *act* in order to actualize the given potentialities.

5.5. Theoretical and observational terms in the empirical sciences

Terms with a *potential* nature primarily belong to the theoretical terms of natural sciences. The existence of theoretical terms which are not explicitly definable by observational terms was of interest already to Carnap in his *Testability and Meaning* (1936). They mostly include dispositional terms, such as the classical term *soluble* – which was the starting point for Carnap's considerations. Their result was that dispositional terms are not defined by observational terms with complete definitions, but only by partial definitions. This kind of dispositional terms implicitly assume their *potential* nature of having their source in the concept of *act* and *potency* by Aristotle. A partial definition in this context may be interpreted as the procedure for actualizing each theoretical term of a dispositional character. This occurs in situations of empirical research, where through the operationalization of the theoretical term, the researcher obtains an observational fact, and hence an observational term, which may be treated as an actualization of the potential reality denoted by the theoretical term which corresponds to it. The observational term is therefore an act for the observational term denoting the *potential* reality (possibilities, potentiality).

As indicated by Przełęcki (1955), who established the concept of a partial definition for theoretical terms, this class of terms also includes several theoretical ones whose dispositional character is not so visible at the first sight. Examples here may include terms expressing physical characteristics and sizes: *the transmission of light, thermal conductivity, electrical conductivity, density of a solution, osmotic pressure, atmospheric pressure, material strength, etc.* Przełęcki (1961) pointed out that the dispositional nature also applies to certain theoretical biological terms, which he exemplified by the term *genotype.*

It is also possible to give examples of theoretical terms in experimental psychology (e.g., *convergent thinking ability on symbolic material, verbal intelligence, emotional intelligence, intro-extraversion)* which denote the psychological reality of a dispositional character. These terms may be actualized in cases of standard psychometric tests as their behavioral results. These dispositions may be defined as sets in the sense of K. Leśniewski's mereology (Biela 1976). The findings of Carnap and Przełęcki are also applicable in behavioral sciences (including psychology, sociology, economics), where empirical methods, such as observation or experiment, are also used.

5.6. Mass as potential energy

Using the terminology of Carnap (1936) and its subsequent developments made by Przełęcki (1955, 1961), the concept of *matter,* known in physics, may undoubtedly be considered a theoretical term which denotes potential energy really existing in a material object or a given system of material objects. This term is a general one and applies to any small element of a material structure (microstructure), any large element of a material structure (macrostructure) or to the entire macrostructure or microstructure system that is available to human perception. Every material object, understood as a *physicalistic mass,* is a really existing reality of a *potential* nature, in terms of the potential energy accumulated in it.

The above fact is clearly expressed by A. Einstein who stated, in accordance with formula (5.5), that the mass of a material object is directly proportional to the total energy potential contained in this object, and inversely proportional to the square of the speed of light in vacuum. This kind of a theoretical interpretation of mass of a material object assumes that there is a certain quantity of *E,* called total energy contained in a material object which is the object of analysis. Einstein was well aware that in addition to the types of energy already known in physics (e.g., kinetic, thermal, electrodynamics, electromagnetic, nuclear, etc.), there are also other types of energy which are not yet recognized by physics at the present stage of its development.

Among the physical terms relating to the relationship between mass and energy, physicists point out the concept of *potential energy.* However, it is actually limited to the physical system's mechanical energy that depends on the mutual arrangement of the system parts (e.g. elastic energy) and on their position in the field of external forces. This term aptly expresses the intuition contained in the concept of the *mass a material object,* expressing the potential energy. Without questioning the conventions in the concept of *potential energy,* known in mechanics, we may still broaden the scope and content of the concept of *mass* and understand it as the total potential energy contained in the mass of the given material object.

If we feel that *mass is* a theoretical term in physics expressing the dispositions of a material object to actualize the potential energy contained in this object, we may expect that in the case of many material objects it is impossible to formulate a complete definition for the concept of *mass of object O,* but in these situations we should be satisfied with partial definitions (see: Przełęcki 1955, 1961). We cannot operationally point to situations where it would be possible to observe all kinds of energy potentially contained in the mass of the given material object.

Relating the notion of *matter* to the concept of *act* and *potency* by Aristotle, it should be noted, however, that the creator of the classic conception of science actually singled out *active possibility* as the source of transformation of the being's existence, and *passive possibility* which is the source for the cognition of this transformation. The active possibility already entails the act of the transformation of being. In this context, in relation to *mass* in physics, we may distinguish two types of mass *active mass* and *passive mass.* By *active mass* we will understand the mass of an active material body that is activating the potential reservoir of energy of a material body or a component of its structure, aimed at a specific alteration of the physical system. This happens within a specific motion of mass, which is a physical process, a chemical reaction, a thermo-nuclear reaction, a phenomenon of quartz, etc. In turn, by the mass of a passive material body or system *(passive mass)* we will understand the processes and phenomena which actualize the given potentiality of the body or of the material system which is the object of observation, research and analysis.

5.7. Energy as an act of a re-arrangement of the material and behavioral potentiality

While we have interpreted *mass* as one of the fundamental theoretical concepts in physics, *energy* should be understood as an elementary concept of physics (in the Carnap sense), and therefore it should have the status of an empirical or observational term. The role of elementary terms in empirical theories does not raise serious doubts. These terms refer to directly observable phenomena, processes and properties (Przełęcki, 1967). Of such character is the term *energy,* which, strictly speaking, is always accompanied by an adjective to determine the type of processes where the energy is observed. Thus, according to the specific processes taking place and observed in the given physical systems, we may talk about energy which is: mechanical, electromagnetic, gravitational, nuclear, kinetic, electrical, thermal, hydro, elastic, quantum, quartz, plasma, bioplasma, solar, air, seismic, volcanic, ice, etc.

As indicated by Carnap (1936) and Przełęcki (1961), the primary hypotheses in the theory of natural sciences are generally formulated using theoretical terms which are defined only partially by elementary terms. Of such character are terms which describe the mass of material systems, and so is very term *mass.* These terms may be defined only partially, indicating the corresponding observational (and often quantitative – using appropriate measurement scales) types or conditions of energy, exposed or liberated (i.e. energy actualized in a given situation) as a result of the given processes or phenomena. The scope of the observation and quantification of the processes and energy-related phenomena in certain physical systems where a given energy is generated from a given energy-mass, may be limited for technical and situational reasons. Therefore, observation grasps only a part of the content of the theoretical term denoting the energy-mass of the given material system which is specific for the given process or phenomenon.

The Einstein's equation, expressed in formula (5.6), allows us to quantify the observed energetic processes and energy phenomena in relation to the given physical system where it is possible to accurately determine the mass of the given energy system and to determine the speed of mass which produces energy in the observed material system. If the speed reaches the speed of light in vacuum, or is close to it, one may also observe the such energy processes as fission or fusion of atomic nuclei, burning, etc. – which is accompanied by the emission of energy.

If we refer the considerations about energy as an act of change in a material system to behavioral sciences (especially, behavioral economics), we may interpret the behavioral formula of *SOR* in terms of this approach. Then, by *S* one should understand the information flow to the decision maker, through a given signal. The mediating variable, *O*, in this situation is understood as the process of signal processing into information in order to make a satisfactory decision. The decision maker's behavior is *R,* which is the sequence of behaviors leading final decision in the given situation. In the energy-behavioral sense, the decision *R* is the decision maker's actualization of the given system of matter and its potentiality, which is related to the emission/to producing energy, i.e. the actualization of energy.

5.8. The ontic-behavioral status of a scientific fact in energetics

We will now look more synthetically on the ontic status of a physical scientific fact in energetics. By *fact* we understand a phenomenon or an empirical process as an object of intersubjectively available observation. Its constitutive characteristic is repetition. Facts which have such features may be treated as following the nomothetic model, typical for natural sciences.

For Aristotle, the creator of the classical conception of science based on the fundamental question 'why?' *(Gr. diati*), explaining the ultimate rules/reasons/rights of the existence of a pluralistic world – being is the reality called *form*, through which another reality, called *substance,* is what it is. The form is the only factor constituting the being in the full sense. In our case the form concerns the being of a scientific fact in energetics. Strictly speaking, the form is about giving an appropriate form to a material system, i.e. giving it energetic substance in a way which is observable and measurable. The occurrence of a fact, which is also an act of starting an energy process (thus, *fact* becomes *act*), may explain the existence of its starter (energy-operator, scientist, decision maker), and the goal which he or she intends to achieve by producing an energy being as a fact. This goal may be cognitive (learning the truth about physical reality), economic (providing energy for industrial production or municipal purposes), military (bombing by an airplane pilot), political (giving an argument in diplomatic negotiations.)

5.9. The information equation

In the physical sense, giving an ontic status of physical energy to a given energy mass, which is a reservoir of potential energy, takes place as a result of certain activities of the operator-energy-decision maker, who (in a behavioral sense), who should first find out (i.e. obtain appropriate information in advance) what action to perform with the energy mass. The essence of this operation in an energetic sense is to change the location of the coordinates from the given point E_o to the given point of E_f in the space of energy mass. If, for simplicity, we assume that this change of location is a movement in the Euclidean type of space, then such situation may be illustrated as in Figure 5.1.

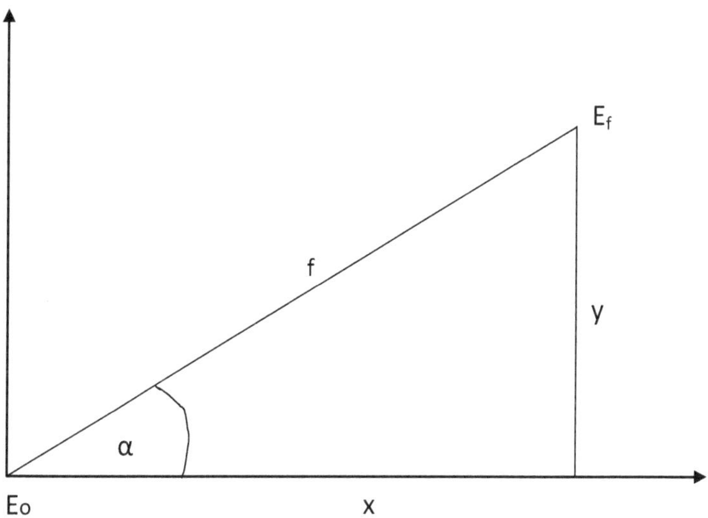

Figure 5.1. Illustration of energetic mass transfer from rest at point E_o to point E_f in Euclidean space.

In the context of the above findings, by information *I* we may understand a possible and deliberate change of the energy state of the mass from the one at point E_o to the state at point E_f, which is accompanied by the mass traveling the distance of *d* from the beginning of a hypothetically assumed setting of coordinates of *0.0* at E_o to point E_f with coordinates of *x, y*. This relationship may be expressed as:

$$I = (E_f - E_o) \times f \qquad (5.17).$$

Substituting formula (5.17) with the appropriate expansions of E_f and E_o, based on formulas (5.3) – (5.6), we receive:

$$I = (m_f c^2 - m_o c^2) \times d = (c^2(m_f - m_o)) \times f = (m_f - m_o)\, c^2 f \qquad (5.18).$$

It is not possible to measure the distance *d* under the Pythagorean theorem as:

$$f = \sqrt{x^2 + y^2} \qquad (5.19),$$

because the information must include an angular measure about angle α at which the mass m_o is to move in space to point E_f, not moving in circular motion with a radius *f*. In this situation, to clarify the information in formula (5.18), we will use simple trigonometric functions of the acute angle α in a right-angled triangle, where:

$$f = y/\sin\alpha \qquad (5.20),$$

$$f = x/\cos\alpha \qquad (5.21).$$

or

Hence, by replacing *f* in (5.18) respectively as in formulas (5.20) and (5.21) we may obtain two alternative formulas for information as a function of a change of energy mass from state m_o to state m_f after the mass has travelled the distance *f* at a speed of light, respectively, as:

$$I = (m_f - m_o)\, c^2\, (y/\sin\alpha) \qquad (5.22),$$

or

$$I = (m_f - m_o)\, c^2\, (x/\cos\alpha) \qquad (5.23).$$

Equations (5.17), (5.18), (5.22), and (5.23) express the elementary regularity in actualizing the energetic potentiality of mass through moving the energy mass from rest to a destination specified by the decision maker in the Euclidean space. Depending on the needs, these equations may be adapted to the situation where we are dealing with the surface of the energy mass on a plane, or a mass which is a block of a certain volume, from any location on a three-dimensional space to the position specified by the decision maker, the operator of the system of energy and matter. We may also use a four-dimensional space of a Euclidean type, where the fourth dimension is time *t*, i.e. space-time. In the Euclidean matrixes the principle of calculating the distance between two objects – points in this space – is determined as:

$$f_{ox}=\{\sum_{s=1}^{z}|m_{xs} - m_{os}|^2\}^{\frac{1}{2}} \quad (5.24),$$

where:

s - any dimension of space, where $s = 1,2, \ldots, z;$

f_{ij} - distance between two points in space $s;$

m_{xs} - the destination of the energy mass in dimension $s;$

m_{os} - the location of mass energy at rest in dimension s.

To solve certain energy problems one may apply the so-called *city block matrix,* where the principle of calculating the distance between points is based on a summation of the absolute differences for two positions of energy mass:

$$f_{ox} = \sum_{s=1}^{r} |m_{xs} - m_{os}| \quad (5.25),$$

where the symbols are as in formula (5.24).

Formulas to calculate the distance between the points occupied by mass m_o at the state of rest, and by mass in m_x (destination), may be generalized in Minkowski's spaces as follows:

$$f_{ox} = \left\{\sum_{s=1}^{r} |m_{xs} - m_{os}|^r\right\}^{\frac{1}{r}} \quad (5.26),$$

where:

r - is a specification indicating the type of the metrics : $r \geq 1$, and the remaining symbols take the sign, as in previous models.

Both the *city block*-type spaces and spaces of the Euclidean type are special cases of Minkowski's space, because for the *city block* $r = 1$, and for the Euclidean space $r = 2$. The characteristics of the metrics also pointed out to the so-called domination or maximization matrixes where the distance f_{xo} has the following form:

$$f_{xo}^{(\infty)} = \max_s (m_{xs} - m_{os}) \quad (5.27).$$

In certain specific issues concerning transport (motion) of energy mass we may use the maximization or the domination spaces of a Minkowski type. In order to determine the content of physical information, i.e. the destination point in space for the energy mass, the operator-decision maker may the use methods of decision analysis, were the possible location points of the energy mass will be treated, according to the decision situation scheme (5.13), as decision options (alternative actions) *D,* and the elements of set *H* will be the projected hypothetical states of the world, whose occurrence may take place in the given situation. The decision analysis in this case will aim at determining the utility of the various hypothetical locations of the energy mass, in the context of the anticipated consequences of these states in the given conditions. The results of these studies may then be presented in the form of the so-called payoff matrix, as a type of Cartesian product, d_i x h_j, which may be presented in the table (see: Table 5.1).

Table 5.1. Payoff matrix defining the utility of a movement of energy mass in space which actualizes the potential energy contained in this mass

D \ H	h_1	h_2	...	h_j	...	h_z
d_1	u_{11}	u_{12}	...	u_{1j}	...	u_{1z}
d_2	u_{21}	u_{22}	...	u_{2j}	...	u_{2z}
⋮	⋮	⋮	...	⋮	...	⋮
d_i	u_{i1}	u_{i2}	...	u_{ij}	...	u_{iz}
⋮	⋮	⋮	...	⋮	...	⋮
d_n	u_{n1}	u_{n2}	...	u_{nj}	...	u_{nz}

In Table 5.1. u_{ij} is to be understood as an abbreviated representation of function $u(d_i,h_j)$, whose first argument is any element of a set of possible locations (options of location) of energy mass m which may be transported from location m_o to location m_x, obtained through action a_i, while the other argument in this function is a hypothetical state of the world h_j, which may occur in the given energy space, but the operator-decision maker does not know which hypothetical state of the world actually occurs.

Typically, function u_{ij} has more than one dimension. It is then possible in the analysis of energy and information to determine the integration of the utility function using a simple formula of a weighted sum type:

$$u_{ij} = \sum_r u_{ij,r} \times w_r \quad (5.28),$$

where:

u_{ij} – the overall utility of the transporting action d_i of energy mass m_o,

$u_{ij,r}$ - the utility of transporting d_i the energy mass m_o in dimension r,

w_r - the weight of dimension r in actualizing the energy potential of mass m_o.

For more complex analyses of energy and information, we may use the method of multidimensional scaling, which might enable to reconstruct the systematizing spaces used by analysts, engineers-designers and operators of energy systems. The data for multidimensional scaling is based on the theory of data by C.H. Coombs (1964), where their relational nature is defined (Biela, 1992).

To determine the utility function in the situation of analyzing the transporting of the energy mass we must determine the balance of the anticipated costs of traveling the distance d_{xo} (due to the resistance of the environment) and the benefits related to the actualization of the energy mass at point E_f (see Figure 5.1). Hence, ultimately the value of d in equation (5.17) may be interpreted as:

$$f_{ox} = u_{ij} \quad (5.29),$$

where:

f_{ox} – is the way d_i of transporting the energy mass m from state m_o at point E_o to state m_x at point E_{fi};

u_{ij} - a balance of utility, taking into account the costs of realizing f_{ox} by choosing d_i and the benefits associated with actualizing the energy mass at point E_{fi}.

Taking into consideration equality (5.29) and the function of information from formula (5.17), the energy-decisional interpretation of information may be expressed as:

$$I_{ij} = (E_{fi} - E_o) \times u_{ij} \quad (5.30),$$

where:

I_{ij} – is the general information about the utility of energy transformation d_i of the energy mass m from point E_o to point E_{fi} in space, with a hypothetical state of the world h_j;

E_{fi} - the destination of the route of the energy mass from the state of rest after the operator-decision maker selected the alternative d_i;

E_o - point of the state of rest of the energy mass m_o, where the possible route of transformation of this mass begins;

u_{ij} - as in formula (5.29).

Formula (5.30) may be called the energetic-decisional or behavioral equation of information. In this context, we may easily see that the general utility matrix in Table 5.1 may be transformed into an energy-utility matrix specifying the route $m_o \rightarrow m_{fi}$, provided that the state of the world h_j occurs, which may also be expressed in Table 5.2.

Table 5.2. The matrix of information about the utility of the transformation d_i of energy mass m from point E_o to point E_{fi} in the energy space, with the hypothetical states of the world h_j

H / D	h_1	h_2	...	h_j	...	h_z
d_1	I_{11}	I_{12}	...	I_{1j}	...	I_{2z}
d_2	I_{21}	I_{22}	...	I_{2j}	...	I_{2z}
⋮	⋮	⋮	...	⋮	...	⋮
d_i	I_{i1}	I_{i2}	...	I_{ij}	...	I_{iz}
⋮	⋮	⋮	...	⋮	...	⋮
d_n	I_{n1}	I_{n2}	...	I_{nj}	...	I_{nz}

The matrix presented in table 5.2 may be a starting point for an analysis aiming to identify which way of actualizing the potential of the energy mass is optimal in terms of the criterion of rationality of the decision.

5.10. Concluding remarks on the integration of concepts of *information, decision, mass* and *energy*

When analyzing the concepts of *mass, energy* and *information,* we tried to focus on the fact that it is possible to overcome the dualism of *energy* and *information*, observed in contemporary science. The Aristotelian concepts of *act* and *potency* were very useful tools for this analysis, as they implicitly refer to the contemporary philosophy of science, built on the foundation of Carnap, and spread by Przełęcki in connection with the discussion on the definability of theoretical terms in scientific disciplines.

The above analysis allowed us to formulate the theoretical outline of the approach to information which we may call a behavioral-decision- energy oriented on, and to formulate an equation as a function of actualizing the energy potential of the mass by the operator for a particular decision as the movement of this mass from rest to a certain point in the energy space. This concept allowed us to tie the concept of *energy-information* with the possibilities offered by the methodology of decision analysis and multidimensional scaling. The analysis, however, requires a more detailed explanation of the issues related to decision, information and energy. Our studies essentially focused on kinetic energy, which is just a starting point of analysis undertaken. One should also specify in what metric units of measure might the theoretical term *information* be presented in order to translate it into a term which is quantitatively observational.

The proposed interdisciplinary conception suggests to integrate the metric physical units with the information-economic approach. The plane for such metric integration may be the behavioral approach. A concrete application of the outlined conception of information may be an interpretation of Tables 5.1 to 5.2 as a basis for the analysis of optimization in various sectors of behavioral economics, including the economics of transport. From this perspective, the system of concepts: *information-energy – decision making* gives a chance to advance economic studies by implementing its elements within the analyses.

6. CONCLUSIONS

Economic events, both at the global macroeconomic and microeconomic level, indicate that the human factor plays an important role in their dynamics. In the monograph I have tried to show that the decision makers – the subjects of these events – are concrete, real people. It is the living persons as decision makers who bring about certain economic crises, not merely in individual companies, but also at the global level.

We have seen the systematic development of the notion of a decision situation as a well-ordered-set of three, called an ordered triple, through a well-ordered-set of four, called an ordered quadruple, to a well-ordered-set of five, called an ordered 5-tuple. Developing this concept was possible thanks to the fact that representatives of such disciplines as formal logic, mathematics, economics and psychology collaborated in the field of decision making. An outcome of such cooperation are new journals, e.g.: *Decision Sciences, Decyzje* (in Polish), *Theory and Decision, Judgement and Decision Making, Journal of Behavioral Decision Research, Information Research, Information Seeking, Behavioral Decision Making.* This kind of interdisciplinary cooperation is an example of the integrative path in contemporary science which studies decision making and information seeking in decision situations. The behavioral approach was suggested as a methodological tool to integrate and develop decision sciences and information sciences. Here, decisions as human behaviors were reflected in the light of the axioms of game theory by J. von Neumann and O. Morgenstern, called classical axioms of the utility theory.

Analyzing the issue of information seeking in a dynamic decision situation, one may formulate the problem of the decision to invest in finding new information in order to reduce the risk of the final decision in this situation. There were presented the issue of optimality of the decision concerning the search for new information. The situation of finding new information and the associated problem of the decision to invest were described as a communication system. The models for an optimal investment decision in search of new information base on the criteria which are well-known in the theory of optimal decision.

The problem of the decision to invest in new information is related to the question whether in terms of the economy it is legitimate to invest, and if so, how much to invest in the search for new information in a situation of an economic decision. A wider context here involves a possible methodology for analyzing the costs and benefits associated with searching and acquiring new information in a particular decision situation. In the case of economic decisions, such methodology may be the pragmatic methodology of accounting, introduced by H. Ronek (1995). This methodology analyzes the relationship between the primary and final expenditures on the one hand, and the finally accounted costs on the other hand, with special attention paid to the time factor in cost accounting. This approach also proposes to distinguish expenditures on strictly economic activities (production, services) that use the factors of production which deteriorate, from expenditures that do not qualify as cost (production loss).

In this context, the primary input, i.e. the collected economic resources, is a potential reality which may be used more or less optimally. Hence, there arises a question how to reach this optimal use, both at the macro scale as well as at the level of a single company. As we have seen, the novelty of the pragmatic approach in methodology of accounting is that it stresses that in the practice of accounting, the primary input only includes the use of the initial resources, while other factors, such as the cost of the decision maker's risk or the cost of information seeking, are not taken into account. Altogether, we may say that production costs should also reflect other costs derived from the primary inputs. For example, considering the investment expenditures related to the primary input with a high risk required of the company owner, the calculation should take into account the degree of risk, as – from the behavioral point of view – there arise costs of abandoning one possible path of investment in order to choose another path. This is a new cost category which should belong to the cost of primary inputs, alongside with consumption. In behavioral accounting, investing in information seeking belongs to this category. This very pragmatic approach to the methodology of accounting, a discipline within economics, has much in common with the interdisciplinary field of decision theory. A behavioral interpretation of mechanisms in accounting lets us conclude that calculating the primary expenditures, which are an accumulation of macro- and microeconomic potentiality, should be modified by taking into account the above economic activities.

After reviewing various aspects of searching for information in decision situations, the monograph focuses on the search for probabilistic information. Various descriptive and normative (ideal) models are confronted with the experimental results, where we also observe how decision makers behave when seeking information in decision situations. Among these behaviors one may distinguish two models of a sequential search for probabilistic information. A. Biela proposed the model called a step by step one, to analyze the optimality of each new investment in searching for new probabilistic information in a dynamic decision situation. . The advantage of this model is its intuitive simplicity and thus greater behavioral operationality. In turn, E. Micał and A. Biela elaborated the other version of this model, called combinatorial, which allows to evaluate the utility of a given informational cycle (e.g. purchasing a fifth signal that carries probabilistic information) without having to perform a calculation after each step of the investment cycle. The advantage of the combinatorial model is t that it is cheaper to use, because applying it we only need information about the last signal.

We have also seen the viewpoint of behavioral economics as a theoretical approach to analyze the behavior of decision makers in a variety of economic situations that are of interest to the various fields within economics and management studies. Our analyses tried to provide examples of such cognitive regularities, called heuristic, fallacies (or cognitive biases), and indicated the need to consider them in the analyses of economic phenomena.

A distinct element in our analysis was a reflection on the significance of the experimental research method in economic sciences, illustrated with examples of experiments on decision making in various areas of economic life. A specific topic of interest are experiments on seeking information in a dynamic decision situation where the decision maker is able to undertake investment activities that involve purchasing new information to reduce the uncertainty of the decision situation. The analysis also allows to point out that the introduction of experiments makes economics a more strict and empirical science. Experimental approaches to economic research are also frequently mentioned, including experiments of V. Smith, a Nobel Prize winner in economics (2002), the author of the experimental method in the economic sciences. Another added value of such approach is that by adopting a more integrated perspective of behavioral economics, the economic sciences come closer to the actual reality of economic life of living people, who perceive the reality around them in their own cognitive categories.

The behavioral approach also allows us to integrate certain theoretical concepts used in different scientific disciplines. This was the case with integrating the concepts of *information* and *decision* in the first part of the monograph, and, in the next step, integrating the concepts of *information* and *energy* – in the last chapter. Such integration enables to create the conception of *energy-decision–information,* for which the formulated equation shows that information is a function of energy as an actualization of mass-energy in an act of decision making by the operator, i.e. the decision maker operating with energy. This conception is in its initial stage of development and requires further clarification and elaboration.

The present monograph offers only a general view on the cognitive and applied potential of the behavioral approach for the economic and social sciences. This potential lies mainly in the theoretical and methodological possibilities of the behavioral concepts and research methods, and particularly experimental studies. Therefore, a continuation of our explorations might concern information seeking in specific areas of decision making. For example, we may ask specific questions concerning the situation of choosing one's own vocation : 1. How many alternative vocations do students or school graduates consider when choosing their vocation? 2. What cognitive and emotional processes are involved in decision making when choosing one's profession? What kind of investments do students and school graduates make when seeking information while making their choosing-profession-decision? How far is choosing one's vocation/profession an economic decision? Answering the above questions would give us orientation for ontological, epistemological and methodological considerations towards a theoretical framework for career guidance practice, as well as for social and economic policy making on a state or regional level. Choosing one's vocation could be interpreted as an economic decision, of long-term socioeconomic consequences, not only for the individual but also for their family, local community, the employer, the region, state and macrostructures such as the European Union.

It is important to be aware of the relationship between vocational guidance and the conceptual framework behind it (Ertelt and Ruppert 2011). Good career guidance needs a good theoretical background ("there is nothing so practical as a good theory" – Kurt Lewin): a clear conceptual framework helps us to make sense of human behaviour in decision making situations, sometimes to influence it, and occasionally even to predict it and help persons who are looking for advice in developing their careers. In order to engage in the real world effectively, one needs to clearly define the conceptual tools that would allow him or her to do it systematically. Unfortunately, theoretical conceptions that counsellors mostly rely on are largely based on a normative-prescriptive rational decision making model that is increasingly alien to the real-world settings, and thus fails to provide the career counsellor and the client with the conceptual tools they need in today's world. Moreover, these normative models are treated not only as methodological tools for orientation in human behaviour, but they are interpreted as the human reality itself.

Similar questions may be asked about other areas of human endeavor where people are individual or collective decision makers and seek new information to update their knowledge about the uncertainty and risk involved in the decision making process. However, under uncertain or risky situations people still make decisions. This is because uncertainty and risk are constitutively related to human decision making. This monograph has presented certain theoretical schemas, methods and accounts which may be helpful in coping with stress in decision making.

Literature

Abramson N. Teoria informacji i kodowania. Tłum. J. Nowakowski, W. Sobczak. Warszawa 1969, PWN.

Adamus W. (red.)(2008). *The Analytic Hierarchy & Network Processes. Application in Solving Multicriteria Decision Problems,* Krakow: Jagiellonian University Press.

Adamus W. (2008a). Wejście Polski do strefy euro w aspekcie korzyści , kosztów, szans i ryzyka. w: T. Guz, ks., R. Mazurkiewicz, R. Tłuczek (red.), Tożsamość narodowa i suwerenność państwa a integracja europejska, Lublin: Katolicki Uniwersytet Lubelski Jana Pawła II, 193 – 222.

Adamus W.(2009) , *A New Method of Job Evaluation*, Scientific Annals of the "Alexandru Ioan Cuza" University of Iasi, Economic Sciences Section, Tom LXVI, 515- 536.

Adamus W.(2010), *Metody ilościowe w zarządzaniu i organizacji.* w:L. Haber(red.), Komunikacja i zarządzanie w społeczeństwie informacyjnym, Kraków: NOMOS.

Adamus W., Gręda A.(2005). Wielokryterialne wspomaganie decyzji w rozwiązywaniu problemów organizacyjnych i menedżerskich, *Badania Operacyjne i Decyzje*, Nr 2, 5-37.

Adamus W., Łasak P. (2010). Zastosowanie metody AHP do wyboru umiejscowienia nadzoru nad rynkiem finansowym, *Bank i Kredyt*, Vol. 41 No.4, 73 - 100 .

Adamus W., Rzońca B. (2008). Wykorzystanie metody VDA w badaniach ekonomicznych ,[w:] *Metody ilościowe w badaniach ekonomicznych IX, Wielowymiarowa analiza danych*, Warszawa: Wydawnictwo SGGW, 9 – 18,

Anderson N. H. A simple model for information integration. W; R. P. Abelson et al.(eds) Theories of cognitive consistency. A sourcebook. Chicago 1968, Rand McNally.

Anker J. N., Townsend J. C., O'Connor J. P. A multivariate analysis of decision making and related measures. *Journal of Experimental Psychology,* 1963, 55, 211-221.

Aristotle (Arystoteles), (1990a), Fizyka, [w:] Dzieła wszystkie, Leśniak K. i in. (przekł.), t.2, Warszawa

Aristotle (Arystoteles), (1990b), Metafizyka, [w:] Dzieła wszystkie, Leśniak K. i in. (przekł.), t.2, Warszawa

Aristotle (Arystoteles), (1993), Fizyka, [w:] Dzieła wszystkie, Paciorek A, Regner L, Siwek P. (przekł.), t.4, Warszawa

Audley R. J. Decision making. *British Medicine Bulletin*, 1964, 20, 27-30.

Beach L. R. Probability magnitudes and conservative revision of subjective probabilities. *Journal of Experimental Psychology*, 1968, 77, 57-63.

Becker G. M. Sequential decision making Wald's model and estimates of parameters. „Journal of Experimental Psychology" 1958, 55(6), 628-636.

Becker G. S. (1990), *Ekonomiczna teoria zachowań ludzkich.* Warszawa: PWN.

Berryman J.(2006). What defines 'enough' information? How policy workers make judgements and decisions during information seeking: preliminary results from an exploratory study, *Information Research*, 11, 2005-2006

Biela A. Rozwiązywanie problemów w aspekcie teorii informacji. *Roczniki Filozoficzne*, 1971, 19, 77-87.

Biela A. Struktura układu komunikacyjnego: źródło sygnałów-decydent. *Roczniki Filozoficzne*, 1972, 20, 151-I60.

Biela A. Struktura procesu informacyjnego w sytuacjach decyzyjnych. *Przegląd Psychologiczny*, 1973a, 16, 445-455.

Biela A. Przetwarzanie sygnałów na informację niezawodną. *Roczniki Filozoficzne*, 1973b, 19, 59-74.

Biela A. (1976). Informacja a decyzja, Warszawa, PWN.

Biela A (1986). Psychological patterns in predicting disjunction and conjunction of clinical symptoms. *Acta Psychologica,* 61, 183-195.

Biela A.(1986a). Towards a Synthetic Approach to Intelligence. *Behavioural and Brain Sciences,* 9, 578-581.

Biela A. (1991). Analogy in Science. Frankfurt am Main: Peter Lang Verlag.

Biela A. (1992). Skalowanie wielowymiarowe jako metoda badań naukowych. Lublin: Towarzystwo Naukowe KUL.

Biela A. (1995). Skalowanie wielowymiarowe w analizach behawioralnych i ekonomicznych. Lublin: Norbertinum.

Biela A. (2001). Wymiary decyzji menedżerskich. Lublin: TN KUL.

Biela A. (2006). A Paradigm of the Unity in Social Sciences. *Journal for Perspectives of Economic, Political and Social Integration,* 12, 167-177.

Biela A. (2007). Kapitał ludzki I kapitał intelektualny jako dobro gospodarcze i moralne, w: B. Piontek, W. Piontek (red.), *Rozwój, godność człowieka – gospodarowanie – poszanowanie przyrody.* Warszawa: Polskie Wydawnictwo Ekonomiczne.

Biela A. (2009). Koncepcja *informacji, masy* i *energii*: w kierunku zintegrowanego podejścia. W: K. A. Kłosiński, A. Biela (red.), *Człowiek i jego decyzje.* Wydawnictwo KUL.

Biela A. (2010). Psychologiczne i społeczne zasoby kapitału ludzkiego w zarządzaniu personelem. W: M. Pawlak (red.). Nowe tendencje w zarządzaniu. Lublin, Wydawnictwo KUL, 57-69.

Biela, A., Chlewiński, Z., Walesa, Cz. (1983). Developmental aspects of decision making. W: L. Sjöberg, T., J.A. Wise (Eds.) (1983). Human decision making. Karlshamn: Bokförlaget Doxa, 291-311.

Blandford A., Attfield S. (2010). Interacting with Information. "Synthesis Lectures on Human-Centered Informatics", 3, 1-99.

Booker D.M., Drake A., Heitger D.L. (2007).New product development: How cost information precision affects designer focus and behavior in a multiple objective setting, *Behavioral Research in Accounting,* 19 (1), 19.

Brichaček V. (1970), Use of subjective probability in decision making. *Acta Psychologica*, 34, 241-253.

Broglie, L. (1966), *Certidudes et inceritudes de la science*, Paris: A. Michel

Bruner J., Goodnow J., Austin G. (1956), *A study of thinking*. New York: J. Wiley.

Bujak F. Subjektywna ocena prawdopodobieństwa zdarzeń prostych przez dzieci z klas I-VIII. *Roczniki Filozoficzne,* 1972, 20, 143-150.

Bujak F. (1974). *Pomiar prawdopodobieństwa zdarzeń i użyteczności działań w sytuacjach decyzyjnych*. Archiwum KUL (nieopublikowana rozprawa doktorska).

Burchell N., Kolb D., (2006) 'Stability and change for sustainability', *University of Auckland Business Review,* 8, 33-41.

Burrows D., Okada R. (1973). Parallel scanning of semantic and format information. *Journal of Experimental Psychology*, 97, 254-257.

Butler R., Davies L., Pike R. (1993). Strategic Investment Decisions: Theory, Practice, and Process.London , Routledge

Butryn S. Pomiar ryzyka w podejmowaniu decyzji. Lublin 1973 (MA dissertation).

Caginalp G., McCabe K., Porter D. (2004). The Foundations of Experimental Economics and Applications to Behavioral Finance: The Contributions of Nobel Laureate Verno

Carnap, R.(1936), Testability and Meaning. *Philosophy of Science*, vol. 3, s.419-471.

Case D.O. (2007). Looking for information: a survey of research on information seeking, needs and behavior. London, Academic Press.

Cattell R. B. (1957), Personatity and motivation structure and measurement. New York:

Chen K-Y, Hogg T. (2008). Modeling Risky Economic Decision-Making with Bounded Rationality, Information Systems Frontiers 5(1):47–61

Cherry C. (1966), On human communication. A review, a survey and criticism. Cambridge: Massachusets Institute of Technology Press.

Chlewiński Z. (1972a), Teoria pobierania próbek z populacji bodźcowych. W: *Sprawozdania TN KUL*, Lublin: TN KUL, 23-27.

Chlewiński Z. (1972b), Trzy modele identyfikacji pojęć. *Roczniki Filozoficzne*, 20, 85-100.

Chlewiński Z. (1975). Cognitive Conservatism and Radicalism I Individual and Group Decisions. *Polish Psychological Bulletin,*6, 139-146.

Chlewiński Z. (1979). Decyzja, W: Encyklopedia Katolicka, Tom 3, Lublin, Towarzstwo Naukowe KUL, 1080.

Cohen J., Meudell P. Strategies of search. *Acta Psychologica*, 1968, 28, 322-343.

Connaway L.S., Radford M.L., Dickey T.J., Willimas J.A., Confer P. (2008). Information-Seeking Behaviors of Millennials and Baby Boomers. *Libri*, 58, 123-135.

Coombs, C.H. (1964). *A theory of data*, New York: J. Wiley.

Coombs C. H., Kao R. C. (1966), Nonmetric factor analysis. *Engineering Research Bulletin* , 38, 426-443.

Cooper R., Johri A. (2002). Learning by doing and Aggregate Fluctuations, , *Journal of Monetary Economics*, 49, 1539-1566.

Davies J., White J., Wright A., Maru Y., LaFlamme M. (2008). Applying the sustainable livelihoods approach in Australian desert Aboriginal development. *The Rangeland Journal* **30,** 55–65.

Davis D.D., Holt Ch.A. (1992). Experimental Economics. Princeton, Princeton University Press.

Davis J. H., Hoppe R. A., Hornaeth J. P. (1968), Risk taking; task, response patterns and grouping. *Organizational Behavior and Human Performance*, 3, 124-142.

De Swart J. J. (1972), Conservatism as a function of bag composition. *Acta Psychologica*, 36, 197-206.

Deway J. (1997). How we think. Boston, Houghton Mifflin (first edition: Lexington, 1910, D.C. Heath.

Diederich A., BusemeyerJ.R. (2003). Simple matrix methods for analyzing diffusion models of choice probability, choice response time, and simple response time. *Journal of Mathematical Psychology, 47,* 304-322 .

Driver J. M., Hunsaker P. L. The Luna I Moon Colony. A programmed simulation for the analysis of individual and group decision making. *Psychological Reports*, 1972, 31, 879-888.

DuCharme W. M. (1969), A reviews and analysis oj the phenomenon of conservatism in human inference. *Interdesciplinary Program in Applied Mathematics and Systems Theory, Raport: Systems* 46-5, Houston: Rice University.

DuCharme W. M., Peterson C. R. Intuitive inference about normally distributed populations. *Journal of Experimental Psychology*, 1968, 78, 269-275.

Durkheim E. (1964). The division of labour society. New York, Free Press.

Edwards W. (1962). Dynamic Decision Theory and Probabilistic Information Processing. *Human Factors in Electronics,*4, 59-73.

Edwards W. (1968), Conservatism in human information processing. W: G. Kleinmutz (ed.) *Format reprezentation of human judgment*. New York: J. Wiley.

Edwards W. (1969), A bibliography of reseach on behavioral decision processes to 1988. *University of Michigan, Report No.7.*

Edwards W. (1971). Bayesian and regression models of human information processing – a myopic perspective. *Organizational Behavior and Human Performance,* 6, 634-648.

Edwards W., Lindman H., Savage L. J. (1963), Bayesian statistical inference for psychological reasarch. *Psychological Review*, 70,193-242.

Edwards W., Slovic P. Seeking information to reduce the risk of decisions. *American Journal of Psychology*, 1965,78,188-197.

Ekel J. (1970), Jak stawiamy diagnozę? *Psychologia Wychowawcza*, 1,501-611.

Ekins, P. (Ed.)(1990). The Living Economy, London, Routledge.

Ekins P., Max-Neef M. (1992). Real Life Economics: Understanding Wealth Creation, London, Routledge.

Einstein, A. (1961), *Relativity. A special and general Theory*, New York:

Ertelt B-J, Ruppert J-J. (2011). Heuristic Theory of decision Making: Evidence and Implications for Career Guidance, In: S. Kraatz, B-J. Ertelt (Eds.), Professionalization of Career Guidance in Europe. Tübingen, dgvt Verlag.

Felton J., Gibson B., Sanbonmatsu D.M. (2003). Preference for risk in investing as a function of trait optimism and gender. *Journal of Behavioral Finance,* 4, 33.

Fisz M. (1967), *Rachunek prawdopodobieństwa i statystyka matematyczna*. Warszawa: PWN

Fleischmann B., Borgwardt K.H., Klein R., Tuma A. (2008). Operation research proceedings. Dordrecht, Springer.

Fried L. S., Peterson C. R. Information seeking: optimal versus fixed stopping. *Journal of Experimental Psychology*, 1969, 80, 525-529.

Gajos T., Hayashi T., Tallon J-M., Vergnaud J-C. (2008). Attitude Toward Imprecise Information . *Journal of Ecocnomic Theory,*140, 27-65.

Gaugler E. (1962), Innerbetriebliche InformInformation als Fűhrungsausgabe. *Untersuchungen und Berichte Verőffentlichungen de AGP, II,4,3-32.*

Gaugler E. (1993), Fűhrungsentscheidungen und Fűhrugsveantwortung in der Wirtschaft, In: N. Glatzel, E. Keindienst (Eds.), Die personale Struktur des gesellschaftlichen Lebens. Berlin, Duncker & Humboldt.263-275.

Geller E. S., Pitz G. F. (1968), Confidence and decision speed in the revision of opinion.*Organizational Behavior and Human Performance* ,3,190-201.

Gettys C.F., Manley C.W. (1968). The probability of an event and estmates of a posteriori probability based upon its occurrence, *Psychonomic Science,* 11, 47-68

Gino F. (2004). The Hidden Cost of Buying Information, w: *Harvard Business School Working Knowledge for Business Leaders Archive,* 11/8/2004

Goode H. H. Deferred decision theory. W: R. E. Machol, P. Gray (Eds.) Recent deuelopments in information and decision proceses. New York 1962, McMillan.

Gottsdanker R. Choice reaction time and the nature of the choice reaponse. *Psychonomic Science*, 1969,14,257-258.

Green P. E., Halbert M. H., Minas J. S. An experiment in information buying. *Journal of Adversiting Reaearch*, 1964,4,17-23.

Green P. E., Sweeta J. A. Signal detection theory and psychophysies. New York 1966, J. Wiley.

Greniewski H. (1969). Cybernetyka niematematyczna. Warszwa, PWN.

Greniewski H., Kłosiński K.A., Lefewr W., Smolan G. (1973). *Tak i nie.* Warszawa, KiW.

Greń J. (1972). Gry statystyczne. Warszawa, PWE.

Grzelak J., Tyszka T. Some preliminary experiments on cooperation in n-person-games. *Polish Psychological Bulletin*, 1974, 5, 81-91.

Guilford J. P. Three faces of intellect, W: J. Jenkins, J. Peterson (eds.) Studies in individual differences. New York 1961.

Hausmann D., Läge D. (2008). *Judgment and Decision Making*, vol. 3, 229-243.

Hintikka J. The varieties of information and scientific explanation. *Logic Methodology and Philosophy of Science*, 1968, 3, 311-331.

Hockey R. Changes in information - selection patterns in multisource monitoring as a function of induced arousal shifts. *Journal ot Experimental Psychology*, 1973, 1, 35-42.

Holt Ch. (2006). Markets, games and strategic behaviour. Boston, Addison-Wesley.

Holt R., 2007. Investment, irreversibility and financial imperfections: the rush to invest and the option to wait, Economics Bulletin, *AccessEcon,* 5(10), 1-10.

Howell W. C. Task characteristics in sequential decision behaviour. *Journal of Experimental Psychology,* 1966, 71, 124-131.

Ilard P., Lipschitz L. (2006). The macroeconomic management of foreign aid. Washington DC, International Monetary Fund, Publication Services.

Irvin W.S., Smith W.A.S. (1956). Further tests of theories in an “expanded judgement” situation. *Journal of Experimental Psychology,* 52, 345-348.

Irvin W.S., Smith W.A.S. (1957). Value, cost and information as determiners of decision. *Journal of Experimental Psychology,*54, 229-232.

Jajuga K. (2004). O pewnych modelach decyzji finansowych. *Decyzje,* 1, 37-54.

Jamison D. T., Kozielecki J. Subjective probabilities under total uncertainty. *American Journal of Psychology*, 1968, 81, 217-225.

Jeffrey R. The logic of decision. New York 1965. McGraw-Hill.

Jungermann H. Einc Unfersuchung des Einflusses der a-priori-Wahrscheinlichkeiten auf die bei Entscheidungen tolerierte Irrtums-Wahrscheinlichkeit. Institut fűr Psychologie der Technischen Hochachule Darmstadt Bericht Nr B9-4, 1969.

Kamiński S. Pojęcie nauki i klasyfikacja nauk. Lublin 1998, TN KUL.

Kamphuis W., Houttuin K. Gaillard A.W.K. (2010). PLATT: A flexible platform for performance in complex environments. *Behavior Research Methods,* 42, 739-753.

Kaźmierczak J. Teoria gier w cybernetyce. Warszawa 1973, WP.

Kietliński R. Empiryczny model decyzji w warunkach ryzyka. *Studia Psychologiczne*, 1974, 13, 7-23.

Kirsch W. (1988). *Die Handhabung von Entscheidungsproblemen. Einführung in die Theorie der Entscheidungsprozesse.*Műnchen, Verlag Barbara Kirsch.

Kłosiński K.A. (1983). Teoria sytuacji decyzyjnych. Wrocław, Ossolineum.

Kłosiński K.A. (1995). Racjolaność decyzji, z myślą o nowych paradygmatach w ekonomii. Instytut Naukowo-Wydawniczy dr Kłosińskiego.

Kłosiński K.A. (2006). Wprowadzenie do miedzynarodowych stosunków gospodarczych. Lublin, Wydawnictwo KUL.

Kłosiński K.A. (2007). Strategia sukcesu. Lublin, Verba.
Kłosińsk-i K.A., Biela A. (red.)(2009). Człowiek i jego decyzje. Lublin, Wydawnictwo KUL.
Kłosiński K.A. (2009a). Racjonalność egzystencjalna świata w XXI wieku. W: Kłosiński K.A., Biela A. (red.)(2009). Człowiek i jego decyzje. Lublin, Wydawnictwo KUL, 83-93.
Kofler E. Wstęp do teorii gier. Warszawa 1968, PZWS.
Kotarbiński T. Traktat o dobrej robocie. Wrocław 1973,0ssolineum.
Kozielecki J. Zagadnienia psychologii myślenia. Warszawa 1968, PWN.
Kozielecki J. Rozwiązywanie problemów. Warszawa 1969, PZW S.
Kozielecki J. Psychologia procesów przeddecyzyjnych. Warszawa 1969a, PWN
Kozielecki J. (1981). Psychological Decision Theory. Warszawa, PWN.
Kranz D. Threshold theories of signal detection. *Psychological Review*, 1969,76,308-324.
Krąpiec, M. A. (1964) Struktura bytu. Charakterstyczne elementy systemu Arystotelesa I Tomasza z Akwinu, Lublin , TN KUL
Krąpiec, M. A. (1973) Akt i mozność. Arystoteles, [w:]Gryglewicz F, Łukaszczyk R, Kuhn, T. (1962), The Structure of Scientific Revolutions, Chicago
Lange D. (1971). Optimal decisions: Principles of Programming, Oxford, Pergamon Press.
Lerner A. J. Zarys cybernetyki. Tłum. S. May. Warszawa 1971, PWN.
Leśniewski S.0 podstawach matematyki. *Przegląd Filozoficzny*, 1930, 4,77-405.
Linkov J., Ferguson E., Magar V.S. (2008). Real-Time and Deliberative Decision Making. Dordrecht, Springer
Lissowski G.(2003) Klasyfikacja informacji pragmatycznej, [w:]Jadacki, J.J. (red.) Analiza pojęcia informacji, Warszawa, s. 95-114
Loewenstein, G. (1995). "Out of Control: Visceral Influences on Decision Making," *Organizational Behavior and Human Decision Processes* 65, 272–292.
Luce R. D., Raifta H. Gry i decyzje. Tłum. J. Kucharczyk. Warszawa 1964, PWN.
Łaguna M. (2010). Przekonania na własny temat i aktywność celowa. Gdańsk, Gdańskie Wydawnictwo Psychologiczne.
Łukasiak-Goszczyńska, M. (1974). Badanie strategii podejmowania decyzji wielowymiarowych. Warszawa: Uniwersytet Warszawski (rozprawa doktorska).
Łukaszewski W. Niezgodność informacji i aktywność. *Przegląd Psychologiczny*, 1971, 21, 35-69.
Makarowski R. (2008). Granice ryzyka. Paradygmat psychologiczny. Kraków, Oficyna Wydawnicza „Impuls".
Malawski M. (2009). Robert Aumann,*Decyzje*, 11,117-125.
Manz W. Experiments on probabitisfic information processing. *Acta Psychologica*, 1970, 34, 184-200.

Marks D. F. The consisfency of subjectiue probability judgments. Proceedinga of a Research Conference on subjective probability and related fields, April 1969,.Hamburg.

Marreiros G., Santos R., Ramos C., Neves J. (2010). Context-Aware Emotion-Based Model for Group Decision Making, *IEEE Intelligent Systems*, 25, 31-39.

Martin D. W., Gettys C. F. Feedback and response mode in performing a bayesian decision

Mazierski, S. (1969).Prolegomena do filozofii przyrody inspiracji arystotelesowsko-tomistycznej, Lublin, Tow. Nauk .KUL.

Mączyński J. (1996). Partycypacja w podejmowaniu decyzji. Warszawa, Wydawnictwo IFiS PAN.

Messick D. M. Learning probabilities of events: a discussion. *Acta Psychologica*, 1970, 34, 172-183.

Micał, E. (2008). Zastosowanie sekwencyjnego modelu podejmowania decyzji zakupu informacji probabilistycznej. Lublin, KUL (MA dissertation).

Middleton M. A., Warren L. Risk-taking effects on group decision making. *The Journal of Psychology*, 1972, 82, 183-196.

Mosteller F., Nogee P. (1951). An experimental measurement of utility. *Journal of Political Economy*, 59, 371-404.

Newell, T. S. (2004). Thinking beyond the disjunctive opposition of information literacy assessment in theory/practice. *School Library Media Research, 7.*

Newell A., Simon H. (1962). GPS, a program that simulates human thought. New York, McGraw-Hill.

Newell A., Show J., Simon H. (1963). The process of creative thinking, w: Contemporary approaches to creative thinking. New York, Prentice Hall.

Nosal C. Rola zdolności poznawczych w procesie rozwiązywania problemów. *Studia Psychologiczne*, 1974, 13, 113-130.

Peterson C. R., Beach L. R. Man as an intuiliue statistician. *Psychological Bulletin*, 1966,68,29-46.

Peterson C.R., DuCharme W.M. (1967). A primacy effect in subjective probability revision, *Journal of Experimental Psychology,* 73, 61-65.

Peterson C.R., Edwards W., DuCharme W.M. (1968). Sampling distributions and probability revisions. *Journal of Experimental Psychology,* 76, 236-243.

Peterson C.R., Swensson R.G. (1968). Intuitive statistical inference about diffuse hypotheses, *Organizational Behavior and Human Performance,* 3, 1-11.

Peterson G. R., Schneidor R., Miller A. J. Sample size and the revision of subjective probabilities. *Journal of Experimental Psychology*, 1965,69,622-527.

Phillips L.D., Edwards, W. (1966). Conservatism in a simple prabability inference task, *Journal of Experimental Psychology,* 72, 346-354.

Piontek F. (2001). Kontrowersje I dylematy wokół rozwoju zrównoważonego I trwałego, w: F. Piontek (red.), Ekonomia a zrównoważony rozwój, Białystok, Wydawnictwo Ekonomia i Środowisko.

Piontek, F. (2007). Podstawy teorii rozwoju, w: B. Piontek, W. Piontek (red.), Rozwój, godność człowieka – gospodarowanie – poszanowanie przyrody. Warszawa, Polskie Towarzystwo Ekonomiczne.

Pitz G. F. Sample size, likelihood, and confidence in a decision. *Psychonomic Science*, 1967,8,267-268.

Pitz G. F. Informalion seeking when available information is limited. *Journal of Experimental Psychology*, 1968, 73,25-34.

Pitz G.F. (1969).Use of response times to evaluate strategies of information seeking, *Journal of Experimental Psychology,* 80, 553-558.

Pitz G. F. (1970). On the processing of information: probabilistic and otherwise. *Acta Psychologica*, 34, 201-213.

Pitz G.F., Downing L. (1967). Optimal behavior in a decision making task as a function of instruction and pay-offs. *Journal of Experimental Psychology,*73, 549-555.

Pitz G.F., Reinhold H., Geller E.S. (1969). Strategies of information seeking in deferred decision making, *Organizational Behavior and Human Performance*, 4, 1-19.

Porter, D. P., & Smith,V. L. (1995). Futures contracting and dividend uncertainty in experimental asset markets. *Journal of Business, 68*, 509-541.

Przełęcki, M. (1955) O tzw. definicjach operacyjnych, Studia Logica, t.3, s. 125-149

Przełęcki, M. (1961) Pojecia teoretyczne a doświadzcenie, Studia Logica, t.11, s. 91-138

Radzicki J. Wpływ niektórych czynników sytuacyjnych na proces formułowania diagnozy probabilistycznej. *Studia Psychologiczne*, 1974,13,95-112.

Ramsey F. Truth and probability. W: Foundations of mathematics and other logical essays. London 1931.

Raven J. (1984). Competence in modern society: Its identification, development and release. Oxford, England: Oxford Psychologists Press.

Raven, J. (1995). The New Wealth of Nations. A new Enquiry into the Nature and Origins of the Wealth of Nations and the Societal Learning Arrangements Needed for a Sustainable Development, New York, Royal Fireworks Press.

Ricciardi V. (2008). The Psychology of Risk: The Behavioral Finance Perspective. *In*: F. Fabozzi, (ed.), *Handbook Of Finance: Volume 2: Investment Management And Financial Management*, Wiley, pp. 85–111.

Rockenbach B. (2004). The behavioral relevance of mental accounting for the pricing of financial options. *Journal of Economic Behavior & Organization,* 53, 513–527.

Ronek H. (1995). Pragmatyczna metodologia rachunkowości. Lublin, Wydawnictwo UMCS

Rożnowski, B. (2009). Przechodzenie młodzieży z systemu edukacji na rynek pracy w Polsce. Lublin, Wydawnictwo KUL.

Schlaifer R. Teacher's solution manual to accompany analysis of dccision under unccrtainty. New York 1969, McGraw-Hill.

Scholtz S.W., Wagner R., (2005). The Quality of Prior Information Structure in Business Planning – An Experiment in Environmental Scanning. W: H. Fluenen, D. den Hertog, P. Kort (Eds.), *Operation Research Proceedings,* Berlin, Springer, 238-245.

Schum D. A., Martin D. V. Human processing of inconclusive evidence from multinomial probability distributions. *Organisational Behavior and Human Performance*, 1968, 3, 335-365.

Scodel A., Ratoosh P.R., Minas J.S. (1960). Some personality correlates of decision making under conditions of risk. W: D. Willner (red.), Decisions, values and groups. New York, Pergamon Press.

Shannon C. E., Weaver W. The mathematical theory of communication. Urbana, Illinois 1949, The Univereity Press.

Shani Y., Zeelenberg M. (2007). When and why do we want to know? How experienced regret promotes post-decision information search. *Journal of Behavioral Decision Making*, 20, 207–222.

Shani Y., Tykocinski O.E., Zeelenberg M. (2008). When ignorance is not bliss: How feelings of discomfort promote the search for negative information. Journal of Economic Psychology.,29, 643-653

Shepard, R.N. (1962). The analysis of proximities: multidimensional scaling with an unknown distance function. Psychometrika, 27, 125-140.

Shepard, R.N. (1972). Psychological representation of speech sounds. W: E.E. Dawid, P.B. Denes (Eds.), Human communication: a unified view. New York: Mc Graw Hill, 67-113.

Silverthorne S. (Ed.)(2004). The Hidden Cost of Buying Information, in: *Harvard Business School Working Knowledge for Business Leaders Archive,* 11/8/2004

Simon, H. (1959). Theories of decision making in economics and behavioral science, *American Economic Review,* 49, 253-283.

Simon, H. (1969). The Science of Artificial Intelligence, Cambridge, MA, MIT Press.

Sjöberg L., Tyszka T. ,Wise J.A. (red.)(1983). Human Decision Making, Lund, Doxa.

Skinner B.F. (1974). About Behaviorism. New York, Knopf

Skulimowski A.M.J. (2009). Formal models of freedom of choice and cognitive aspects of multicriteria decision support. W: Kłosiński K.A., Biela A. (red.)(2009). Człowiek i jego decyzje. Lublin, Wydawnictwo KUL, 47-59.

Smith V.L. (1976). Experimental Economics: Induced Value Theory". American Economic Review 66 (2): 274–279.

Smith V.L. (1982). Markets as economizers of information: Experimental examinations of the "Hayek hypothesis". *Economic Inquire,* 20, 163-179.

Smith V.L. (2004). Behavioral economics research and the foundation of economics, *Journal of Socioeconomics*, 34, 135-150.

Snapper K.J., Peterson C.R. (1971). Information seeking and date dignosticitcity. *Journal of Experimental Psychology*, 87, 429-433.

Stachowski R. Modele liniowe przeddecyzyjnego procesu integrowania informacji. *Przegląd Psychologiczny,* 1973, 16, 335-359.

Stachowski R. Badania nad przeddecyzyjnym problemem integrowanio informacji w sytuacji bayesowskiej. *Studia Psychologiczne*, 1974, 13, 49-71.

Streufert S., Streufert S.C. (1968). Information load, time, *Psychonomic Science,*13, 327-328.

Strojna E., 1974). Porównywanie podejmowania decyzji w sytuacjach ryzykownych o różnych źródłach niepewności: losowym i sprawnościowym Journal of Marketing Research. *Studia Psychologiczne,* 13, 25-36.

Sweets J.A., Tanner W.P., Birdsal T.G. (1961). Decision processes in perception, *Psychological Review,*68, 301-340.

Szaniawski K. Kryteria podejmowania decyzji. W: J. Kozielecki (red.) Problemy psychologii matematycznej. Warszawa 1971a, PWN, s.303-324.

Szaniawski K. Pragmatyczna wartość informacji. W: J. Kozielecki (red.) Problemy psychologii matematycznej. Warszawa 1971b, PWN, s.325-347.

Szaniawski K. Przedmowa do polskicgo przekładu G. Jahody Psychologia przesądu. Warszawa 1971c.

Szaniawski K. Two concepts of information. *Theory and Decision*, 1974,1,9-21.

Szeloch Z. Kultura organizacyjna i klimat organizacyjny, Centrum Kreowania Liderów, Kłudzienko, 1991

Szeloch Z. Podstawy zarządzania strategicznego przedsiębiorstwem, WSB-NLU w Nowym Sączu, 1996

Szopiński J. (2004). Kreatywność menedzerów a ich funkcjonowanie rodzinne, zawodowe i osobowosciowe. Kraków, Wydawnictwo Uniwersytetu Jagiellońskiego.

Tatarkiewicz, W. (1990) Historia filzofii, t. 1, wyd. 12, Warszawa, PWN.

Tichomirow O., Bielik j., Poznjanska E., Turczenkowa N. (1964). Opyt primienienija tieorii informacji k analizu processarieszienija myszlitielnych zadacz czełowiekom, *Woprosy psichołogii*, 4, 21-38.

Tolman E. (1932). Purposive behavior in animals and man. New York: The Century Co.

Tosi, H. L., Mero, N.P., Rizzo, J.R. (2000), Managing Organizational Behaviour. Oxford: Blackwell Publishing

Tversky A.,Edwards W.(1966). Information versus reward in binary choices.*Journal of Experimental Psychology,* 71, 680-683.

Tversky, A. and Kahneman, D. (1982) "Judgments of and by representativeness". In D. Kahneman, P. Slovic & A. Tversky (Eds.), *Judgment under uncertainty: Heuristics and biases*. Cambridge, UK: Cambridge University Press

Tversky, A. and Kahneman, D. (October 1983). "Extension versus intuitive reasoning: The conjunction fallacy in probability judgment". Psychological Review 90 (4): 293–315.

Tyszka T. (1968). Podejmowanie decyzji. Badania nad prawdopodobieństwem subiektywnym. *Psychologia Wychowawcza*, 11, 376-395.

Tyszka T. (1970). Subiektywna interpretacja prawdopodobieństwa, zagadnienie wyboru w warunkach niepewności. *Przegląd Psychologiczny*, 20, 19-40.

Tyszka, T. (1983). Contextual multiattribute decision rules. W: L. Sjöberg, T. Tyszka, J.A. Wise (Eds.), Human decision making. Karlshamn: Bokförlaget Doxa, 243-256.

Tyszka, T. (2010). Decyzje. Perspektywa psychologiczna i ekonomiczna. Warszawa, Scholar

Vlek C.A.J. (1965). The use of probabilistic information in decision making. Psychological Institute, University of Leiden, Report No 009-65.

Vlek C.A.J.(1970). Learning probabilistic of events. An analysis of the problem and its relevance for the study of decision making. *Acta Psychologica,* 34,160-171.

Vlek C.A.J., Beintema K.A. (1967). Subjective likelidoods in a posteriori probability estimation. Psycholological Institute, University of Leiden, Report No E 014-67.

Vlek C.A.J., Van der Heijden L.H.C. (1967). Subjective likelihood Functions and variations in the accuracy of probabilistic information processing. Psycholological Institute, University of Leiden, Report No EDA, 7-67.

Vlek C.A.J., Van der Heijden L.H.C. (1970). Aspects of suboptimality in a multidimensional probabilistic information processing task. *Acta Psychologica,* 34,300-310.

Vlek C.A.J., Cvetkowich G. (Eds.)(1989). Social Decision Methodology for Technological Projects, Dordrecht, Kluwer Academic Press.

Vohs K.D., Baumaister R.F., Loewenstein G. (2007). Do emotions help or hurt decision making? New York, Russel Sage Foundation.

Von Neumann J.,Morgenstern O. (1944). Theory of Games and Economic Behavior, Princeton NJ, Princeton University Press.

Wald A. Sequential analysis. New York 1947, J. Wiley.

Wald A. Statistical decisions functions. New York 1950, J. Wiley.

Walesa Cz. (1972). Rozwój procesów decyzyjnych u dzieci, Badania eksperymentalne dzieci z klas od I do VIII. *Roczniki Filofozoficzne – Psychologia,* 20, 101-142.

Walesa Cz. (1975). Geneza ryzyka. *Roczniki Filozoficzne – Psychologia,* 23, 71-86.

Walesa Cz. (1988). "Gain-Loss" – Balansing self in existential risk taking. W: A. Biela, Z. Uchnast (red.). Problems with the self in psychology. Lublin-Bielefeld, 92-101.

Walesa Cz. (2005). Zasady dokonywania decyzji życiowo doniosłych. *Zeszyty Naukowe Wyższej Szkoły Ekonomii i Innowacji w Lublinie,* 1, 149-165.

Walesa Cz. (2011). The cognitive – dynamic issue of important and vitally significant decision. A psychological study. W: D. Musiał, E. Rydz (red.). The psychology of human development – Selected study. Lublin, Towarzstwo Naukowe KUL, 65-91.

Wallach M.A., Kogan N., Burt R.B. (1967). Group Risk Taking and Field Dependence- Independence of Group Members, *Sociometry*, 30, 323-338.

Watson J.B. (1930). *Beheviorism*. Chicago, The University of chicago Press.

Wiener N. (1965). Udział w dyskusji opublikowanej w: *Perspektywy cybernetyki*, Warszwa, Książka i Wiedza.

Wiener, N. (1971). Cybernetyka, czyli sterowanie w zwierzęciu i maszynie. Warszawa, PWN.

Williams D., Hall T., Kennedy M. (2000). A framework for improving the requirements engineering proces management. *Software Quality Journal,* 8, 1-15.

Wolf C. R. (1995), Information seeking on Bayesian conditional probability problems: A fuzzy-trace theory account. Journal of Behavioral Decision Making, 8,85–108.

Wu S.W., Delgado M.R., Maloney L.T. (2009). Economic decision-making compared with an equivalent motor task ,106(15),6088-6093.

Zaleski, Z. (1987). Motywacyjna funkcja celów w dzialalności człowieka. Lublin: Redakcja Wydawnictw Katolickiego Uniwersytetu Lubelskiego.

Zaleski Z. (1991). Psychologia zachowań celowych. Warszawa, PWN.

Zaleski Z. (2003). Psychologia własności i prywatności. Lublin, Żak Wydawnictwo Akademickie.

Żylicz, T. (2009). Suwerenność człowieka w ekonomii, w: K.A. Kłosiński, A. Biela (red.), Człowiek i jego decyzje. Lublin, Wydawnictwo KUL, 131-144.

DEUTSCHE ZUSAMMENFASSUNG

Translated from English by Bernd-Joachim Ertelt

Die Wissenschaft hat sich zunächst als ganzheitlicher Ansatz entwickelt, später kam noch eine fachgebietsspezifische Betrachtung hinzu. Heute ist es geboten, beide Ansätze gleichzeitig wahrzunehmen: Den fachgebietspezifischen Ansatz, der den Forschungshorizont bestimmter Fachgebiete erweitert, zum Aufbau von Wissen beiträgt und den Fortschritt der Menschheit ermöglicht und den integrativen Ansatz, der die interne Kommunikation des angereicherten Wissens vertikal unterstützt und eine Betrachtung der Wissenschaft oder ihrer Teilgebiete als System ermöglicht. Das Nebeneinander dieser beiden Entwicklungstrends, also dem fachgebietspezifischen, horizontalen und dem integrativen, vertikalen Trend, kann in vier Bereichen der Methodologie beobachtet werden: 1) in den Konzeptionen der Wissenschaft selbst, 2) in der Systematik der Wissenschaft, 3) im Konzept eines wissenschaftlichen Paradigmas und 4) in der Entwicklung von wissenschaftlichen Konzepten (Biela 1991).

Neben den unbestrittenen Vorteilen des fachgebietspezifischen Trends für die Entwicklung der Menschheit und der Wissenschaft können aber auch Risiken beobachtet werden, die aus der Fokussierung auf nur eine Entwicklungsrichtung resultieren. Ein Anzeichen für ein solches Risiko ist die immer schwieriger werdende Kommunikation unter Fachleuten, die verschiedene Schulen und Forschungsansätze vertreten, selbst wenn sie alle zum gleichen wissenschaftlichen Fachgebiet gehören. Ganz zu schweigen von den Unstimmigkeiten zwischen den Vertretern unterschiedlicher Fachgebiete. Dies wird greifbar bei wissenschaftlichen Konferenzen, bei denen normalerweise Vorträge von Vertretern eines Fachgebiets parallel stattfinden. Diese Repräsentanten haben häufig keine Vorstellung von der Arbeit, der Herangehensweise oder dem Bezugsrahmen des jeweils Anderen. Der integrative Trend in der Wissenschaftsentwicklung bildet ein Gegengewicht zu diesen Schwierigkeiten in der Kommunikation, wie sie beim fachgebietsspezifischen zu beobachten sind. Das wichtigste Merkmal der integrativen Richtung besteht darin, dass ein bestimmter Forschungsaspekt, ein bestimmtes Forschungsobjekt oder -schema nicht nur Vertretern eines einzelnen wissenschaftlichen Fachgebiets, sondern Vertretern mehrerer Fachgebiete geläufig ist (Biela 1991).

Mit seinem verhaltensorientierten Ansatz bei der Informationssuche im Rahmen der Entscheidungsfindung repräsentiert das vorliegende Werk den integrativen Trend in der Wissenschaft. Informationen und Entscheidungen gehören zu den wichtigsten Konzepten, die es ermöglichen, Situationen zu verstehen, in denen Menschen verschiedene Rollen mit sozialem, professionellem, politischem, wirtschaftlichem, spirituellem oder existentiellem Charakter spielen.

In Kapitel 1 wird die Entwicklung des Konzepts einer Entscheidungssituation dargestellt, von der wohlgeordneten Menge „drei" (geordnetes Tripel) über die wohlgeordnete Menge „vier" (geordnetes Quadrupel) bis hin zur wohlgeordneten Menge „fünf" (geordnetes Quintupel). Diese Entwicklung bei der Forschung zur Entscheidungsfindung und Informationssuche in Entscheidungssituationen ist das Ergebnis einer engen Zusammenarbeit von Wissenschaftlern aus Fachgebieten wie formale Logik, Mathematik, Wirtschaftswissenschaften und Psychologie und ist Teil des integrativen Trends in der Wissenschaft. Der verhaltensorientierte Ansatz wird als methodologisches Werkzeug empfohlen, mit dem sich Entscheidungs- und Informationswissenschaften miteinander verbinden und entwickeln lassen. Daher werden Entscheidungen, die als menschliche Verhaltensweisen zu betrachten sind, aus der Sicht der Axiome der Spieltheorie (klassische Axiome der Nutzentheorie) von J. von Neumann und O. Morgenstern diskutiert.

In Kapitel 2 wird der Aspekt der Informationssuche in einer dynamischen Entscheidungssituation analysiert, in der Personen möglicherweise vor dem Problem stehen, eine Entscheidung treffen zu müssen, ob in die Beschaffung neuer Informationen investiert werden soll, um das Risiko der endgültigen Entscheidung in der gegebenen Situation zu reduzieren. In diesem Kapitel wird der Frage einer Entscheidungsoptimierung durch die Suche nach neuen Informationen nachgegangen. Die Situation des Suchens nach neuen Informationen wird als Kommunikationssystem dargestellt und das damit im Zusammenhang stehende Problem der Entscheidung hinsichtlich der Investition ebenfalls diskutiert. Die herangezogenen Modelle basieren auf den Kriterien der Theorie der optimalen Entscheidung.

Unser Interesse an der Entscheidungsfindung hinsichtlich der Investition in die Beschaffung neuer Informationen basiert auf der Frage, ob diese im Sinne der Ökonomie begründbar erscheint, und falls ja, wie viel in einer gegebenen wirtschaftlichen Entscheidungssituation zu investieren sei. Um diesen Aspekt in einem größeren Zusammenhang zu sehen, ist eine angemessene Methodologie erforderlich, um Aufwand und Ertrag dieser Beschaffung zu analysieren. Einen sehr hilfreichen Ansatz für wirtschaftliche Entscheidungen bietet die pragmatische Methodologie des Rechnungswesens nach Ronek (1995), der die Beziehung zwischen den anfallenden Primärkosten und den Gebrauchsgütern, die aus der Aktivierung/Nutzung des primären Inputs (durch den Prozess der Herstellung oder das Erbringen von Dienstleistungen) resultieren, auf makro- und mikroökonomischer Ebene untersucht. Angesichts der Gründe für die Schwierigkeit bei der Bestimmung von

Angemessenheit und Vergleichbarkeit der Kosten und deren Effekte werden die Verfahren zur Feststellung der Angemessenheit und Vergleichbarkeit kritisch hinterfragt. Diese Schwierigkeit ist eine Folge der Annahmen innerhalb der Methodologie des Rechnungswesens, da weder die angefallenen Kosten noch die Herstellungskosten entsprechend den anerkannten Abrechnungszeiträumen verlaufen (Ronek 1995). In diesem Ansatz werden außerdem die primären und finalen Inputs in Bezug auf die letztendlich berechneten Kosten analysiert. Dabei konzentriert sich der Ansatz auf den Zeitfaktor bei der Kostenrechnung und unterteilt Ausgaben in strikt wirtschaftliche Aktivitäten mit sich verbrauchenden Produktionsfaktoren (z. B. bei der Herstellung oder bei Dienstleistungen), und in Ausgaben, die nicht als Kosten gelten (z. B. Produktionsausfälle).

Die wirtschaftlichen Ressourcen des primären Inputs sind ein Potenzial, das mehr oder weniger optimal genutzt werden kann: Die Herausforderung besteht deshalb darin, diese so zu nutzen, dass daraus der größtmögliche Vorteil sowohl auf der Ebene des einzelnen Unternehmens als auch auf makroökonomischer Ebene entsteht. Die Neuartigkeit des pragmatischen Methodologieansatzes zeigt sich in der Empfehlung, auch andere Kosten aus dem primären Input in die Produktionskosten aufzunehmen, anstatt nur den Verbrauch bzw. die Verwendung der anfänglichen Ressourcen in die Gesamtberechnung des Inputs einzuschließen, ohne andere Faktoren, wie die Risikokosten des Entscheidungsträgers oder die Kosten für die Beschaffung von Informationen, zu berücksichtigen. Im Falle der Investitionen im Zusammenhang mit einem primären Input, bei denen ein hohes Risiko für den Unternehmer besteht, sollte bei der Berechnung auch das Risikoausmaß einbezogen werden. Denn wenn der primäre Input auf eine bestimmte Weise investiert wird, kann er nicht mehr an anderer Stelle investiert werden, auch wenn andere Optionen effizienter wären. Aus verhaltensbezogener Sicht entstehen Stilllegungskosten oder entgangene Gewinne aufgrund der nicht gewählten Option. Dies ist eine neue verhaltensorientierte Kostenkategorie, die zum primären Input zählt, jedoch nicht als Verbrauch angesehen wird. Das verhaltensorientierte Rechnungswesen zählt Investitionen für die Suche nach neuen Informationen zu dieser Kategorie. Eine solche Interpretation des verhaltensorientierten Rechnungswesens führt zu der Schlussfolgerung, dass der primäre Input (eine Ansammlung wirtschaftlicher Möglichkeiten auf makro- und mikroökonomischer Ebene) so angepasst werden sollte, dass auch die oben genannten Aktivitäten eingeschlossen sind. Im Rahmen des pragmatischen Ansatzes im Rechnungswesen findet eine Annäherung zwischen den Wirtschaftswissenschaften und dem interdisziplinären Feld der Entscheidungstheorie statt.

Die Darstellung des Konzepts einer wirtschaftlichen Entscheidungssituation (Kapitel 1) und des Problems der Optimierung einer Entscheidung, in die Suche neuer Informationen zu investieren (Kapitel 2), geht einher mit der Behandlung verhaltensorientierter Studien hinsichtlich des menschlichen Verhaltens in dynamischen Entscheidungssituationen, in denen eine Möglichkeit besteht, nach neuen Informationen zu suchen. Diese in Kapitel 3 dargelegten Studien sind Teil des Mainstream in der Verhaltensökonomik und befassen sich mit der Entscheidungssituation als dynamische Stimulus-Situation, die den Entscheidungsträger beeinflusst. Die Hauptmodelle bei der Suche nach neuen Informationen im Entscheidungsprozess – das deskriptive und das normative Modell – bilden die Basis für die Forschung hinsichtlich der Informationssuche in der Verhaltensökonomik. Die vorliegende Schrift stellt die eigene Forschungssystematik zum Thema wirtschaftliches Verhalten als Teil der Forschungsrichtung zu Informationsprozessen in einer dynamischen Entscheidungssituation dar; dazu werden die grundlegenden Forschungsergebnisse präsentiert. Die informationelle Funktion wird definiert als *Informationssuche (information seeking)* und *Erwerb (purchasing), Sammlung (gathering), Erlangen (reaching), Erhalt (obtaining) von Informationen*. Im umfassenden Sinne bezieht sich jeder dieser Begriffe auf dasselbe Konzept, konzentriert sich jedoch auf unterschiedliche Aspekte der Informationssuche. Auch wenn einige Autoren die Begriffe synonym verwenden, scheint es doch so, dass die Begriffe *Informationsaktivität* und *Informationsverarbeitung* am besten geeignet sind, die Totalität der Informationsprozesse in einer dynamischen Entscheidungssituation auszudrücken und sich dabei zu ergänzen. Daher werden sie generell als die zentralen Begriffe betrachtet. Ein weiterer Begriff ist *Meinungsänderung*, welcher sich auf das Endergebnis von Informationsprozessen bezieht. Der experimentelle Ansatz der Wirtschaftsforschung wird von V. Smith (Wirtschaftsnobelpreis 2002) vertreten, dem Verfasser der experimentellen Methodik in der Wirtschaftsforschung.

Nach der Diskussion verschiedener Aspekte der Informationssuche in Entscheidungssituationen, konzentrieren wir uns auf die Untersuchung probabilistischer Informationen. Die Rationalität von Entscheidungen hängt in hohem Maße von den für den Entscheidungsträger verfügbaren Informationsressourcen ab. Anhand einer Analyse verschiedener deskriptiver und normativer (idealer) Modelle und experimenteller Ergebnisse wird außerdem erörtert, wie sich Entscheidungsträger bei der Informationssuche in Entscheidungssituationen verhalten. Unter diesen Verhaltensweisen können zwei Modelle einer sequenziellen Suche nach probabilistischen Informationen unterschieden werden. Das erste Modell von A. Biela bietet eine Optimierungsanalyse jeder weiteren Investition in die

Beschaffung neuer probabilistischer Informationen in einer dynamischen Entscheidungssituation. Mit der anderen Version dieses Modells von E. Micała und A. Biela, das als kombinatorisches Modell bezeichnet wird, lässt sich die Nützlichkeit eines gegebenen Informationszyklus (z. B. Erhalt eines fünften Signals, das probabilistische Informationen enthält) bewerten, ohne nach jedem Schritt des Investitionszyklus eine Berechnung durchführen zu müssen. Der Vorteil der ersten Version liegt in der intuitiven Schlichtheit und somit der größeren verhaltensorientierten Operabilität, während die kombinatorische Version den Vorteil gegenüber dem sequenziellen Modell hat, dass sie einfacher zu nutzen ist, denn für die Anwendung sind nur Informationen zum letzten Signal erforderlich.

Die Untersuchung stellt die Sichtweise der Verhaltensökonomik als theoretischen Ansatz zur Analyse des Verhaltens von Entscheidungsträgern in verschiedenen wirtschaftlichen Situationen dar, die für die unterschiedlichen Bereiche der Wirtschaftswissenschaften und Unternehmensführung von Interesse sind. In Entscheidungssituationen treffen Menschen Entscheidungen hinsichtlich bestimmter Investitions-, Finanz-, Führungsstrategie-, Marketing- und Konsumentenbelange und wenden dabei nur sehr selten die aus den Wirtschaftswissenschaften bekannten normativen Modelle an. Sie verwenden eher solche kognitiven Schemata, die ihren Ursprung in der intuitiven Wahrnehmung und der Alltagssprache haben. Mit unseren Untersuchungen haben wir versucht, Beispiele solcher kognitiven Regelhaftigkeiten (Trugschlüsse oder kognitive Verzerrungen genannt) aufzuweisen, und die Notwendigkeit betont, diese in den Analysen wirtschaftlicher Phänomene zu berücksichtigen.

Ein entscheidendes Element unserer Arbeit ist die Betrachtung der Bedeutung der experimentellen Forschungsmethodik in den Wirtschaftswissenschaften, illustriert durch Beispiele von Experimenten zur Entscheidungsfindung in verschiedenen Bereichen des Wirtschaftslebens. Von besonderem Interesse sind solche Experimente zur Informationssuche in einer dynamischen Entscheidungssituation, bei denen der Entscheidungsträger Investitionsaktivitäten im Zusammenhang mit dem Erwerb neuer Informationen zur Reduzierung der Unsicherheit tätigen kann. Anhand der Analyse lässt sich auch betonen, dass die Einführung von Experimenten die Wirtschaftswissenschaften zu einer strengeren und empirischeren Wissenschaft macht. Ein weiterer Mehrwert eines solchen Ansatzes besteht darin, dass sich die Wirtschaftswissenschaften durch eine stärkere Integration der verhaltensökonomischen Sichtweise den Menschen im Wirtschaftsleben, die die Realität um sich herum ja in ihren eigenen kognitiven Kategorien wahrnehmen, eher annähern.

Der verhaltensorientierte Ansatz ermöglicht es uns auch, bestimmte theoretische Konzepte, die in verschiedenen wissenschaftlichen Fachgebieten verwendet werden, zu integrieren. Dies betrifft die im ersten Teil des Buches diskutierten Konzepte zur *Information* und *Entscheidung* sowie die im abschließenden Kapitel angesprochene Integration der Konzepte *Information* und *Energie*. Eine solche Verknüpfung ermöglicht es, die Konzeption *Energie-Entscheidung-Information* zu generieren, für die die formulierte Gleichung zeigt, dass Information eine Funktion der Energie als Aktualisierung von Masseenergie im Rahmen einer Entscheidungshandlung durch den Entscheider ist, d.h. der Entscheidungsträger handhabt Energie. Dieser Ansatz befindet sich erst am Anfang seiner Entwicklung und erfordert weitere Abklärung und Ausarbeitung.

Schriftenreihe Arbeit und Bildung
des Heinrich-Vetter-Forschungsinstituts e.V.

Herausgegeben von Franz Egle und Carl-Heinrich Esser

Band 1 Tobias Hagen: Langzeitarbeitslosigkeit in der Metropolregion Rhein-Neckar. Unter Mitwirkung von Sonja Hamberger. 2010.

Band 2 Walter A. Oechsler / Eva M. Müller: Arbeitsmarkt und Beschäftigung in der Metropolregion Rhein-Neckar. 2010.

Band 3 Bernd-Joachim Ertelt / Andreas Frey / Christian Kugelmeier (Hrsg.): HR zwischen Anpassung und Emanzipation. Beiträge zur Entwicklung einer eigenständigen Berufspersönlichkeit. 2012.

Band 4 Franz Egle / Hermann Genz (Hrsg.): Fit für Arbeitsvermittlung, Beratung und Integration. 2012.

Band 5 Adam Biela: Information and Decision in Behavioral Economics. 2012.

Band 6 Thomas Fohgrub: Qualitätssicherung von Arbeitnehmerüberlassung durch systematische Evaluation. Ein theoriebasierter, praxisorientierter Ansatz. 2012.

www.peterlang.de

www.ingramcontent.com/pod-product-compliance
Ingram Content Group UK Ltd.
Pitfield, Milton Keynes, MK11 3LW, UK
UKHW021009120926
8556IPUK00029B/297

9 783631 633809